HOW
TO
INFLUENCE
CHILDREN

HOW
TO
INFLUENCE
CHILDREN

A Handbook of Practical Child Guidance Skills

**Completely Revised and Expanded
Second Edition**

Charles E. Schaefer, Ph.D.

JASON ARONSON INC.
Northvale, New Jersey
London

THE MASTER WORK SERIES

First softcover edition 1994

Library of Congress Cataloging-in-Publication Data

ISBN: 1-56821-273-9
Library of Congress Catalog Card Number: 94-71312

Manufactured in the United States of America. Jason Aronson Inc. offers books and cassettes. For information and catalog write to Jason Aronson Inc., 230 Livingston Street, Northvale, New Jersey 07647.

To My Family

Mom and Dad,
My wife Anne,
Children Eric and Karine

A WORD ABOUT PRONOUNS

I have attempted to eliminate sexist language by alternating the gender of personal pronouns throughout the book. Consequently, you will read "she" in some sections and "he" in others. Please consider that the child mentioned is the one you have in mind, even though the sex reference doesn't always agree.

FOREWORD

In the decade since the publication of the first edition of *How to Influence Children* there have been rapid advances in the field of child guidance. This all-new, revised edition reflects these exciting developments. The book has been completely revised and updated. With the exception of the Appendix, every section of the book has been improved and expanded. More than a standard revision, then, this second edition is virtually a new book!

The enthusiastic acceptance of the first edition confirmed my conviction that such a comprehensive, practical handbook of effective child guidance skills was needed. Although *How to Influence Children* has now come of age, it should be recognized that the contents of this book are neither final nor complete. New and better ways of raising children will be discovered. I hope to aid these advances in future editions of the book.

Charles E. Schaefer, Ph.D.

PREFACE

If you feel some responsibility for the behavior of a child or a group of children, this book is designed for you. You will find in this book a comprehensive approach for teaching children to behave. If you are a parent, teacher, or child care worker, you will find this to be a useful guidebook. But the same basic influence strategies will also be valuable for psychiatrists, psychologists, social workers, school counselors, pediatricians, parent educators, and others who want to help parents help their children behave better.

According to psychologist Lee Salk, there is a pressing need for scientifically based child care information written by experienced clinicians who can translate information into a language that is easily understood by parents. The goal of this guidebook is to provide a clear, concise description of the basic skills involved in effective childrearing. The ideas are based upon an extensive review of the literature, common sense, and my thirty years experience as parent, parent educator, and child psychologist.

Influencing children toward good behavior is not a natural ability all of us are born with, but there is now a large body of knowledge based on sound laws of human nature to guide us to effective practices. Dealing skillfully with children is just as much an art, just as much a science as any other occupation or profession. Unfortunately, most parents and teachers receive little or no training in child guidance skills.

Child Guidance Skills

There are many skills involved in guiding or influencing children toward good behavior. Influence skills include talking, listening, ordering, persuading, challenging, loving, reasoning, rewarding, punishing, and so on.

Seventy specific child guidance skills are contained in this guidebook. The skills are grouped into two major sections. The first part of the book concerns ways of establishing effective discipline. The second part of the book relates to the formation of close parent–child attachments and describes ways parents can foster positive family relationships. The approach described in this book has been field tested by numerous researchers across the country and has proven effective in enabling parents to reduce noncompliance in their children.

An added feature of this volume is the appendix that reviews basic principles of child development. A primary goal of raising children is child growth and development. The focus of this appendix is on the development of the personality, sociability, and morality of children.

This handbook provides a broad overview of child guidance practices. The definitions and descriptions of each skill are meant to offer a frame of reference or structure for organizing and clarifying the reader's thoughts. The succinct "how-to" format is designed to provide a blueprint for action, and allow for quick and easy retrieval of information. Although kept to a minimum, the reference notes point to the scholarly foundation of the book.

The comprehensive scope of this guidebook is based on the fact that there are many ways to influence children. Like the master woodcarver who has over 300 special tools to work with, adults who assume responsibility for children must be knowledgeable of, and proficient in, a wide variety of social influence techniques. As a result, one will be less likely to resort to the use of yelling and hitting. Some methods, of course, will be more useful than others, but all should prove helpful on specific occasions. I have included in this book only "positive" child care practices. In my judgment, a positive technique must meet a threefold criteria: it must be effective in stimulating a child to action, it must not lower the child's self-esteem, and it must not harm one's relationship with the child.

The techniques in this book are suitable for use with children of all ages, except infants. This guidebook has been used as a text or supplementary reading for parent education groups and courses on childrearing, child management, parenting, and social influence.

Charles E. Schaefer
April 1994
Teaneck, New Jersey

CONTENTS

HOW
TO
INFLUENCE
CHILDREN

Part I
Ways to Establish
Effective Discipline

INTRODUCTION

For the very true beginning of wisdom is the desire of discipline; And the care of discipline is love.

—*Apocrypha*

A central core of childrearing is discipline. Discipline, in this book, is used in the broad sense to mean the teaching process by which adults help children learn to live as socialized beings and achieve their optimum growth and development. The essence of discipline is to teach and it is derived from the Latin word for pupil, meaning one who follows the teachings of a leader. The immediate goal of discipline is to control and direct children so they can get along in society. Children must learn to perform desirable acts and avoid undesirable ones if they are to live in harmony with others.

The long-term goal of discipline is the development of *self-direction* or *inner control*. Internal control means governing one's own behavior by using explicit norms, standards, and rules that have been internalized. The self-disciplined person has the inner controls necessary for constructively meeting the frustrations and demands of daily living. Parents, then, should be continually striving to work themselves out of the job of disciplinarians by gradually developing this skill in children.

Discipline is probably the one aspect of childrearing about which parents feel most concerned and insecure. Fortunately, there have been thousands of scientific research studies which shed light on how best to teach children discipline. In the first part of this book I will discuss a number of ways for you to become a more effective disciplinarian or teacher.

The first part on effective discipline is subdivided into "Child Management" and "Child Guidance." The management section refers to specific practices for directly influencing a child to do something the parent desires, or to stop performing an inappropriate act. The guidance section presents methods for teaching children to cope with the outside world while developing their abilities and discovering their true identity. The management section, then, describes ways of directly applying external controls on children, while the guidance section contains more indirect methods of promoting self-control and self-development in children.

Section A
Child Management Skills

By the term child management or control techniques, I mean those strategies employed by parents to change the ongoing course of a child's behavior. These techniques are designed to have an immediate effect, to regulate a child's activity in the here and now. Their function is to channel behavior in certain directions, inhibiting some tendencies and encouraging others.

Child management techniques encompass both positive approaches (e.g., praise, persuasion, rewards) and negative approaches (e.g., physical punishment). A positive approach is one in which your intention is to teach a child more adaptive ways of behaving while you show respect, acceptance, and support. With a positive approach, you view and treat your child as a friend rather than an adversary. As a result, the child feels that you are with him rather than against him. A negative or punitive approach, on the other hand, has as one of its goals hurting a child by inflicting severe physical or psychological pain, e.g., loss of self-esteem, intense fearfulness, anxiety, or guilt. Punitive techniques devalue a child and belittle his importance as a human being. Hit and yell are dreary old punitive methods in many parents' bag of child-management tricks. Parents need to know a whole array of alternative methods (such as distraction and using positive rewards) which are not abusive to children. The use of punishment has its place in childrearing and its proper application will be described in this section. While discipline and punishment are interrelated they are far from being synonymous. Punishment is just one aspect of the multifaceted disciplinary approach advocated in this book.

The negative or crisis approach to parenting is mainly concerned with behavior control rather than with behavior management. It mainly consists of punishing misbehavior. Behavior management, on the other hand, emphasizes that parents should teach and reinforce desired behaviors more frequently than punish misbehavior. Behavior managers try to prevent misbehaviors and crises from occurring; behavior controllers tend to overlook good behavior and respond to children only when they show problem behaviors.

WINNING YOUR CHILD OVER BY PERSUASION

Thought convinces; feeling persuades.

—Theodore Parker

If there is any one secret of success, it lies in the ability to get the other person's point of view and see things from his angle as well as your own.
—Henry Ford

We flatter ourselves by claiming to be rational and intellectual beings, but it would be a great mistake to suppose that men are always guided by reason. We are strange, inconsistent creatures, and act quite as often, perhaps oftener, from prejudice or passion. The result is that you are more likely to carry men with you by enlisting their feelings, than by convincing their reason.
—John Lubbock

Persuasion means to motivate children to do something by arousing their emotions, drives, and ideals more than their intellect. Persuasion is an ancient art. Greek and Roman orators, for example, tried to sway their listeners' decisions by stirring up their emotions. The origin of the word "persuasion" is the Latin term *per* meaning *through* and *suasio* signifying *sweetness*. So a persuasive person takes the time and effort to *win* people rather than *dominate* them.

A parent's job is not only to lead children to water but to make them thirsty. Basically those who supervise others are salespeople. It's their task to sell good attitudes and good behaviors. A good salesperson knows the basic wants and needs of people and has the ability to see things from their point of view.

Some specific persuasive strategies follow:

1.   Buttering Up

This technique involves doing someone a favor in order to make them feel obligated to return the favor. The selling power of "taking the client to lunch" is widely recognized in the business community. Moreover, research has shown that the extraneous gratification of eating while listening to appeals by others, increases the effectiveness of the appeals. So try fixing your child a special meal before you attempt to persuade her.

Another "buttering up" technique involves rewarding a child in one area prior to requesting his compliance in another. For example, you would first excuse a child from one of his daily chores and then tell him that you now expect him to study longer.

This technique also includes being as friendly, helpful, and pleasant as possible to a child in order to get him in a good frame of mind. Once he is in a positive mood, you would then make a request of him, e.g., to study, write a thank-you note, and so on. Children are especially skilled in being extra nice before they request a favor. Parents would be well advised to learn from their children how to apply this technique.

2.   "Foot-in-the-Door" Technique

Persuading people to make a large commitment by asking them for a smaller commitment first is an old sales technique. Research has now firmly established the effectiveness of this foot-in-the-door approach.[2] If a child is persuaded to perform some small act in behalf of a parent, the child will subsequently be more likely to perform a bigger favor for the parent. It seems that once someone says yes the first time, subsequent yeses come a lot easier.

So you should give easily fulfilled requests to your child the first time, then give more difficult but the same type of requests. For example, you might first say, "Margaret, please put your Raggedy-Ann doll away." Later ask her to put more and more of her toys away. When baking a cake, first ask the child to come and help by pouring the milk in the bowl; once the child is there, you might ask for other assistance. In brief, you initially use a behavior that seems easy or attractive to get the child initially involved and then you gradually try to get the child to do other more complex behaviors.

Car salesmen are very familiar with this technique which they call "Selling Up." They will first try to get you to buy a lower priced car or a stripped-down version—and then they will point out how many other features you could get for just a few dollars more.

3.   Appeal to the Child's Desires

A key way to motivate a child is to ask first, "What's in it for the child?" Put yourself in the child's shoes. For example, instead of saying to a child, "You need to get a college education," try arousing a need in the child by saying, "College graduates earn more money," "College graduates are respected more than high-school graduates," "College graduates are better able to think and express themselves," or "College graduates are more interesting to talk to."

So an effective way to get a child to do something is to point out the positive aspects of that behavior from the child's point of view. The advantage of the behavior for the child can be highlighted by associating it with one of the child's needs, desires, emotions (e.g., joy, fun, status), or values (e.g., to be good or to be grown-up). In other words, you induce a child to do something by talking about what the child wants and how this behavior relates to it, rather than talking about what you want or what the facts dictate. Rather than feeling pushed by you, the child feels pulled toward the behavior by its own attractiveness.

Further examples of increasing the value of some behavior by appealing to the basic desires of the child are: "This is fun and it's so easy"; "That looks like an exciting thing to do."; "You're probably tired of eating the same food all the time. This new dish will be a nice change from the ordinary."; "This book looks interesting. I always wondered what it was all about."; "John, I know making the football team means an awful lot to you. I think you'll find that if you eat everything on your plate you'll have the strength and energy to go full steam the whole game!"; "If you keep hitting other kids like that, nobody will want to play with you. You'll be so lonely."

Parents should also appeal to the ego-ideals and values of the child (to be competent; be good). Since most young children want to appear grown-up and acquire status, you might try saying: "You're getting so grown up, I don't think you need a babysitter anymore." Other examples of appealing to the ego-ideals of the child are: "Is that the way an eagle scout would behave?"; "Charles, you've always been so smart and curious, especially in school. I wonder if the college you're interested in will be stimulating enough for you? It would be a shame to waste real intellectual talent like yours."

In making appeals, try to hook them into the child's emotions, imagery, desires, and personal values rather than calmly using reason to convince.

4. "Bandwagon Effect"

You can capitalize on a child's need to belong and be accepted by others by using the "bandwagon effect." When children feel that everyone is doing it or not doing it, there is a tendency for them to want to jump on the bandwagon and join the crowd.

5. Change Self-Image

You can change a child's self-image by attributing to him positive qualities he did not know he had. For example, if you keep telling a child he is neat and tidy, he will probably begin to show more cleanliness behavior. In one research study a group of fifth graders were repeatedly told by their teacher that they were a neat and tidy class (when in fact there was evidence to the contrary). This technique resulted in less littering in the classroom. In other studies when students were told that they had good mathematical ability or were highly motivated in math, they later showed gains in math achievement and self-esteem.

So try attributing positive qualities to your child on occasion: "I know you want to do the right thing."; "You're not the kind of boy who enjoys being mean to others."

6. Be Dramatic

Merely stating a truth usually isn't enough to convince people. Thus, a good advertising company will try to make a truth vivid (appealing to the senses and the imagination), and dramatic (use of dialogue). Moreover, a good ad man will make a truth come alive by the use of illustration, novelty, and humor. With these techniques in mind, you might want to show your child a color photograph of the lungs of a heavy smoker to induce him to stop smoking. Or you might create an image by showing him a picture of a highly successful college graduate to motivate him to attend college.

Rather than nagging your child to feed his dog, you might post a picture of a starving dog with a caption signed by the child's pet: "Please don't let this happen to me!" One picture can indeed be worth a thousand words. In lieu of lecturing the kids about bickering and fighting, you could try posting signs on the dining room mirror saying "Make peace not war!" "Brotherhood begins at home," or "Would you like to have yourself as a brother?"

Other examples include pinning a sign to a bike left outside: "I'm lonely and afraid of getting wet. Please take me to the garage." Or you might leave this note in a messy room: "I'm a mess. I feel awful like this and I'm afraid nobody cares about me. Would someone please clean me up."

You can try other novel means of capturing a child's attention, e.g., ring a cow bell to make an important announcement. Another effective way to arouse attention is to try to determine how the child expects you to react and do just the opposite. For example, rather than trying to calm a child down when he is in the midst of a temper tantrum, you could say, "Hey, that looks like fun," and stage a temper tantrum yourself. By being unpredictable and using surprise tactics, you can release tension, arouse children's interest, and inspire children to modify their usual way of responding (just as you have) or at least discuss possible new ways of solving problems.

7.   Get a Commitment

People are more likely to change or do something if they give their word and thus commit themselves. So ask a child, "Will you do it?" and occasionally ask the child to sign a written agreement. When a child commits himself to something publicly, i.e., in front of others, he feels even more obligated.

8.   Appeal to Norms

If you want a child to do something you can appeal to a value or norm that is beyond the individual ("It's for the group," "It's the rule".) rather than appeal to your personal interests ("Do it for me".). This may reduce the extent to which the other person views compliance as a matter of giving in to you and thus may reduce his resistance.

9. Door-in-the-Face-Technique

In this procedure you start with a request for action that is sure to be rejected, followed by a subsequent message requesting a more moderate outcome. Of course, the second moderate behavior is what you desired of the child from the beginning. This procedure works because we tend to make concessions to those who previously made concessions to us. For example, if you want your child to vacuum his room, you might first request that he vacuum all the upstairs bedrooms. When he balks, scale down your request and ask your child to give in a little too.

10. Give Some Freedom of Choice

Try to help children feel that what they are doing is their own idea. People like to feel that they are in control of their behavior, free to behave as they wish. If this feeling is reduced or threatened, the person may show resistance. Many studies have shown that a person with pressure on him to act a certain way not only may refuse to comply, but—to assert his freedom—may actually do the opposite. A child may purposefully foul up a piano recital when forced to perform in front of relatives.

Thus, whenever possible ask a child "What would you rather do, wash the dishes or take out the garbage?"—rather than saying, "Please take out the garbage." Giving a child *choices* conveys a feeling of more freedom.

11. Use Expert Testimony

You can sometimes persuade a child by the use of quotations from an authority or specialist. This principle is employed in testimonial advertising. It is clear that the testimony of certain respected individuals is accepted by children with less skepticism than that of others. For example, you might leave around the testimony of a child's athletic hero concerning the negative effects of drug abuse.

12. Appeal to Fear

Fear-producing communications have been found to be a relatively useful technique in effecting attitude change in teenagers, particularly in regard to cigarette smoking and drug abuse. Generally speaking, the more disastrous the predicted consequences, the more likely the attitude change. But this can be overdone. If you exaggerate the facts in order to intimidate a child, there is a high probability the child will discount your message as a "scare" tactic.

So be sure the harmful effects are not so extreme as to appear very unlikely, e.g., showing decaying mouths to children to promote tooth brushing. Also, be sure you know your facts so that children will perceive your information as highly credible. Moreover, clearly point out something the child can do to avoid the negative consequences.

13. Use Guilt

People who feel guilty about a recent wrongdoing, are more likely to perform a good behavior to expiate the guilt. Thus they are more likely to comply with a request for a good deed than people who do not feel guilty.

So you can increase the likelihood a child will comply with a request by first arousing feelings of guilt in her. You might say, for example, "Maureen, your sister feels very bad about your accidentally breaking her toy. Why don't you use your allowance money to buy some ice cream for you both?"

14. Have Your Child Pretend

Sometimes it is helpful to ask your child to pretend he is someone else, to put himself in another's place. You might ask the child how he would feel if he came to a new school and everyone ignored him. In this way he may act more friendly to a new classmate.

Also getting your teenager to pretend he has experienced cancer as a result of smoking can be a powerful influence on him to quit smoking.

THE EXTRAORDINARY POWER OF SUGGESTION WITH CHILDREN

To know how to suggest is the art of teaching.

—Amiel

Since children are especially suggestible, it is of vital importance that parents be familiar with the extraordinary power of suggestion. To suggest means to bring a thought to a child's mind for consideration. It often leads to an action which the child otherwise would not have taken. A suggestion carries practically no pressure to comply so that the freedom to act or not is left with the child. The power of suggestion depends, in large measure, on the blind faith that most children have in authority figures, especially their parents. Children tend to uncritically accept what their parents say as "the truth." This is particularly true if a positive relationship exists between parent and child.

Good parents learn to cut down on giving orders by using suggestions. They make suggestions by saying:

"You might want to consider this . . . "
"Maybe if we tried it this way . . . "
"You seem much stronger than you have ever been."

Questions can also be used as indirect requests:

"Must you play the piano?"
"Can you answer the phone?"

Accentuate the Positive, Eliminate the Negative

Positive Suggestions.   By positive suggestion you induce a child to engage in positive behaviors. Some examples are:

"If you try real hard you will do better. Everyone who has tried real hard has done better the second time and I'm sure you can too."
"You're going to feel better after you take this medicine."
"You're very tired and will probably go right to sleep now."
"I know you're going to be very brave when you get the shot from the doctor."

Instead of phrasing a question negatively (You don't want apricots, do you?"), ask it in a positive way (You do want apricots, don't you?"). The positive approach will result in much more compliance by the child. You might also try asking in an either/or way ("One dish of apricots or two?").

Negative Suggestions. A negative suggestion directs a child's thoughts to undesirable behaviors. Try to stop yourself before you give a negative suggestion to your child. Examples of negative suggestions are:

"Girls don't do well in math."
"John, you are going to drop that milk bottle."
"Stop playing with matches, you are going to set the rug on fire."
"You're just like your uncle; he came to a bad end."
"You're a bad child."
"You're going to end up in reform school."
"You'll never be a tennis player."
"You'll make a fool of yourself."

When you make a negative suggestion you will find that quite often the undesired behavior comes true. The child feels you know what you are talking about and tries to make your prediction come true. Negative suggestions lower a child's self-esteem by teaching him, "I can't do that," or "I'm no good."

Concluding Remarks

Even more effective than a direct suggestion with an older child is an indirect suggestion, i.e., the idea is not obviously the product of another but appears to arise within the mind of the child himself. For example, you might say to your child, "John, from what you've said I gather that you feel the best way to settle this is for you to ask your sister to return your toy?" In this regard, suggestions that seem to strengthen ideas already present in a child usually produce action.

People in crisis situations are particularly open to suggestion. So when under extreme stress your child may well accept a suggestion he would otherwise reject.

Also noteworthy is the fact that you can make a suggestion more effective by capitalizing on natural changes in a child's life development. For example, with an immature child, you might suggest that he will act more socially mature right after he has had a birthday or has gone away to camp.

Finally, physicians have long been aware of the power of suggestion to relieve certain psychosomatic disorders. A noted dermatologist, for example, reports that he often removes warts on children by having the child paint the wart with a harmless colorful dye while repeating this incantation:

> *"Every time I put this potion on, it is going to find the mother wart and the rest will die."*

If the child openly believes in magic this technique almost always works in five to seven days. The power of this suggestion procedure seems to derive from two sources, an authority figure and the magical chant.

SHOULD YOU REWARD YOUR CHILD FOR BEING GOOD?

> *Incentives are spurs that goad a man to do what he doesn't particularly like, to get something he does particularly want. They are rewards he voluntarily strives for.*
> —*Paul G. Hoffman*

> *Call it what you will, incentives are what get people to work harder.*
> —*Nikita Krushchev 1960*

> *Mankind has two masters: pleasure and pain.*
> —*Jeremy Bentham*

I never cease to be amazed by the power of rewards in influencing children. This power is derived from a basic law of human nature that you can put right to work for you in raising children. People tend to repeat acts which bring them pleasure or enjoyment while avoiding those they find unpleasant. So behavior rewarded tends to be repeated. Psychological studies have clearly shown that proper use of this principle can dramatically improve the behavior of even the most difficult child. Rewards are called "positive reinforcers" because they strengthen the behavior they follow. So a reward is anything that increases the likelihood a behavior will reoccur.

Although the use of rewards or incentives for good behavior sounds like an obvious, basic principle, many parents fail to use it. They either attend more to what is wrong with their children and fail to "catch them being good," or they believe children should not be rewarded for "doing what they're supposed to do."

It would be nice if children behaved appropriately all the time just because they are supposed to, but it just doesn't work that way. Children, like adults, need incentives to improve their behavior. Indeed, adults make frequent use of incentives in their daily interactions. Businesses give bonuses or merit pay for superior performances; police departments offer rewards for information leading to the capture of criminals; the IRS grants tax rebates for those who invest in energy-saving devices; and mail-order companies give premiums to customers who enclose payment with an order.

Types of Rewards

There are two types of rewards: social and nonsocial. Social rewards involve praise and approving attention from people. A nonsocial reinforcer includes either a tangible thing or a privilege, such as food, money, a toy, or a special activity. For example, being able to stay up late, going to a movie, or getting an ice-cream cone are all examples of nonsocial positive rewards. The use of nonsocial rewards will be discussed here, while a following section will describe the use of parental praise and approval.

Grandma's Rule.   One type of reward that parents often use has been called "Grandma's rule." Basically, this rule states that work must come before pleasure. Thus the everyday rewards or pleasant events in the home are made contingent upon the performance of work or unpleasant activities in the home. Examples of this rule are the following statements to a child: "Eat your vegetables and then you can have dessert," "You may visit your friend after you take out the trash," or "When you finish cleaning your room, we'll make cookies."

The Difference Between a Bribe and a Reward

A reward is a compensation for good, meritorious, or desired behaviors, while a bribe is a payoff to stop inappropriate behavior. For effective rewards, *first* the appropriate behavior occurs, and *then* the reward is given. Bribery reverses this order—the payoff comes *before* the appropriate behavior. So a bribe is given to stop misbehavior (a child is given 25 cents to stop fighting) or to prevent misbehavior from occurring ("I'll give you a cookie now if you promise not to throw a tantrum in the supermarket.")

Guidelines for Giving Rewards

1. Be systematic in giving rewards by using the following three-step approach:

    Be Specific. Pick only one or two very specific, concrete, and observable behaviors to reward. Don't reward a child for some vague, global trait such as being good; rather reinforce more specific behaviors such as sharing his toys with others or sitting quietly in a restaurant.

    Contingent Rewards. Make the reward *contingent* upon the desired behavior by a "when-then" statement: "When you eat your vegetables then you can have dessert."

    Evaluate. Keep a record. The more you monitor a child's progress by counting and making a record of the frequency of the desired act the more you will be able to note progress or lack of it. Check off on a calendar every day in which the desired behavior occurs. Regularly review your success or lack of it and revise your procedures as necessary, i.e., find a more powerful reward; try for a small behavior change. A common error most of us make is to demand too much for too small a reward when we begin to teach something new to a child. The first little steps by a child need big rewards!

2. Use anything the child likes as a reward—any high-frequency behavior. Thus if your child likes to read but forgets to wash dishes, use "Grandma's rule" and make reading in the evening contingent upon washing dishes. If your child likes to eat vegetables but not meat, make a portion of vegetables the reward for eating a portion of meat.

The more you know your children and their individual interests, likes, and activities, the more skillful you will be in finding effective rewards. So observe what your child likes, and what he spends his free time doing. Knowledge of child development is also helpful. For instance, candy has been found to be a more effective reward with 4–5 year olds than praise. Older children will not be as motivated by food or games but will work for special privileges and extra money.

How much of a reward should you give? Try to match the amount to the difficulty level of the desired behavior.

3. *Give Sparingly.* Don't reward a child for everything he does or else he'll expect to be rewarded for anything and everything. He'll develop the habit of thinking "What's in it for me?" Children need to learn that some things must be done because they are a necessary part of life. They also need to develop internal sources of self-satisfaction, i.e., virtue and success are sources of rewards in themselves. As with anything else, rewards should be used with moderation and should be faded out as soon as possible.

Rewards should be reserved for situations where you need to give your child a boost to perform a difficult or new behavior. So rewards are for motivating children to make an effort to improve their behavior. They are not for maintaining past standards of performance.

4. Sometimes it is a good idea to give the child an immediate token reward, such as a star on a chart, for good behavior. The tokens are later traded in for tangible rewards (7 stars for a special toy) or special privileges (12 stars for a trip to the movies.)

A rough rule of thumb is that one generally moves from tokens (stars, smiling faces, poker chips) for very young children, to points for children just before and at the beginning of adolescence, then on to the contingency contracts for teenagers and young adults.

5. To first establish a behavior in your child you should reward continually. Once the behavior is firmly established you should give the reward only sparingly, e.g., only reward after 2–3 good behaviors. Occasional rewards have been found to have more lasting effects on behavior than rewarding every time.

6. Concrete rewards should always be given in conjunction with social reinforcers, i.e., praise, affection, appreciation, individual attention.

In this way the concrete reward can be gradually phased out and replaced with just the social rewards. Frequent use of both primary (tangible) and secondary (social) reinforcers helps create a positive orientation in the home, that is, a feeling that there are numerous rewards and satisfactions for appropriate participation in family life. In subsequent sections the use of social rewards will be discussed, i.e., praise, adult attention.

7. There are three general conditions for rewarding children. In the first case, you tell the child in advance that he will receive a reward only if he performs a certain desired behavior. In the second case, you say nothing in advance but give a reward after you notice a child performing the desired behavior. The third situation involves giving a reward for no specific behavior but just because you like the child or the way he generally behaves. The first condition is advisable when the child rarely if ever performs the behavior you desire because of low motivation, fear, anxiety, or special difficulty. The second condition works well when you wish to increase the frequency of an appropriate behavior that already occurs with some regularity. The third condition is best when you want to show general approval or appreciation of the child's behavior.

8. Reinforce Only Desired Behavior. A common pitfall of parents is to take good behavior for granted and to pay attention to those behaviors they really don't like in their children. To scold a child you must pay attention to him; this attention may actually reinforce the misbehavior. The solution here is to give the positive reinforcement (attention) to support only desired behavior. If your child is playing quietly, go over and praise him for doing so, or maybe even give him an edible treat, such as popcorn. Ignore the times he plays noisily.

Families with problem children often reinforce deviant behaviors at a high rate while prosocial behaviors are often ignored or rewards are given in a noncontingent manner.[3]

PRAISE AND APPROVAL: POSITIVE WAYS TO BRING OUT THE BEST IN CHILDREN

Words of praise, indeed, are almost as necessary to warm a child into a congenial life as acts of kindness and affection. Judicious praise is to children what the sun is to flowers.

—Bovee

I could live a week on one good compliment.

—Mark Twain

I praise loudly; I blame softly.

—Catherine II

Praise is like champagne; it should be served while it is still bubbling.
—Robins Reader

Any fool can criticize, condemn, and complain—and most of them do.
—Dale Carnegie

Censure cramps the soul and makes the imperfect task forever hateful; praise expands every cell, energizes every organ and makes even the most difficult undertaking an adventure and a victory.

—Will Durant

I. Praise

Praise means to give a realistic, positive appraisal of a child's performance. So by praising children you point out and validate the worth of their achievement. The goal of praise is to show in a clear, objective way that there is cause for the child to feel proud of her work. An observing parent will find many opportunities during the day to give positive feedback. For example, you might say, "That was a very thoughtful thing you just did."; "You really know a lot about science."; "You were really patient while I was on the phone."

Importance.   The educator John Dewey said that the deepest urge in human nature is the desire to feel important. Praise gives children the needed sense of worth, competence, and confidence. This positive feedback is particularly important for inferiority-prone or shy children. When parents change their feedback from being primarily negative to being mostly positive, a new atmosphere develops in the home. Interpersonal vibrations change and family members are drawn closer to one another. Somehow a child's ability to absorb failure and take risks increases.

An observation of daily parent-child interactions often reveals that words of praise and approval are usually few and far between.

Many parents feel funny giving praise for behaviors a child is "expected to do." When behaviors are taken for granted, however, the child either slows them down or performs them without enthusiasm and they die out. Parents appreciate a word of recognition from each other when they have worked long and hard around the house preparing a meal, cleaning the yard, fixing up a room, etc. Children, too, need to hear from others that their efforts and accomplishments are noticed and valued.

Rather than praising, parents tend to blame and punish a lot. Parents with a "red pencil mentality" take good behavior for granted while frequently criticizing and finding fault with their children. However, improvement in behavior elicited by blame has been found to dissipate over time, while that elicited by praise persists. So instead of "kicking your children in the pants," aim higher and give them a "pat on the back."

Guidelines for Praising Children.

1. *Be Specific.*   In praising children avoid vague, general words such as "terrific," "good," "wonderful." When you use such global evaluative adjectives you tend to exaggerate which makes children feel uneasy since they know they did not really do that well. Rather, zero in and describe specifically what worthwhile behavior you observed. So instead of saying "What a terrific drawing!" you might say "That drawing really gives me a feeling of being at the beach."

    Be sure to praise observable actions of the child, not the whole child. Haim Ginott, the noted child psychologist, once observed that "Direct praise of personality, like direct sunlight, is uncomfortable and blinding." Thus we should not praise a child's total personality ("You're a great kid!") but rather the child's specific behaviors. Statements which describe in a very specific way the commendable aspects of a child's behavior ("It takes a lot of strength to move that heavy workbench."), then, are more informative, realistic, and more apt to prompt self-praise. Research studies have verified the fact that young children show more positive changes in their behavior as a result of descriptive rather than "person-oriented" praise. They seem able to draw positive inferences about themselves from descriptive comments about why you admire their behavior, i.e., they learn to praise themselves. Clearly, it takes both thought and subtlety to praise well.

2. *Be Sincere; Avoid Flattery and Manipulation*
   A. *Flattery.*

> *Whenever you commend, add your reasons for doing so; it is this which distinguishes the approbation of a man of sense from the flattery of sycophants and admiration of fools.*
>
> —*Steele*

> *As the Greek said, many men know how to flatter; few know how to praise.*
> —*Wendell Phillips*

When you flatter your goal is to make the child think well of you or to make the child like you. Sincere praise, on the other hand, does not seek to ingratiate oneself to another; it seeks to make the other more aware of their worthwhile behavior.

B. *Manipulation.* Manipulation means using praise as a way of getting a child to do something you want. For example, I know of one father who always wanted to become a big-league baseball player but never did. He started telling his son who was on a Little League team how great a player he was and how one day he'd be a big leaguer. This type of praise was perceived as a subtle form of pressure by the boy who soon lost interest in playing baseball. So don't magnify or overemphasize a child's accomplishment as a way to boost your ego or the child's personality. If your expectations or image of a child are too high, most likely you will frighten a child. So a compliment should be objective and given without ulterior motives.

3. *Don't Mix Praise and Criticism.* Avoid using praise as a form of implied criticism:

> "You did a good job—at last."
> "You played very nicely this afternoon for a change."
> "That's good, now why didn't you do that before?"
> "Well, *finally* you've done it right."

4. *Give Immediately.* In general, it is best to give praise immediately, preferably while the child is still in the act. However, it is also effective to tell a child that you have been thinking about something he or she did a while ago and then give a compliment.

5. *Indirect Praise.* Often it is effective to praise a child indirectly and casually by talking about him at a time when the child can hear it. In this way, there is no implied demand on the child to behave in a certain way—it is just a statement of fact and respect.

6. *Use in Moderation.* Give praise in moderation. Like frosting on a cake—if you give too little it is not sweet enough; if you give too much it is too sweet. Freely give praise when it is due because of effort or achievement, but do not overuse praise by giving it for every little thing a child does.

7. *Evaluate the Effect of Your Praise on a Child.* Parental praise can either please a child or turn a child off. If a child has low self-esteem, praise loses credibility because the child can't believe it and feels unworthy. Also a perfectionistic child will find fault with your praise because he is not satisfied with his work.

   With some children you need to reaffirm the compliment if they have difficulty believing it. Say, "Maybe you don't feel that way, but this is the way I feel."

8. *When to Praise, When to Use Concrete Rewards.* Children under the age of 5 seem most receptive to concrete rewards such as candy, toys, or pennies. Children over 12 years of age are as responsive, if not more so, to social rewards such as praise from parents.

9. *Likelihood of Acceptance.* Children will be more likely to accept your praise if you have a positive relationship with them, if they believe you are trustworthy, and if they regard you as quite knowledgeable about the praised behavior.

10. *Overjustification.* What happens if you reward something a child

likes to do for its own sake, like drawing. One study found verbal praise enhanced the desire to draw for the fun of it; but concrete rewards (e.g. money) decreased the children's intrinsic motivation (overjustification effect).

11. *Self-Praise.*   Encourage your children to evaluate their own performance. In the last analysis the value and meaning of an experience is up to the child. One way to get your children in the habit of praising themselves after they have behaved well is to describe how good the act must make them feel. The following examples illustrate an attempt to foster self-evaluation in a child by imaginatively putting yourself in the child's shoes and expressing the feeling:

> "Looks like you had a good time painting that!"
> "You worked hard on the poster and it must make you feel proud to gain recognition."
> "I imagine it was hard for you to tell the truth when your teacher was yelling so loud."
> "You really fixed that for me quickly. How did you think of doing it that way?"
> "This is a good report card. You must be proud of your ability to learn so well."

By giving positive feedback of this nature you not only let children know you are aware of their efforts and achievements but you are helping them become independent by reinforcing their own judgment and self-confidence. You are assisting children to develop an internal locus of evaluation that is realistic and verifiable.

12. *Modeling Self-Praise.*   Studies have shown that parents with low self-esteem tend to foster the same attitude in their children.[4] So open up and make positive comments about yourself to your children. Appreciating your own work is not being proud or vain.

In order to create a family climate in which self-encouragement and self-praise are acceptable, try praising yourself in front of your children whenever you do something well or are proud of it. Since children learn best by imitation and modeling, they will learn to develop a positive attitude about their own accomplishments.

The use of this technique will be difficult because most adults have been taught that it is inappropriate to praise yourself or toot your own horn.

To begin using this procedure, practice self-praise internally, then vocalize praise of your work, and then move on to praising your personal qualities. You might explain to your children that you are praising yourself because you want to teach them how to be appreciative of their own efforts and qualities; that it is important for everyone in the family to value themselves and their efforts; that use of self-praise usually results in one performing desired behaviors more often in the future.

Noteworthy is the fact that research has indicated that self-praise and praise of others are positively correlated. It seems that one learns the general skill of praise-giving. It also seems logical that the more you can accept praise from yourself, the more comfortable you will be receiving it from others.

A complete description of the self-praise technique is contained in the book by D. W. Felker, entitled, *Building Positive Self-Concepts,* Burgess Publishing Co., 1974.

II.   Approval

The deepest principle in human nature is the craving to be appreciated.
—*William James*

Appreciation is like an insurance policy. It has to be renewed every now and then.
—*Dave McIntyre*

Approval refers to the expression of your personal liking of a child's behavior. Approval says, "I like what you did." Praise says, "What you did is truly exceptional and worthwhile." Thus, praise has a more objective standard of evaluation. Approval indicates that what a child does, although not extraordinary, is valued.

Examples of approval statements are:

"I'm glad you changed your shirt—you look neat."
"I appreciate your hanging up your clothes even though you were in a hurry to go out to play."
"I like the way you come in for dinner without being called."

Nonverbal approval messages include smiles, head nods, winks, a gentle squeeze of the hand or pat on the back, and turning "thumbs up."

THE IMPORTANCE OF SETTING A GOOD EXAMPLE FOR CHILDREN

Example is not the main thing in influencing others. It is the only thing.
—Albert Schweitzer

What you are thunders so loudly I cannot hear what you are saying.
—Emerson

Whatever you would have your children become, strive to exhibit in your own lives and conversation.
—Mrs. Sigourney

Children have more need of models than of critics.
—Joubert

A. Modeling By Parents

How we parents behave probably does as much or more than anything else to shape our children's character and behavior. Thus, studies show that if parents smoke there is a higher probability their children will also. If parents overuse drugs or act violently, their children are more likely to exhibit similar behaviors. Good parents appreciate the fact that the power of a good example is one of their most valuable tools. They know that children observe them as they go about their daily life, and that their own example will influence children far more than verbal advice or preaching.

Modeling refers to the example parents set for children by their daily actions. Children are the world's greatest mimics. They continually imitate what they see and absorb what they hear. Modeling tends to be more effective than words alone since your actions provide a clearer example to copy.

Sometimes parents don't practice what they preach. If you have temper outbursts when frustrated but punish children for this reaction, you set a double standard that confuses the child. It's very difficult—sometimes impossible—to expect children to behave more maturely than you do. If you are usually late or messy yourself, how can you insist that children be on time or neat? The words will go in one ear and out the other. So when you have difficulty getting children to measure up to the moral or behavior standards you insist on, take a close look at yourself. Do you measure up to these standards? Are you practicing them wholeheartedly or just preaching for the benefit of the children? If you don't believe in something enough to practice it yourself, preaching seldom does much good. It is important to become more aware of situations where your actions contradict your words to a child.

Accentuate Positive Behaviors.   Mature parents will strive to set positive examples for their children in a variety of ways, including: facing daily problems with good judgment, common sense, and a willingness to accept the consequences of their actions; maintaining control over their emotions; applying themselves diligently to tasks and taking pride in their work; exhibiting an optimistic outlook on life; finding joy in present activities rather than becoming overly concerned about past deeds or future projects; deepening their close, loving relationships; expanding their circle of friends and acquaintances; searching for additional knowledge throughout their lifetimes; and endeavoring to become more aware of the ideals and values which give meaning and direction to their lives.

Decrease the Negatives.   Fears are extremely contagious. There is a considerable body of psychological literature which indicates that most of the fears of children are learned—either from their parents or from other children. Thus, if you readily reveal your fears in front of your children, e.g., fear of strangers, of the dark, of snakes, of big dogs, of heights, of dying, then the odds are greater that your children will acquire them by imitation. As far as possible, then, parents should summon up their courage and keep their fears under cover when children are around.

If you're not able to really conceal your fears, you should openly acknowledge them, e.g., "Gee, that scared us both, I guess." By admitting fears, you can strip away some of their sinister qualities and help relieve the obvious tension in children.

Apart from fears, you should try to control your negative attitudes, prejudices, and personal dislikes. If, for example, a mother has a negative attitude towards housework and continually complains while doing these tasks, there is a good chance that her children will develop an adverse outlook towards their household chores and possibly to work in general. Similarly, if a parent has a personal dislike for certain foods, that parent is well advised to keep these dislikes to herself.

In addition to keeping your fears, prejudices, and undesirable attitudes to yourself, you should also avoid using fear threats as a means of disciplining a child or even in jest. Examples of fear threats are:

"The boogey man will get you if you do that."
"There is a witch (monster) outside who will eat you if you ever talk to me like that again."
"Something terrible will happen to you for that."

Increase Your Modeling Power

Research indicates that the following behaviors will increase the likelihood that children will imitate your behavior:

1. Display any positive feelings you have toward desired behaviors. For example, show the enthusiasm and interest you have for certain tasks by saying, "This is really fun and it is so easy!" In short, you can make an activity more appealing and attractive to kids when you make it seem enjoyable. The best teachers are the ones who are enthusiastic about what they are doing.
2. If you have a close, warm, and caring relationship with a child, the child will be more likely to follow your example.
3. Imitation of your behavior is more likely if the child views you as possessing a high degree of competence, status, and control over resources.
4. Behavior that is followed by some positive reinforcement, e.g., praise, material reward, is more apt to be imitated.
5. The use of several models exhibiting similar behavior is more effective in influencing behavior than the use of a single model.

B. Modeling By Others

Although parents are by far the most influential models in a child's life, children will also imitate other persons for whom they have respect, admiration, and/or affection. Thus, effective models for your children include older siblings, baby-sitters, neighborhood friends, teachers, public figures, highly successful people, and fictional heroes. To assist your child in attending to these models, try pointing out features of the model's behavior that you want emulated. For example, you might observe, "Gee, your friend Maria always leaves promptly when her mother calls her!" Praising or rewarding a model for desired behavior in front of your child is another way to get your child to attend to the behavior. Once your child exhibits the desired behavior, be sure to praise the act.

Television is a medium that has the potential to expose your child to considerable prosocial or antisocial modeling, particularly if your child is a heavy viewer, i.e., over four hours a day. There is a great deal of evidence now to indicate that you would be wise to monitor your child's viewing so as to minimize exposure to shows of violence and programs which are designed to produce fear or fright.

The characters in books can also act as models for your children. By choosing books that convey meaningful morals and lessons, you can help your child learn important values and coping skills.

Discussion

In regard to prosocial modeling by others, it is noteworthy that a model can influence your child's behavior in two ways.

1. The model can engage in a behavior that your child has never experienced before and thereby induce your child to do something new, e.g., attend sleep away camp.
2. The model can do something already familiar to your child and thereby induce your child to engage in this particular behavior rather than some other behavior, e.g., being respectful rather than discourteous to adults.

HOW A "CONTRACT" CAN IMPROVE YOUR CHILD'S BEHAVIOR

A contract is a formal written agreement which spells out specifically what you want from a child and what you are willing to give in return. A contract is a very useful tool with children for three reasons:

1. It makes *crystal clear* your expectations and intentions about desired behavioral changes in a child. It is surprising the degree of ambiguity that exists in many homes as to what behavioral changes are expected of children and what the consequences will be for changing or not changing these behaviors. Contracts spell out *who* is to do *what* for *whom* under what *circumstances*.

2. The emphasis is on the *positive reinforcement* the child will receive for improving her behavior. So rewards are used as incentives, rather than punishment. Often parents get into the habit of showing little positive feedback towards a troublesome child. Consequently, the relationship between parent and child is marked by coercion rather than cooperation. Contracts can reverse this vicious cycle of conflict and alienation by emphasizing the positive, rewarding exchanges that can cement a parent-child relationship.

3. Both parties make a commitment to fulfill the agreement. Most children believe that because they have *signed* the contract, they have the responsibility to carry it out. Also, the parents' signatures give a child more faith that the parents will fulfill their part of the agreement.

   There are two types of contracts you can use with children. A "reward contract" specifies the rewards you will give a child for changing his behavior. Examples of rewards are an extra allowance or the privilege of staying up an hour later at night. In a "reciprocal contract" you agree to change some aspect of your behavior that the child finds unpleasant, e.g., stop nagging, if he agrees to change some aspect of his behavior for you, e.g., start attending school regularly. Older children and teenagers sometimes prefer reciprocal contracts.

Behaviors you might ask your child to change by means of a contract are:

1. Do 90 minutes of homework a night from 7:00 to 8:30.
2. Make his bed and hang up his clothes before he goes to school.
3. Less talking back or arguing when given a directive.
4. Improve her grades in French from failing to passing.
5. Attend classes at school every day with less than two tardies per month.
6. Be home by 10 o'clock weekday nights and midnight on weekend nights.

Behavior changes your child might ask of you in return are:

1. Stop nagging about . . .
2. A private phone.
3. Give $____ per week.
4. Use of the family car (to) ____.

Guidelines for Contracts

1. *The negotiation of a contract must be open and honest, free from explicit or subtle coercion.*   Mutual respect and voluntary agreement must characterize the important negotiation process.
2. *The terms of a contract should be as specific as possible.* Responsibilities and rewards should be described in terms of specific, observable behavior. The contract should state, "Earn a C grade or better on the weekly quiz," rather than "Do better in class." Doing better in class is vague and will mean different things to different people. A common mistake in writing contracts is to use vague, general terms so as to ease the negotiation between parents and children. Each party can interpret a vague statement in ways advantageous to himself. When everyone is clear about each clause of a contract and agrees to abide by all the clauses, they should sign a statement to indicate their commitment.
3. *The contract must provide advantages to each party over the status quo.*   Each party should be able to get more for his involvement in the contract than he is currently getting. Creative problem solving is needed so each derives a net gain from the agreement. Be sure there are no loopholes in the contract which allow one person to take advantage of the other.

4. *The child must be able to perform his part of the contract without undue hardship.* Parents often make the mistake of asking too much from a child. The task you ask of a child must be easily achievable. A contract should set the stage for success and accomplishment.

SAMPLE CONTRACTS

CONTRACT

Date_____

This is an agreement between <u>Eric Smith</u> and <u>his mother</u>
                                      (child's name)   (parent's name)

The contract begins on _____ and ends on _____.
                                 (date)   (date)

It will be reviewed on _____.
                            (date)
The terms of the agreement are: I, Eric Smith, will ____

_____

_____ .

I, Eric's mother, will _____

_____ .

If Eric fulfills his part of the contract he will receive the agreed upon reward from his mother. However, if he fails to fulfill his part of the contract, the rewards will be withheld.

Child's signature _____

Parent's signature _____

CONTRACT

Effective dates: October 15–
October 22

I, Eric Smith, agree to complete my homework assignments each day (Sunday through Thursday).

I, Eric's father, agree to allow Eric to extend curfew hours to 10:00 P.M. on weeknights and 12:30 A.M. on weekend nights if he has completed his homework assignments each day.

We agree to the above conditions.

_____

Child's signature, date

_____

Parent's signature, date

This contract will be reviewed on the ending date of agreement.

CONTRACT

I, John Adams, do hereby agree to wash the boat, keep the motor greased, and make sure that all gear is treated and stored. These tasks will be done promptly after each use during the months of July and August. In payment, I will receive $5.00 per week—it being understood that this is half pay because I enjoy the boat too.

Signed _____
       (child)

Signed _____
       (parent)

Date _____

ADDITIONAL READING

DeRisi, W. J. and Butz, G. *Writing Behavioral Contracts.* Research Press, 1974.

"SHAPING UP" A CHILD'S BEHAVIOR

Often the behavior you desire from your child is a rather big, complex task that is difficult to achieve all at once. Children tend to become discouraged when too much is expected of them in too short a period of time. They tend to learn slowly by taking small steps. It is often advisable, therefore, to break a complex task down into its component parts and to ask a child to perform only a small segment of the whole at first. Thus, rather than asking your child to perform the complex task of cleaning her room, you might ask her initially to put all the toys in her room in the toy box. The following week you might request that she also dust the furniture and window sills in her room. The next week you might ask her to vacuum the room as well. The idea in shaping is that you *gradually* move a child toward a desired behavior, rather than requiring a total behavior change.

After identifying the desired behavior goal, list all the steps the child needs to do to reach the goal. For example, to get a B+ in math your daughter (who is failing the subject) would first have to get a passing grade, then a C, then a B, and finally a B+. Then tell your child of the initial change you desire (passing grade) and reward the achievement of this goal. Then reward further steps toward the final goal. Slow down if the child isn't able to reach a step. Make the learning steps smaller. The most common error of parents is in trying for too big a behavior change in the child.

Guidelines

1. Begin the shaping procedure by analyzing the task to determine the various steps or parts of which it consists. Then arrange these parts of the task in a series. Place them in a natural order proceeding in a step-wise fashion from the most basic or elementary part of the task to the most complex or difficult behavior. Each step should require a little more of the child than the one before. After the child performs each step easily be sure to reward him and then require that he perform the next step. Continue in this manner until he is performing the complex behavior task. For example, if you want your six-year-old to make her bed, begin by teaching her to pull the sheet up over the pillow; then ask her to pull the blanket up over

the sheet; then tuck in the blanket; and so on until the child has mastered the complex task of making a bed.

2. Sometimes you have to reward your child for performing acts that are, at first, only remotely similar to your final goal. Suppose, for example, that you wish to have your child play cooperatively with others. First you would reward him for not teasing or being verbally abusive to his peers, then for sharing his possessions with others, then for playing by the rules of a game, and so on. This principle of "successive approximations" involves rewarding your child for behaviors that, at first, are only slightly related to your goal. Once the child learns these remote behaviors and they seem firmly established, you then reward behaviors that are successively closer and closer to the final goal. The point is you have to start somewhere and that somewhere may be quite a distance from the final goal when dealing with children. Shaping desired behaviors, then, requires considerable patience which is difficult for parents living hectic lives.

3. In teaching young children new skills, e.g., combing hair by a four-year-old, you may first have to reinforce the attempt. Then reward a better attempt next time. In teaching a young child to tie his shoes you might initially reinforce pulling the strings tight; then pulling a string through one hole, etc. Reward the child with praise, attention, stars, toys (whatever is meaningful) for meeting each step towards the goal. If the child is unable to meet your request, return to the level where success can be attained. This only means that you are going too fast and must slow down.

4. By setting the difficulty level of tasks just below your child's felt competency, you ensure that the child tastes success immediately and regularly. This will, of course, nurture a child's self-esteem and self-confidence.

5. By careful planning and execution, parents should be able to achieve step-by-step growth in a variety of new child behaviors, such as throwing a ball, table manners; and in eliminating unwanted behavior such as dawdling, and so on. The key is to think small and reward large. Usually we require steps that are too large. Remember that it is better to have steps toward a final goal that are too small rather than too large.

CHALLENGING YOUR CHILDREN TO DO THEIR BEST

A challenge involves striving for something just beyond easy reach so you have to stretch in order to achieve it. The purpose of challenging your children, then, is to motivate them to raise their sights and reach a little higher level of achievement. Hopefully children will internalize this striving for improvement and will become ambitious. Ambition can be defined as the setting of increasingly challenging goals for oneself.

We parents tend to expect too little of children. We fail to realize when they are ready for growth and mastery.

The challenge aspect is often crucial for a child's growth. As the noted psychologist Piaget has pointed out, unless there is disequilibrium or imbalance between some aspects of a child's environment and himself, there will be no motive for change nor movement to a higher stage of development.

How do parents know when to expect more from their child? The truth is no simple formulas exist for determining a child's readiness to perform a specific task. Children develop at different rates. We need to study each child as objectively as possible to learn what they are capable of and when they are ready for new experiences and new learning. Observing other children of a similar age and ability can give us general norms which we can adapt to a particular child. Don't assume that if a child balks or resists that he is not ready. To challenge children to grow often means to endure their resistance.

Set Standards

Children need their parents to set standards of behavior. The standards of behavior should be low enough to reach but high enough to strive for. They must challenge and stretch them to attain their full potential, to put out their best effort.

For children with above average ability in some area, doing their best will involve striving for excellence, that is, for superior achievement. In recent decades there seems to have been a decline in the quality of work in American society.[5] Slipshod craftmanship by adults and lowered academic achievement by students are clearly in evidence. A new egalitarian attitude has emerged which adopts a mediocre standard of performance for everything and everybody. No person or thing is deemed superior or inferior to any other. In reality, some people possess superior talent to others and parents should expect and insist that their children perform at the highest level possible.

The more clearly you set up excellence as the goal, the more your children will respond to the message. Though not every child is equipped to excel, you will be establishing a climate that encourages those who have ability. This means avoiding comparisons between one individual's achievements and another's. When children understand that your focus is on excellence, not on competition, they will begin to follow suit.

Parents set standards of excellence and high achievement by expecting and insisting that their children meet certain achievement levels from an early age, by showing an interest in and monitoring a child's progress, and by giving children explicit feedback as to their performance. You give a child evaluative feedback by reacting to her successes with warmth and approval, and with disappointment when the child performs poorly.

Various studies have shown that parents of children who demonstrated high achievement in school and in their careers had set achievement standards for the children which were high and explicit.[6,7] These parents had strict requirements for their children in terms of homework, school attendance, library work, and reading. Also, the parents tended to model high achievement in their own lives. One study[8] asked parents of highly successful children how important it was for their child to "grow up to attain a standard of excellence." A total of 71 percent of the parents rated this as very important. Also noteworthy is the fact that a recent survey of teachers revealed that they were almost unanimous in favoring requiring higher standards of performance from students in schools. This was a nationwide teacher opinion poll conducted by the National Education Association in 1978.

> *Few things in life are as important as the pride of craftsmanship, at whatever level it may occur—the pride in a job well done.*
> —*Brooke Allen*

The Competitive Edge

To compete means to enter into a rivalry by trying to surpass something, whether it be your own past level of performance, or the performance of others. You might challenge a child to compete with himself by saying, "I bet you're too young to do this!"; "Do you think you could build a bigger tower?"; "Can you get dressed before the sand in this egg timer runs out?"; or "Can you push the peanut butter into all the corners of the bread without getting any on the table?" These challenges are effective when a child is clearly able to do something but is poorly motivated to attempt it. Preschool children, in particular, respond well to such challenges. Be sure to be appropriately surprised, impressed, and pleased when your child accepts the challenge and accomplishes the task.

Appealing to a child's drive to compete with others, to do as well or better than other people, is another effective way to motivate children. Thus, rather than telling your children to stop slouching at the dinner table, you could say, "Let's see who can sit the straightest" Or you might suggest, "Let's have a race to see who can pick up the most books from the floor." Seeing other children perform tasks she is capable of will stimulate your child to exert a greater effort to succeed.

Since American children have been found to be more competitive than children of other nations, competition must be used with discretion in this country. It should only be employed when winning or losing does not produce a great deal of anxiety. Competition can be used effectively to increase performance on simple, relatively unimportant tasks, such as stacking firewood, driving a golf ball, shooting pool, or developing good posture. It is particularly appropriate when there is no set criterion to evaluate individual performance so that comparison with others is the only source of evaluatory feedback.

Encourage Risk Taking

If children are to grow they need to leave their safe physical, emotional, and intellectual existence and take prudent risks. A risk involves facing the possibility of failing, losing, or encountering danger. Opportunity for growth and risk-taking are often unseparable. Research has indicated that people who achieve at high levels take moderate risks[7]. They are not "risk avoiders" nor do they take reckless chances.

When children lack genuine challenges and adventure in their daily lives they often seek excitement elsewhere. Some turn to violence for this excitement, while others choose to abuse drugs or sexually act out.

CELEBRATE FAMILY LIFE BY RITUALS AND CEREMONIES

Rituals or ceremonies are what make certain days different from all the other days. Family rituals are special ceremonies which are observed by the family at certain times, in accord with prescribed rules. It is helpful to establish a number of rituals in the home. In addition to traditional observance of national holidays and religious events, many families have added their own special rituals, such as a festive meal and entertainment by talented family members on special occasions. Rituals bond a family together and give it pleasure.

Children gain in many ways by taking part in special ceremonies. Rituals mark the passage of time and thus give stability and predictability to life. They offer children a chance to give, as well as to receive. They relieve the monotony of everyday living.

Parents who want their children to be guided more by ideas and ideals than by dollar signs and things should make a point of discussing the true meaning of national and religious holidays with their children. Parents should also join fully with the children in observing these holidays. Homemade decorations and mementos can cut down on costs and increase your family's sense of personal involvement in the occasion.

Rituals to Honor Individuals

Ceremonies honoring individual family members can be used to add zest and enthusiasm to family living. A ceremony is an interesting, exciting event that makes a child the center of attention. It can be used to reward children, or show approval, or caring.

The use of ceremonies as a technique for motivating children to achieve or perform desirable behaviors has held a prominent place in many character-building projects, e.g., girl and boy scouts. Moreover, churches have long used rites and ceremonies to inspire awe and reverence, as well as to celebrate or commemorate special occasions.

Parents should make regular use of ceremonies to give their children added incentive to achieve, e.g., recognize a child's intellectual, emotional, or social achievement by a special cake, trophy, speech, party, or family gathering. Ceremonies can also be used to express general love and caring for a child, e.g., a "nonbirthday" party.

In addition, they can serve to give public notice of a child's "rite of passage" into a more advanced developmental level, e.g., becoming a man or a woman (puberty or reaching the voting age). The purpose of such family rituals is not only to foster pride by publicly recognizing and celebrating the event, but also to notify all concerned to expect more mature behavior from the child.

Ceremonies make an event memorable by their novelty, the intensity of emotion, and the feeling of family sharing and camaraderie.

WHY YOU SHOULD "GET AWAY" FROM YOUR CHILDREN FOR A WHILE

Strategic withdrawal is sometimes the best tactic when you are in conflict with your child. Rather than allowing a conflict to escalate when either or both of you are upset, try leaving the scene for a while. Retire to the bathroom or bedroom and lock the door. Be sure to stock your retreat room with a magazine rack filled with literature and a radio to shut out the noise of a child who is crying or yelling. You will often find that the disturbance dramatically ends when you do this and that the children were quite able to cope with the situation themselves. A temper tantrum, for instance, is no fun unless there is an audience. It is also very difficult to continue complaining, arguing, or whining when no one is listening.

When you take a "time-out," your child will probably increase his misbehavior to get you to return. Be firm and ignore these tactics. Only return if the safety of the child is endangered or the child is doing something that absolutely cannot be tolerated; in this case, calmly punish without comment, and again return to your place of withdrawal. The chances are the child will stop acting up in the future when he sees that his efforts are not worth the undesirable outcomes.

The distancing technique is very similar to the time-out approach discussed later, except that instead of removing the child from the situation you remove yourself. The effect tends to be essentially the same.

More extensive forms of parent-child distancing, e.g., a child attending summer camp, visiting relatives, or living at a boarding school, are sometimes effective in relieving explosive parent-child conflict situations.

Case Illustration

Mary, the mother of a hyperactive four-year-old boy seldom got through a day without screaming.[9] Since her son gave up naps more than a year ago she didn't have time for a break all day long.

As each day progressed, tempers would flare, voices would rise, and soon they would be screaming at each other. On the verge of child abuse, the mother sought advice. She learned to go into another room to cool off instead of screaming. Also when she threatened punishment she now made sure she followed through so her son learned she meant business. At the end of the first nonscreaming day her son said, "This was a good day, wasn't it Mommy? I love today!"

"Couple" Time

It's important for a husband and wife to get away by themselves sometimes. If people had to work at a job seven days a week, they would be likely to hate it or become stale at it. The same goes for being a parent. Some parents arrange to have a date with each other once a week and regularly schedule a baby-sitter for the children. This not only helps them relax but keeps their romance alive. Brief or extended vacations are especially important for parents who wish to avoid becoming "burnt out" in the parenting role after periods of severe crisis or extended stress. It is important to be able to spot the early warning signs of becoming psychologically run down, i.e., irritability and impatience, feeling the "blues and blahs," sleeplessness, increased proneness to accidents and illnesses, difficulty controlling hostile outbursts, hypersensitiveness to criticism, decline in your socializing, little enjoyment of the children, a feeling of being "tied down," and an inability to relax.

A common practice for parents in Britain and Canada is for parents to go away on vacations and leave their children with relatives or neighbors, or when the children are old enough, by themselves. American parents often feel guilty when they do this and in anticipation of their guilt, commonly forego the trip. Contributing to the problem is the breakup of the extended family, so that relatives are often not accessible for watching the children. Wise parents will overcome these obstacles and regularly schedule time together away from the children.

"Alone" Time

Every parent deserves some time apart from the demands of caring for children and spouse. Personal, private time is needed for one's well-being. Privacy is like sleep. It is restorative and refreshing, and some people seem to need far more of it than others. In solitude you are not trying to please or impress anybody, to conform to their ideas and patterns of behavior; you are completely your own self, free to follow your inclinations and listen to your inner thoughts. Parents spend so much of their lives bending and stretching themselves to meet the needs of others, that it is immensely important to be able to stop now and again and to forget about everybody except ourselves.

On a daily basis be sure to escape for a few minutes to be by yourself to read, listen to music, take a walk, or do whatever pleases you. Learn to be an effective "escape artist" who can disappear for a time before tensions build up.

The psychologist Dr. Kurt Lewin has made it clear that we all need a certain amount of "personal space" to move about in, and that if you put two people too close together, and give them no chance to move away from each other, any tension that arises in their relationship may become quite severe.

When parenting becomes a chore or a sacrifice you have to find a way to take a few days off to renew yourself. Your spouse or your relatives can take care of the children while you take a mini three-day vacation. During this break you may decide to be alone, to attend a conference or school reunion, or visit with an old friend in a distant city. You should not feel guilty about this since it is a basic human need to relax and be off duty at times. Words cannot describe the energizing relief people feel when they get away from the daily grind for a while. They usually come back with a greater appreciation for their loved ones. How much time is enough for you? The answer is that it varies from parent to parent and situation to situation. If you believe you can't afford to take a vacation by yourself, consider what it will cost if you have a mental or physical breakdown. The truth may well be that you can't afford not to get away for a brief period.

LETTING CHILDREN LEARN FROM THE "NATURAL CONSEQUENCES" OF THEIR ACTIONS

The school of hard knocks can teach children a great deal about life. Lectures by parents often cannot make a point as well as personal experience. So allow your children to experience the unpleasant consequences of their acts as a motive for real change. As long as the natural result of a behavior is unpleasant rather than seriously harmful to a child you can let her learn for herself not to repeat the behavior.

The importance of natural consequences cannot be overestimated. Children will learn for themselves that if they push somebody their size they will probably be pushed back, and that if they don't bother to study for a test they will probably receive a poor mark on it. They will also learn by themselves that if they walk barefoot on a hot pavement, their feet will regret it, and that if they eat too much popcorn and candy their stomach will invariably complain.

By standing back and permitting your children to learn from their mistakes, you will be fostering independence, self-reliance, and self-learning. Your children will see you as less negative, controlling, and intrusive. So let your son walk to school if he dawdles and misses the school bus; if your daughter is 20 minutes late for dinner, let her eat a cold meal; if they spend their allowances too quickly, they'll have to wait until next week for treats; if they hit a bigger child they'll probably get hit back; if they spill milk they have to clean it up and thus learn to be more careful; if they damage the car due to drunk driving they have to pay for it themselves.

"Tough" Love

Teaching youths 12 years old and up to take the natural consequences of their misdeeds is the official policy of Families Anonymous (FA). These parents of youths with drug, alcohol, and other problems simply refuse to bail their children out of jail, pay their fines, or show any sympathy when their child is sent to jail. The parents take the attitude, "We love you, but as we have told you repeatedly, we can no longer be responsible for your actions. You will always have a home and a family to return to, but you must learn to straighten yourself out—we can't do it for you." According to FA officials this is called "tough love" and it's tough to learn, but it works!

Many children will never face up to a problem unless they fall on their face and have to get up by themselves.

ADDITIONAL READING

Dreikurs, Rudolf. *The Challenge of Child Training.* Hawthorne Books, 1972.

HOW TO "PROMPT" CHILDREN TO BEHAVE BETTER

The world does not require so much to be informed as to be reminded.

Prompting means to remind a child to either begin a desired behavior or stop an inappropriate action. Telling a child at 7 P.M. that it is homework time is a simple example. Reminders are often needed when a child is first learning a new behavior. Preschoolers, in particular, need reminders because of their limited memory capacity. Even adults like to be reminded about certain things, like dental appointments and overdue bills. The goal of a prompt is to increase the probability that a particular behavior will occur. If a child fails to respond to prompts, you need to back them up with automatic rewards and/or penalties.

Verbal Prompts

Examples of verbal prompting are:

1. "Dinner in five minutes."
2. "Jimmy, what do you do at 5 o'clock?" (If child fails to remember, you state for him "Feed the dog.")
3. "Louise, do you recall our past discussion in which we came up with what to do now?"
4. "Joan, what is the rule when we are in the library?" (If child cannot remember, state: "No talking.") Most libraries have found it helpful to provide their own visual prompts, i.e., signs, of this rule.

5. "What do you say?" (If you want the child to say "Thank you.")
6. "Remember Pat, we agreed that there will be no TV until all home-work is completed."
7. "Dog." (Take the dog out.)
8. "Thumb." (Take your thumb out of your mouth.)
9. "Karine, what are you doing?" (Implies the child is doing something wrong.)

Nonverbal Prompts

Among the silent, nonverbal signals you can give to prompt or cue your child towards desired behaviors are:

1. A motionless stance or one hand raised can mean attention is wanted.
2. A hand palm down and lowered by degrees can indicate the need for lowered voice or taking a sitting or lying position.
3. A finger in front of one's lips can signal "Quiet please!"
4. Tapping the side of your head can mean the child's behavior is unacceptable.
5. To signal disapproval of a child's misbehavior you can also use eye contact, facial frowns, coughing, and body posture. Standing close to your child when he begins to act up is another effective technique. Sometimes it may be necessary to use physical contact, e.g., putting your hand on the child's shoulders.
6. You might post or display around the home some printed evocative words such as calm, patience, think. These words trigger attitudes and call forth the quality they symbolize.
7. In one classroom where chewing gum was prohibited, the teacher gave reminders by sign language. She rapidly closed and opened her thumb and forefinger (imitating jaw motion) and then, like a baseball umpire calling out the runner, she motioned with her thumb towards the wastepaper basket! Other teachers have used as cues red lights which go on when a child is talking out of turn or otherwise acting inappropriately. Switching lights on and off can also signal children to stop misbehaving.
8. Written notes can be used as reminders. Kids love them. An example of such a note is: "Hello—This is a note from your dog. You

have forgotten to take me out the last three nights. I hope you still love me as much as I love you."

9. Signs or checklists relating to desired behavior can be posted on bulletin boards (very effective with 8 to 12 year olds.) A sample sign follows:

ATTENTION!

HOUSE RULES
1. Phone me as soon as you get home.
2. All chores must be done by 5 o'clock each day.
3. If you eat——*CLEAN UP!*
4. If you go out, tell each other where you are going.
5. No playing in the living room.

Dear Kids:
    These rules are only just a few—set up because
                                                    I LOVE YOU
                                                    Your Mom

Prompt, Don't Nag

Prompts should be given in a pleasant or neutral tone of voice. Nagging refers to the persistent, unpleasant urging that parents make of children: "I have told you a 1000 times . . . " Nagging tends to be delivered in an impatient or angry tone of voice.

The vast majority of young children need frequent reminders if they are to learn a sense of responsibility. Preschoolers and children in the primary grades tend to be impulsive, forgetful, distractible, and unreliable. What then is the difference between nagging and frequent reminders? The first difference is that a reminder, no matter how frequent, remains friendly and there is no tone of impatience or anger. Nagging on the other hand, is given in an unpleasant tone and sounds like a punishment. If you and your child become irritated, you are probably nagging rather than reminding. Another difference is that frequent reminders lead to learning whereas nagging often does not since children tend to tune it out. Nagging makes children resentful because parents tend to exaggerate ("Why do you never do as I say?" "I must have told you a thousand times."); to humiliate ("What's the matter, can't you understand simple English?"); or to use sarcasm ("I guess it's too much to ask you to clean your room.")

HOW TO USE "GRANDPA'S RULE" TO TEACH YOUR CHILD A LESSON

Excess generally causes reaction and produces a change in the opposite direction, whether it be in the seasons or in individuals, or in government.
—Plato

Too much of anything can become unpleasant and undesirable. Too much ice cream, for example, will cause discomfort. At times, you will find it beneficial to satiate your child with an undesirable behavior before it becomes a habit. To satiate means to overindulge your children with more than enough of something they want so that they become sick of it or disinterested as the result of fatigue or boredom.

Thus, when your child first says a curse word at home you might insist that he say it again and again and again until he is tired of it.

When your child first expresses an interest in smoking you might give him a cigarette and encourage him to smoke the whole thing by inhaling. While the child is still a little queasy from the first cigarette, you might recommend that he or she have another.

The famous "Grandpa's rule," in this regard, is that any child who wishes to smoke must first smoke five large cigars in succession. This usually produces a bored-and-weary or sick-and-disgusted reaction on the part of the child to a formerly attractive object. If your child refuses to go to bed, make a deal with him. Ask if he wants to stay up as late as you. If yes, keep the child up much longer than he really wanted. Then wake him up at the usual time. Repeat this procedure until the child learns not to stay up as late as parents do.

As another example, if your child will eat only mashed potatoes at dinner, give him a heaping plate of just mashed potatoes. Later for a snack serve warmed potatoes and nothing else. Continue this approach until your child requests some other foods for supper.

Final Thoughts

Encouraging satiation does not mean you condone or recommend the undesirable behavior. You are simply encouraging your child to overdo so that all pleasure and desire is lost—at least temporarily. Be sure to encourage or insist upon satiation in a calm, friendly tone of voice. It may be necessary to repeat the overindulgence of the behavior several times after the initial effects wear off.

HOW TO DISTRACT A CHILD WHO IS HEADED FOR TROUBLE

Distraction means to turn a child's attention from an objectionable pursuit to a neutral or more socially desirable activity with the goal of inducing the child to lose interest in the troublesome activity. So a skilled parent will often propose a substitute activity rather than constantly saying "no" or "stop that" to the child's current behavior.

The key to success with this strategy is your ability to create an equally attractive substitute activity for the child. On a long car ride, for example, you might try diverting the attention of squabbling children to counting the number of out-of-state license plates.

You will find that the behavior of older children is not as easily diverted as is that of younger children. However, we can still redirect their behavior at times by appealing to other interests or needs.

A parent can use a variety of distraction strategies in order to steer a child to a more desirable behavior.

Questions

Often asking a simple question will suffice as a distraction. The question serves to interrupt the undesired act and simultaneously redirects the child's energy along more acceptable lines. If your child, for example, has the undesired habit of openly masturbating at home, you might try asking her in a calm and positive way about her day in school. If this is unsuccessful you might ask her to get you a glass of water. Your goal is to distract her from what she is doing without making her aware of what you are doing. Thus, you act as if you had a sudden thought—not that you are reproaching her. After repeated distracting incidents, your child may lose interest in the undesirable activity.

Suggestion

Children frequently engage in troublesome behavior because they are bored or tired of the old routine. Just suggesting or providing a new activity or game can work wonders. In this regard it is a good idea to have some games or activities (popping corn, baking cakes) saved up for rainy days when the children have nothing to do and seem headed for trouble.

Examples of suggesting alternate activities for children are:

1. If a child is silly and has the giggles you might send him to the store for you so he can settle down.
2. Suggesting that it's time to bake cookies is an excellent way to stop two siblings from squabbling.
3. You might lift a child into a whirl-around hug in the midst of his charge across the floor to hit another child.
4. If you see that children are playing wildly in the house, you may direct them outside to run off some of their steam. Or you may decide that they are playing wildly because they lack ideas for other challenging activities. Perhaps you would suggest that some of the children help you prepare lunch, while the others play with clay at the table.
5. A child threatening to hit you might be directed to pummel a pillow instead.

Discussion

Distraction has been found to be one of the best management strategies for infants and preschoolers. Young children are more easily distracted than older children, and they cannot be reasoned with as well. Offering a shiny spoon to an infant, for example, is an example of nonverbal suggestion.

It is interesting to note that chimpanzees often practice discipline by distraction in raising their infants. Instead of punishing an infant when troublesome, the chimp mom amuses the child by giving her undivided attention.

Whatever your suggestions, they should be as much in keeping with the child's needs at the time as possible. It isn't really effective to tell an emotionally upset child to go read a book when he really needs some-one to talk to about his painful experiences. After talking with an upset child, you might direct the child to an activity where feelings can be released, like finger painting or play dough.

Rechanneling

Rechanneling, a form of suggestion that seeks more enduring changes in a child, refers to the encouragement of a child to express socially unacceptable impulses in substitute ways that are more constructive or socially acceptable. Basically it involves a sublimation of youthful ener-gies and impulses. Sublimation means to direct the energy of an impulse from the primitive aim to one that is culturally or ethically higher.

It is truly surprising how many troublesome behaviors of children can be rechanneled into constructive, ego-building pursuits. The active, aggressive child, for example, can be encouraged to release his energy in such socially approved activities as physical contact sports (football, soccer, boxing), carpentry (hammering and sawing), drawing or paint-ing, and playing the drums. Building and racing cars may provide a subsequent outlet for these energies. Scouting and club activities offer other constructive outlets. The child with compulsive habits (i.e., ten-dency to repeat the same behavior over and over or to impose a rigid order or arrangement on things) can be encouraged to perform tasks requiring care and orderly precision. For instance, the child might make model airplanes, or construct elaborate objects with matchsticks. These precision products will bring the child praise and also broaden his or her range of interests.

A youth who seeks excitement and independence by constantly run-ning away from home could be allowed to visit relatives in a distant city by himself, attend a sleep away camp, or participate in a survival, back-packing hike in the wilderness. For rechanneling to be successful, it is obviously important to make the substitute activity as satisfying as the maladaptive one, and to offer a variety of outlets for the tremendous energies of youth.

ARE YOU GIVING YOUR CHILDREN TOO MANY ORDERS AND TOO FEW REQUESTS?

All the sleeping dogs of pride are aroused against us when we give orders; at every imperative we stir up armies of defense. Ask and it shall be given you, command and you shall be refused.

—*J. E. Davis*

A request means asking a child to do something while allowing the child the option of saying "no." Children will readily comply with requests when you have a friendly, positive relationship with them. Examples of requests are: "I need your help on this very badly, will you do it for me?" or "I really have this 'thing' about long hair so will you cut it a little shorter as a personal favor to me?" Even very small children respond favorably to the pleasant request: "John, will you help me?" Requests come in two forms, direct ("Could you put out the napkins?") and indirect ("Would you like to put out the napkins or shall I?"). Be sure to *praise* your children when they comply with your requests!

Requests vs. Commands

A request is asking. A command is telling. So the difference between a request and an order is that when you make a request you are willing to accept a yes or no answer. Too often parents will tend to confuse a child by making a request when they are really giving an order or command. If a child has no choice in a situation make this clear by giving him a firm directive: "Mary, come to the table now!" rather than a request; "Would you like to eat with us now?"

Fortunately, parents can allow children freedom of choice in most situations and thus they can get in the habit of saying, "Please do this," rather than "Do this." This tends to foster cooperation in children and to create a positive home atmosphere. A responsible parent gives as few orders as possible but makes frequent use of requests, suggestions, and persuasions. By giving a child as many choices as possible you promote decision making and prevent a child from feeling like a little robot who has little control over his life.

Reciprocity is extremely important in regard to requests; you must be willing to meet most of a child's requests if you expect him to comply with most of your requests.

CHANGING THE HOME ENVIRONMENT TO HEAD OFF CHILDREN'S PROBLEMS

Preventions of misdeeds are far better than remedies, cheaper and easier of application, and surer in result.

—*Tryon Edwards*

An effective way of stopping many misbehaviors is to change the child's environment, as contrasted to efforts to change the child directly. Analagous to preventive medicine, environmental control means changing your household so that your child's disturbing behaviors are less likely to occur. Wise parents have been using this principle for centuries.

The three main ways of altering the physical environment are to add to it, subtract from it, or rearrange it. Adding to the home environment means making it more interesting, stimulating, and responsive to the child's needs. Some examples are:

- When children are bored they are more likely to get into trouble or become whiney. So provide your children with a variety of interesting activities, including games, toys, puzzles, arts and crafts, record player, and musical instruments.
- Try painting your child's room in warm, bright colors to give a warm feeling. Yellow and orange colors give a feeling of vitality, freshness, and excitement. They lead to more optimism and better feelings about oneself.
- Encourage learning at home by providing a variety of books, magazines, encyclopedias, and dictionaries.
- Provide a small table with chairs around it to encourage eye contact and social interaction among shy, withdrawn children.
- Give an alarm clock to a child who has difficulty waking up in the morning.
- Put a fence around the yard to keep the children off the street.

Reducing or taking away environmental stimuli can prevent trouble as well. Some examples are:

- Make the time just before bed a calm relaxing time for a child by restricting wild, exciting play.
- Childproofing the house for a toddler is another example of impoverishing an environment to prevent trouble. So remove all breakable, fragile, or dangerous objects from the reach of young children, cap electrical outlets, and put guards on sharp table corners. Many of these safety devices are available from: The Safety Now Co., Box 567, 202 York Road, Jenkentown, Pa. 19046.
- There is a simple way to train a young child to stop banging on the family piano: lock the piano.

By rearranging the schedule of daily events or simply using physical space differently you can avoid many conflict situations between children. For example, if two of your children cannot be together for any length of time without fighting, try separating them physically (putting up a partition or divider in the playroom, or imaginary line in the living room, or having them play in different rooms) or try rearranging their schedules so that they are not together (one does homework in the evening, one after school). If your child and your best friend can't stand each other, try rearranging your schedule so that your best friend only visits when your child is in school or in bed.

Discussion

An environmental or ecological approach can expand your perspective on and conceptualization of a child's problem. Ask what it is in the home that is triggering off or maintaining the problem, and consider if some change (physical, schedule, or activity) could reduce the misbehavior. If you carefully analyze situations in which discipline breaks down, you may discover certain patterns. You may find, for example, that your preschool child becomes extremely irritable in the late morning when he misses his naps. Just before dinner time has been found to be a troublesome time for school-age children because they are hungry and tired at this time. Knowledge of these patterns should help you prevent them next time, e.g., provide more snacks, naps, or quiet times. Also, consider the time and type of day (rainy weather), previous activities of the child, and what new activities were beginning; if during a transitional period, you might want to provide more supervision or structure.

WHY DAILY ROUTINES ARE SO IMPORTANT FOR YOUR FAMILY

> Routine is to a child what walls are to a house; it gives boundaries and dimensions to his life. Routine gives a feeling of security.
> —Dr. Rudolf Dreikurs

> Traditions, customs, habits, routines are all the arrangements which make everyday life self-starting and self-regulating.
> —Eric Hoffer

> An indication of the child's need for safety is his preference for some kind of undisrupted routine or rhythm. He seems to want a predictable, orderly world.
> —Abraham Maslow

> Habit is the beneficent harness of routine which enables silly men to live respectably, and unhappy men to live calmly.
> —George Eliot

Children thrive best on order and regularity. They are happier when they know what to expect. By setting up regular, unchanging timetables and procedures for conducting daily events, parents provide an environment that is both dependable and predictable. To an immature child, a predictable world is a safe world, free of confusion and uncertainty. Routines also promote efficient learning by supplying a script of expected actions. They prevent disorganized, chaotic households. The quiet execution of ordinary routines of daily living is the earliest form of discipline for children. A routine is not onerous; it is liberating. It doesn't take time; it *makes* time. But children don't realize this. Parents must help them discover this fact. While all children need routine, this structure is all the more important for hyperactive, impulsive, slow-learning, and anxious-fearful children.

Routines help you sidestep the power struggles that so often occur between parents and kids. A child will talk back to and argue with a parent who reminds or orders him to do something. It is hard to argue with an impersonal routine.

When asked what they would do differently if they had to raise children over again, a number of parents have said:[10] "I would insist upon a routine." However, it is a great temptation for parents to deviate from daily routines to suit their own convenience. Thus, one night you might be inclined to put your child to bed a little earlier, while the next night you would keep him up a little later than usual. Don't fall into this trap. 7:30 P.M. bedtime means just that; it should not be 8 P.M. one night, 7 P.M. the next night, 6:30 P.M. another, and so on. Children raised in homes with fluid schedules find it difficult to adjust to the fixed routines of school and business, e.g., a 9 to 3 school day with clearly scheduled events. Apart from other considerations, then, implementation of daily schedules is simply good habit training.

Daily routines should be carefully set up and consistently carried out for such regular events as bedtime, wake-up time, meal times, toilet times, chore times, free play times, play time with Daddy, or for the older child, homework time. It helps to pin the schedule of daily events on a wall near the child's bed or on a kitchen bulletin board.

A bedtime routine might consist of one hour of quiet TV watching, followed by a prompt ("Five minutes till bedtime, dear.") bathroom visit, bedtime story, goodnight kiss, and then lights out. The same procedure would be conducted every night starting at the same time. No nonsense, stalling, or arguing by the children would be tolerated.

A sample routine for children ages 1–3 is as follows:

7–7:30 A.M.	Toilet, wash, dress
7:30–8:00	Breakfast
8–8:10	Toilet
8:10–9:30	Nap or play alone after age 3
9:30–9:45	Snack: orange juice and crackers
9:45–12 noon	Play—outdoors when possible
12–12:30	Toilet and lunch
12:30–3:00	Nap
3–3:15	Toilet; fruit juice and crackers
3:15–5:00	Play, outdoors
5–5:30	Bath
5:30–6:00	Quiet time (helps relax for dinner)
6–6:30	Dinner with family
6:30–7:00	Preparation for bed (quiet time, story)
7:00	Sleep

Guidelines for Routines

1. Be Consistent.   Children are happiest when the same thing happens at the same time every day. If you have to change your plans, let children know ahead of time if possible and they will adjust to your plans.
2. Allow Few Exceptions.   Make an exception to a routine only when something extraordinary happens. During a grandparent visit, for example, the 7:00 bedtime can be pushed back. As long as you explain that it's a special occasion, the normal pattern won't be disrupted.
3. Your attitude towards a routine should be impersonal and unemotional, but interested. It should be clear to a child that it is his or her responsibility to conform to a routine, not yours.
4. Make it clear which of the daily routines are requirements that will be enforced.

Routines for Infants

For infants, it's the order or sequence of daily events that counts, not the timing of the events. The timetable will vary to suit the needs of the individual child. Some babies need to be fed every four hours, some more often. However, for all infants, the daily happenings in a baby's life, such as naps, feedings, play periods, baths, walks, and bedtime, should follow each other in a regular pattern. Almost any order is fine, as long as it becomes a routine and seems to suit both baby and parent. The regular sequence of events for the baby builds security and aids in the development of the child's memory.

DON'T EXPECT YOUR CHILDREN TO ACT LIKE ADULTS

Children are naturally noisy, impulsive, unruly, and inconsiderate. They challenge an adult's expectations of order, cleanliness, and propriety. Since children are not miniature adults we cannot expect them to act with perfect maturity at all times. Some of the behaviors of children, while unpleasant for parents, must be tolerated with good grace and without reproach. Permitting means accepting the harmless childishness of children even though this behavior makes us uncomfortable at times.

Among the normal childhood behaviors that you must expect and permit at times are:

Stepping and playing in mud puddles.
Yelling and shouting during physically active games.
Messy floors while children are playing.
Continual physical activity by school-age children, e.g., running, jumping.
Dirty clothes after playing.
Carelessness, forgetfulness, and tactlessness.
Silliness and joking.
Bickering among siblings.
Crying when hurt.
Negativism of two-year-olds and teenagers.
Not saying "Hello" or "Thank you" on occasion.

Unrealistic expectations for cleanliness, quiet, conformity, and politeness can make a home a jail for a child. Tolerating certain of these behaviors with composure in no way implies that you approve of them or expect them to continue over the long run, e.g., carelessness or thanklessness. Nor is it a license for children to do whatever they wish with no regard for the rights of others.

Permitting also means suspending the house rules on special occasions. If a neat house is the general rule, the neatness rule can be suspended during finger-painting time, for Christmas decorating, or other special circumstances such as a birthday party.

HOW TO IGNORE YOUR CHILD'S MISBEHAVIOR

Ignoring a child's misbehavior is one of the simplest ways to control it. There is now considerable evidence that many kinds of troublesome behaviors can be eliminated by systematically withdrawing your attention.[11]

A basic assumption of ignoring is that parental attention is reinforc- ing and thus maintaining the child's misbehavior. Even unpleasant attention from parents, such as yelling or scolding, can strengthen mis- behavior since the child may regard negative attention as better than no attention.

Ignoring means to deliberately pay no attention to a child when he is misbehaving in a certain way. So avoid looking at or talking to the child when you ignore and give absolutely no attention. The key to ignoring is to either leave the scene or to pretend that the child does not exist. For example, four-year-old Pamela often exhibited temper tan- trum behavior, e.g. yelling, stamping her feet. Her parents decided to completely ignore this behavior and persuaded her siblings and grand- parents to ignore it as well. The tantrums began to quickly disappear after two weeks of ignoring.

"Burst" of Misbehavior

Typically an ignored behavior will get worse, before it gets better. Stud- ies show that children will "test" your resolve when you first begin the ignoring technique. Thus you should expect the child to substantially increase the misbehavior immediately after you start ignoring. So if you decide to ignore a child when she says "I hate you," you can expect a burst of "I hate you" statements at first. In one case I know of the child actually increased these statements from a previous level of 20 to over 30 per day.

Alerted to this likely phenomenon, the mother continued to ignore the increased misbehavior, and after about 10 days the "I hate you" statements began to subside until they were almost nonexistent a month later. So it is very important to patiently and steadfastly "weather the storm" by not giving in when a child starts to test your new approach. It takes time to convince children that you mean business.

A vending machine analogy seems appropriate to explain why people escalate their behavior when ignored. You put a coin in and if nothing happens you jiggle the knob several times. If still nothing happens, you bang or kick the machine since it is ignoring you. If the machine still does not respond to this tantrumlike behavior you give up and walk away.

Spontaneous Recovery

After a behavior has been successfully reduced by ignoring, it often reappears automatically for no apparent reason. It seems the child is trying to get attention by her "old tricks." If this occurs, ignore the behavior again and it should quickly disappear.

Provide Alternate Source of Attention

Ignoring misbehavior does not teach the child to do anything, but rather simply teaches her what not to do. It is wise, then to point out acceptable ways for a child to gain your attention. Ideally you should teach alternate ways to earn attention before you start the ignoring procedure. One way you might suggest for getting your attention is for the child to say in a nice way, "Mom, can you play with me now?" Be sure to praise the child when he asks for attention in an appropriate way.

Guidelines for Effective Ignoring

1. *What to Ignore.* Ignoring is effective with a variety of attention-seeking behaviors which you can tolerate but don't like. Such behaviors include clowning, temper tantrums, nagging (e.g., "Mommy I want to go home now"), bad language, excessive dependency on adults (clinging, crying), sibling rivalry, and interrupting.

   You can't ignore destructive or dangerous behaviors or behavior which is self-rewarding (sneaking cookies).

2. *Simple but Not Easy.* Because ignoring is a simple procedure, many parents assume that is will be easy to carry out. Unfortunately it is not easy to implement. One has to ignore the misbehavior each and every time it occurs. Just paying less attention is not effective and may actually strengthen the misdeed since behavior that is occasionally reinforced is very difficult to extinguish. Also it may be that the child's behavior is being reinforced by other family members such as siblings or grandparents. In these situations you have to insist that the whole household ignore the child's misbehavior.

3. *Record.* It is a good idea to record the frequency of the misbe-

havior prior to and during the ignoring period. In this way you will be best able to evaluate whether the procedure is working.

4. *Praise.*   Remember to praise the child for behavior which is opposite of the undesired act, e.g., being pleasant rather than whiney.

5. *Will Power.*   Ignoring is a slow but effective method of eliminating certain problem behavior in children. It not only requires a lot of patience, but also willpower since it is hard to consistently ignore behavior that you don't like, e.g., a young child in the supermarket who whines over and over, "Please Mommy, can I have just one candy bar?"

6. *Time Out.*   If ignoring proves unsuccessful, use the time-out procedure described in a later section.

HOW TO CONFRONT YOUR CHILDREN WHEN THEY CAUSE YOU TROUBLE

Think not those faithful who praise all thy words and actions, but those who kindly reprove thy faults.

—*Socrates*

Man will become better only when you make him see what he is like.
—*Anton Chekhov*

How do you tell a child that her behavior is bothering you? Confrontation is a process of bringing to a child's attention a behavior of hers that is causing you a problem. Confronting a child is like holding up a mirror and saying, "This is how your behavior is troubling me, please change." If the confrontation is accurate and if the child cares about you, she will usually try to change the behavior. Often you will have to confront a child more than once before a lasting change is made in the behavior.

How Not to Confront

Some parents are either too passive or too hostile in confronting children.

Too Passive. If you "keep in" your grievances toward a child, no matter how minor they are, you will accumulate inner anger and resentment that may eventually get out of control. Living with another person inevitably results in conflict. If the issues are never brought up there is no possibility of their being resolved.

The tendency to withhold bad news from others has been called the "mum" effect. In ancient times the bearer of bad news was often killed. Since bad news still arouses negative feelings, parents tend to overlook or water down confrontations with children when they cause problems. Nevertheless, an essential aspect of socializing children is to teach them the lesson of "reciprocity" i.e., all human relationships are based on mutual responsiveness to each other's needs and feelings. Children cannot just take, they must learn to be considerate of others.

Too Hostile. Hostility means that you see the child as an enemy at that moment and you try to hurt the child by verbal or physical means. Verbal abuse or "psychological karate" includes name calling, threats, and insults; physical abuse includes hitting, kicking, and throwing things. Aggressive confrontations not only increase the potential for counterattack, e.g., a "shout-out" where you scream at each other, but hinder the development of a close relationship.

How to Confront

The best confrontation is one that is assertive rather than passive or hostile. Basically, assertion means standing up for your personal rights and expressing your thoughts and feelings in a direct, honest way that does not violate a child's rights, that is without being domineering, or humiliating or degrading the other person.

One needs to convey a feeling of respect and liking when confronting, of wanting to teach and help rather than seeking to hurt or get back at a child.

Research[12] has found that assertive responses, as compared with aggressive responses, have less likelihood of provoking anger in others and a higher probability of producing the desired change in another's behavior.

Two Effective Methods

The following procedures provide effective models for assertive confrontation.

Gordon "I-messages".[13] A key to effective confrontation is a self-focus rather than other-person-focus. A self-focus means concentrating on expressing your own feelings and needs by means of "I" statements, e.g., "I really feel annoyed when you don't feed your pet as you agreed to do. This means more work for me." An other-person-focused confrontation results in a "you" message which tends to be fault-finding, threatening, or blaming in nature, e.g., "You really ought to be ashamed of yourself for neglecting your pet," or "How cruel you are to let your pet go hungry," or "You'll be sorry if you ever do this again."

An "I-message" has three components:

1. A nonblameful description of the child's behavior that is causing you a problem, e.g., "Jane, when you walk in the house with wet feet it makes the floor a mess."
2. The tangible effects on you now or in the future, e.g., "A messy floor means more work for me to clean up."
3. A descriptive statement of your feelings about the problem, e.g., "I really get annoyed about this." In initial confrontations your emphasis is on teaching the child the specific reason you are distressed, e.g., "When you interrupt me like this I cannot finish what I have to say to your father." In later confrontations about the same problem you should stress more your escalating annoyance or anger, e.g., "I'm becoming really angry about your continuing to interrupt me!"

Notice that you have not given an order or told the child how to solve the problem; rather you have left the responsibility for resolving the difficulty with the child.

ABC Model. This confrontation model also has three parts. In Step A, you briefly share your feelings about the troublesome behavior of the child ("I'm uncomfortable."). This step is similar to the expression of feelings in Gordon's "I-message." Step B involves giving a warm, supportive statement such as "I love you very much," and showing empathy for the child's presumed feelings or motivations, ("I know you mean well."), ("You seem to be feeling down today."). Communication of support and understanding tends to lower the child's resistance to change. Step C involves a specific request that the child modify his bothersome behaviors ("Please stop yelling at me.").

To illustrate the ABC model you might say the following to your teenager who has started to smoke in the house: "I'm upset" (Step A). "You know I care about you and I imagine that smoking makes you feel good." (Step B). "But I'd appreciate it if you didn't smoke in the house."

General Guidelines for Confrontation

1. Be sure your tone of voice is firm and deliberate rather than hostile, contemptuous, or belittling.
2. If you confront too frequently, the child will feel you are nagging or picking on him.
3. Don't exaggerate the child's fault to boost your case. So avoid using the words *never* or *always* ("You never do what I tell you," "Why do you always have to come home late?"). Few things in life are all or none, black or white. Instead be more realistic in your statements ("It happens all too often that your . . . ").
4. A confrontation should address a specific behavior that the child can do something about, such as a messy room, rather than a general personality trait such as sloppiness.
5. Avoid "character assasination" wherein you characterize the child in a negative way, e.g. "You bad boy."
6. Reinforce compliance with appreciation ("Thank you for picking up your clothes.").
7. Make only one confrontation at a time so you can discuss it fully.
8. If the child fails to respond to a confrontation, you must escalate the intensity of the confrontation; that is, put more energy into it than the child is putting into remaining passive.
9. Confrontations are particularly appropriate when a child engages in a bothersome behavior that he is unaware of or indifferent about.
10. Sometimes in confronting children they will respond by confronting you with the inappropriateness of your behavior and you may discover that you both have to give a little to solve the problem (see following section on resolving family conflict.)

TEACH YOUR CHILDREN A POSITIVE WAY TO RESOLVE FAMILY CONFLICTS

The first duty of a wise advocate is to convince his opponents that he understands their arguments, and sympathizes with their just feelings.

—Coleridge

The best argument is that which seems merely an explanation.

—Dale Carnegie

In quarreling, the truth is always lost.

—Publileus Syrus

It is better to debate a question without settling it than to settle a question without debating it.

—Joseph Joubert

Family tensions and conflicts are inevitable. When people rely heavily upon one another and interact frequently, they are prone to rubbing each other the wrong way. If disagreements are not resolved in a positive way, hard feelings, resentment, irritation, and misunderstanding will smolder. A conflict occurs when two or more individuals believe that what each wants is incompatible with what the other wants. The issues over which parents and children disagree are many. It may be over a messy room, or the permissible age of a first "date," or the hour a teenager is expected home from dates. In most cases, one party is not completely to blame for the problem. The responsibility for solving a conflict is usually shared by two or more people.

Because conflict is a process rather than a result, it is intrinsically neither good or bad. The value of conflict depends on whether the results are productive or destructive. Resolving disagreements in a cooperative manner can result in personal growth and bring you "closer" to the other person. Maturity is not the absence of problems, it is the ability to cope with them.

The problem is that most people react to conflict with the wrong kind of procedures. From the beginning of time humans have tended to deal with conflict by either fleeing from it or responding in an aggressive way (force of arms or verbal abuse).

Families today continue to have difficulty handling interpersonal conflict. They tend to quarrel, that is, they have angry, discordant disputes, rather than discuss problems in a calm, rational manner. Thus, family quarrels are reported to be the chief cause of homicides and violence among people. When conflict resolution skills are weak, it is likely that daily living in the family is full of open arguments and/or quiet hostility or coldness to each other.

Not surprisingly, research[14] indicates that families go to mental health clinics because they have more conflicts among family members and fewer means of resolving these conflicts due to the breakdown in communication in the clinic families. Studies also indicate that in families with delinquent children, there is typically poor conflict resolution skills. There tends to be a competitive (vs. cooperative) attitude between parent and child wherein each strives to gain a superior position over the other. One-up-manship by means of aversive control seems to be the goal.

A most critical and pressing aspect of positive parenting, then, is the effective resolution of parent-child conflicts.

Wrong Ways of Resolving Conflict

There are two extremes in the ways people choose to deal with conflicts, namely, withholding or erupting.

Erupters. Basically these people have never really learned to control their childhood temper. They get angry and explode when in conflict situations. The aggressiveness may involve verbal assault (yelling, cursing, insulting, threatening) or physical assault (hitting, throwing things).

Withholders. These people believe it is best to keep quiet when they have a conflict with another. Keeping quiet avoids saying or doing things in anger which will only come back to haunt you. Conflict is confused with violent confrontation. The cost of keeping the peace at any cost is usually unhappiness, ulcers, and feelings of low self-worth. For historical reasons, many females are uncomfortable being in conflict with others. Withholders often resort to coldness or not speaking to another when they have a conflict. When asked if anything is bothering them they will respond "Nothing" or "I don't want to talk about it."

A Positive Method of Conflict Resolution

Most of us do not solve conflicts in a calm, reasonable way. The hallmark of mature conflict resolution is a calm, rational, open discussion of the issues with a problem-solving emphasis rather than personal attack. There should be a spirit of cooperation, mutual acceptance of responsibility or fault, and mutual trust. This is much easier to do when you like one another because then you are more likely to be cooperative and trusting, as well as less likely to use coercion against one another.

Some families fall into the trap of dealing with disagreements on a competitive win-or-lose basis. They do not realize that the idea of "winning" a conflict is an illusion—that one person's "victory" inevitably turns into a loss for both. The best approach is a cooperative one wherein both parties try to find a solution that is mutually acceptable.

The cooperative method has been found to be the most effective way to resolve conflicts. It takes time and requires a lot of self-control and maturity by both parties. The basic procedures is as follows:

FIVE-STEP APPROACH TO SETTLING CONFLICTS

1. State the Problem
2. Generate Solutions
3. Select the Best Solution
4. Implement the Solution
5. Follow-up

1. *State the Problem.*   Each person should state the problem as they see it, keeping the discussion relevant to the conflict issue. A statement of the problem should get right to the significant issue without beating around the bush. It should contain three parts: a specific description of the behavior of the other that you find troublesome; the tangible effects on you now or in the future; and your feelings about it. Thus, you might say, "When you leave your toys and clothes around the house and I have to pick them up it means more work for me. This makes me very annoyed." As a general rule, try to use "I" statements in describing the problem rather than "you" statements. For example, say "I get upset when you interrupt me because I can't finish what I have to say," rather than "You're so inconsiderate for interrupting me." "I" messages focus on your

needs and feelings so that they make others feel less defensive. "You" messages tend to find fault with others which often produces a counterattack on you. So avoid "you" messages, including insults ("You act like a pig."), overgeneralizations ("You always do this to me. "), and assumptions about a child's motives ("You just want to get me angry."). The "I-message,"[15] on the other hand, provides an effective model for being assertive without being aggressive.

After you have expressed your thoughts and feelings directly and briefly you should make a point to listen to and understand the child's point of view. Be an attentive, nondefensive listener who avoids interrupting, contradicting, or passing judgment on the child's statements. Put yourself momentarily in the child's shoes and try to understand her position. Listening sounds both simple and familiar; but in reality it's difficult and rare. Active listening means putting aside your personal beliefs to really understand the other person's position. When you build bridges of understanding you are well on your way towards solving the problem.

In listening look for areas of agreement. Dwell first on the points or areas on which you both agree. Also look for areas where you can admit a mistake. Apologize for your errors. It will reduce a child's defensiveness.

2. *Generate Solutions.*   If we want solutions to a problem we have to work at it; not just sit and complain, blame others, or say it's "impossible." Ask your child to join you in trying to think up at least 10 possible solutions (no matter how extreme they seem). Seeking many solutions forces you to become creative in your problem solving, and often results in an acceptable solution to a seemingly unsolvable problem.

3. *Select the Best Solution.*   Consider the advantages and disadvantages of each proposed solution and come to a mutual agreement on the best solution. The best solution is the one that everyone involved thinks is as fair as possible. When your needs are far apart then you will probably have to compromise, that is, both of you give up something of value in order to get something of value. This process is called negotiation. For example, if both parents and their children like to make active use of the telephone during the evening hours, a compromise might involve giving the children telephone rights from 7:00 to 8:30 and the parents rights from 8:30 to 10:00

On occasion you will find that a child is unwilling to negotiate when it is clearly called for. In these situations you will have to exert your authority and impose a reasonable solution for the good of the family.

4. *Implement the Solution.*   Step four involves spelling out the details of the solution, i.e., what should be done by whom, when, and where. It may be helpful to write down this agreement as to how the decision is to be carried out and have both parties sign the contract.

5. *Follow-up.*   Set up a time in the near future when you and your child sit down to check on how the agreement is working. Some changes may be needed to improve the plan so as to ensure mutual compliance with the responsibilities.

Some Additional Guidelines for Handling Conflicts

1. Avoid using a hostile, irritated tone of voice. Much of the friction of daily life is caused by the wrong tone of voice. To be calm and civil when we disagree is a goal most of us have to keep working at.

2. It is very important that the time be right for problem solving, i.e., both parties are calm, unhurried, and willing to negotiate. The time usually allotted is inappropriate, namely, the evening after a hard day's work when everyone is tired from other pursuits. Mealtimes, bedtimes, and in front of others are also poor times to resolve conflict.

3. Don't try to settle a problem with the following attitudes:

   "You're wrong, I'm right."
   "It's a catastrophe."
   "It's your fault."
   "It's not a problem."

4. Focus on what you could do to solve a problem, not what others should do. It's much easier to change ourselves than others.

5. Don't bring up more than one problem at a time. If you present a "gunnysack" of past grievances, none of them are likely to get resolved.

HOW TO SET LIMITS ON YOUR CHILD'S BEHAVIOR

Freedom is moving easy in harness.

—Robert Frost

The power to make progress comes in large measure from having freedom and an assured path along which to go.

—Maria Montessori

One of the most important tasks of parenting is to control children's behavior by means of rules. We all have to live with rules if we are to live in harmony with one another. What would happen to motorists, for example, if there were no traffic lights or stop signs? At times our personal desires and impulses must be curbed in favor of the common good or for our own welfare. Even though they sometimes grumble, children basically want direction and are grateful to be shown how to behave. However, giving orders is a neglected aspect of parenting. Few parents have been trained to do it well or enjoy it.

Any demand made on a child is a rule. A long-term rule is one that must be enforced again and again over a long period of time, e.g., "Make your bed every morning." A short-term rule or command is a spontaneous directive given a child about a particular situation, e.g., "Don't make those loud noises!" A rule serves the purpose of defining exact boundaries or limits for your child's behavior so that it is clear what is expected.

Apart from clarity, long-term rules offer the advantages of advance notice, consistency, fairness (rules apply to everyone), and the depersonalization of conflicts, i.e., it is the child's behavior in conflict with a rule, not you against the child.

The following guidelines should assist you to be more effective in setting limits on children's behavior and thus increasing the likelihood of their compliance.

Guidelines for Giving Orders

1. *Be Firm in Tone and Manner.*   In giving an order you have to learn how to come on strong without sounding hostile or nasty. Giving an

order in a wishy-washy manner may leave a child with the impression that you do not really care whether she does what you ask. Be firm and speak as if you mean it and expect to be obeyed. A forceful stare and loud voice will get attention. There is no need to shriek or use harsh, angry words.

One study[16] of difficult-to-control children revealed that they tended to ignore their parents' orders because their commands were given in a weak tone of voice. The authors of this study concluded that a parent's tone of voice in giving an order mirrors that person's personal beliefs about his effectiveness as a source of influence. So your tone of voice, which is difficult to self-monitor, should not be so weak as to be ignored, nor so loud as to sound hostile.

If you give an order with conviction and expect compliance from children you will most likely get it. Most of the time children do obey adult directives—especially from parents. Even during the first year of life, for instance, studies have indicated that infants comply 67 percent of the time to their mother's commands. A similar compliance rate is evidenced during the "terrible two's."

Be certain you are right before setting a limit. If you are at all uncertain, feel guilty, or lack confidence in yourself, the child will sense this and probably balk at complying.

Be Firm in Wording.   If a child has no choice in the matter, be honest by giving a direct order, i.e., an imperative statement that cannot be construed as a question, such as:

"Go to your room right now!"
"Stop hitting your sister!"
"Eat your vegetables!"
"It's time to go to bed now!"

Of course there will be many situations where you can allow your children to make a choice and thereby give them valuable experience in decision making. In these situations you can use either requests ("Please rest for a while."), or a suggestion put in the form of a question ("Do you think it's bedtime now?" "Why don't you play a game?" "Wouldn't you like to call your grandmother?" "Help me put these toys away, OK?") By making greater use of requests/suggestions than of commands you avoid giving children the feeling of being continually "bossed around." But don't confuse a child by using a request or suggestion when something must be done right away and a direct command is needed.

2. *Be Specific.* Avoid vague subjective rules which will probably mean different things to different people. A specific rule tells a child exactly what is expected of him and when it must be done. So spell out the details to avoid misunderstanding.

Vague	*Specific*
"Be neat!"	"Put all your toys away before bedtime."
"Come home early."	"Come home by 6 o'clock."
"Be quiet!"	"Don't slam the door. Keep your hand on the knob and close it quietly."
"Your job is to take out the trash."	"Every day your chore is to empty the trash. This means the baskets in the kitchen, bathroom, and laundry room. This must be done before you go to bed."
"You two be good."	"No hitting one another."

3. *Positive Wording.* In making demands of children, parents often phrase their directions in negative terms, such as "No talking with your mouth full," "Don't be messy." Instead, try to make your rules refer to what the child should do (prescriptive) rather than what not to do (proscriptive). Thus, you might say, "Talk in a quiet voice," rather than "Don't shout." or "Blocks are for building things, not for throwing." In this way you teach children alternate ways of behaving that are acceptable to you.

Continual use of prohibitions such as "No," "Don't," "Stop that," not only sets a negative tone in the house but fails to give a child a clear idea of what it is he is supposed to do. It takes thought and practice for parents to get in the habit of saying "Do" rather than "Don't." Some additional examples of how to accentuate the positive in giving orders are:

Negative Wording	*Positive Wording*
"Don't jump on the couch!"	"You must sit down if you want to stay on the couch!"
"If this room isn't picked up, then you can't play outside."	"When your room is picked up, then you can go outside to play."

"If you don't eat your peas, you can't have dessert."

"When you eat your peas, you can have dessert."

"Don't run."

"Walk."

"Don't drag your coat on the ground."

"Hold your coat higher so it doesn't drag."

"Don't squeeze the kitten."

"Carry the kitten gently."

"You can color on this paper, not on the table."

"Don't color on the table."

"Yes, you can have a cookie as soon as we have our snack time."

"No, you can't have a cookie."

"No smoking in your bedroom."

"You can smoke in the bathroom or family room."

So when restricting a child's behavior try to give an acceptable alternative. Don't just say no and leave the child with no idea how to satisfy his wishes. When you close a door, try to open a window for the child. Remember how frustrated you are when you come to a roadblock for which no detour has been provided.

4. *Impersonal Wording.* Rules should be impersonal in the sense of being no one person's rules. The most effective rules are the ones which grow out of the situation and are dictated by those situations rather than by the whims or feelings of a parent.

So make the conflict between the child and an impersonal rule, not between you and the child. For example, don't say "I don't want you to hit your sister" (personal); say, "The rule in this family is no hitting each other."

5. *Explain the Reason for the Rule.* When you tell a child to do something be sure to state the reason it must be done. It is easy for parents to fall into the habit of simply telling children to do things without further explanation. But by taking the time to explain why you want something done you sound less "bossy" and more logical or reasonable. By so doing you increase the likelihood of children complying with your instruction.

Also, blind obedience does not develop the ability to think. When children understand why a rule is necessary they are more apt to conform to it of their own accord, without external pressure. Self-discipline is based on understanding the reasonableness of rules. So only in an emergency or when the child obviously knows the reason say, "Do it because I say so."

Examples of giving reasons for rules are: "Don't put the knife in your mouth, it may cut you." "It is important to study and do homework so you do well in school and get a good job later on." "The stove is hot, keep away so you won't get burned."

6. *Be Sure the Rule is Enforceable.*   Before giving a direction, be certain you can enforce it consistently. Throw out any rule you do not intend to enforce 100 percent of the time. Ask yourself if you will know every time a child breaks the rule, without relying on someone else's testimony or surveillance. If the rule is no TV right after school, and you do not get home until 5 P.M., you will have a difficult time enforcing this rule.

7. *Review Regularly.*   Families should sit down together on a regular basis to review their rules with a view towards making necessary changes. As children mature you will want to relax some regulations while instituting others. Discuss the rules together and make adjustments as needed. Every year should see more areas in which your child is given increased responsibility and freedom. This is a gradual process that cannot be hurried.

With teenagers you will have to change and negotiate the rules quite often so as to balance their need for protection with their growing need for autonomy. Adolescents who are able to realize the risks involved in certain situations, such as football or skydiving, should make more and more decisions for themselves, even potentially dangerous ones. As one teenager expressed it, "Mother, I can't live my life by what you're afraid of."

8. *Allow Children a Choice and a Voice.*   When children have helped create a rule they are more likely to feel some responsibility for it, understand better what is expected, and comply with the rule. They will also feel more control over their own behavior, which is a step toward growing up. Thus, family council meetings are advisable wherein the children are encouraged to express their opinions about a difficulty and help resolve it by establishing a rule.

9. *Advance Notice.*   Be sure to discuss a rule with your children before you start to enforce it. Avoid ex-post-facto laws such as sud-

denly announcing "Since you left your clothes around, you can't go to the movies this weekend."

10. *Give Sparingly.*   Don't put children in a prison of rules and regulations. You will be more effective if you set only a few household rules. Not only will children remember them better but it is just not possible for you to enforce a large number of limits. It takes a lot of time and effort to enforce a single rule. So rules that are not that important should be dropped, such as requiring little children to shake hands with strangers, or insisting that adolescents wear a certain style of dress. Save the rules for the really important duties or areas which are a habitual problem or which involve safety, such as not allowing a young child to cross the street alone, or to take medicine without permission.

It is better to enforce five rules 100 percent of the time than ten rules 50 percent of the time! Most parents and parent-surrogates set too many limits and don't enforce any of them consistently. So be sure that all your rules are important and essential for harmonious living. Studies have shown that the more you increase your rules and commands, the more opposition you will receive from your children. Commands tend to set up automatic resistances in children. Allow children the opportunity, then, to learn from the natural consequences of their behavior, i.e., if they hit a bigger sibling, they will probably get hit back; if they spend their allowance they will have to do without for awhile.

For other matters try routines (brush teeth at bedtime), suggestions ("Wouldn't you like to. . . . ?"), and requests ("Please. . . .").

11. *Have Realistic Expectations.*   In making a demand on a child be sure that he is physically or developmentally able to do it and that you are not infringing on his needs for rest, relaxation, and study. Thus, you would not require a five-year-old to fully make her bed, a seven-year-old to mow the lawn each week, or an eight-year-old to study for two to three hours each day just after returning home from school.

Being realistic also means being tuned in to the present emotional and physical state of the child. Studies show that children who are tired, hungry, ill, or emotionally upset, are less likely to comply with parental commands. Thus, minimal demands should be placed on children at these times. The more legitimate your command, i.e., involves the needs or rights of others, the more obedience you will get, especially by adolescents. Also, children will obey rules more readily when both you and they benefit from the rule. If only you or other adults derive benefit from the rule, you can expect more resistance to the rule.

Another aspect of being realistic is not to set too high a standard of performance. Consider the age of the child and his present way of looking at things. A neat room may just not be important to a teenager. Rules should not be used as your way of imposing your values on a child, e.g., very high standards of cleanliness, quiet, or neatness. You can avoid many battles if you learn to accept different standards in some activities.

12. *Give a Leeway.*   Since children, especially younger ones, find it difficult to change their ongoing activity, give them a forewarning about a time limit. In other words, if you want them to come in from play, allow them a few minutes to finish playing by saying, "Five minutes more, then come in."

13. *Give a Choice.*   Directives which allow a child some freedom of choice tend to result in less opposition. Thus, instead of telling a child, "Put that food back," you might say, "You can either put some of the food back in the bowl or on my dish, whichever you prefer."

14. *Be Sure Your Child Understands.*   Children are more likely to comprehend an order if you state it concisely, and give only one order at a time. Also, have your children explain to you their understanding of the what and why of the proposed rule. This is the only way you can know for sure that your children understand the rule. If a rule is not completely understood, there is little likelihood it will be complied with to your satisfaction. So after giving a new rule ask the children to restate the rule in their own words. Correct any misunderstandings or omissions. Many children are hesitant to admit that they don't understand something, especially if a parent tends to be impatient.

15. *Prompts.*   The next time your child forgets a rule ask, "What's the rule about slamming doors?" Have the child state the rule in its entirety. Remind him if he has forgotten. Once is usually not enough for children to learn something. It takes many repetitions of the information for learning to be firmly established.

Some parents help children remember new rules by writing them down and posting them in a conspicuous place for children to look at each day.

16. *Be Consistent.*   Don't one day say "yes" and another day say "no" for the same thing. Also have private discussions with your spouse about possible rules and reach a binding agreement as to the ones you will both implement. Unless parents agree on house rules the children will divide and conquer.

ARE YOUR CHILDREN CLEAR WHO IS THE BOSS IN THE FAMILY?

Where love rules, there is no will to power; and where power predominates, there love is lacking. The one is the shadow of the other.
> —*Carl Jung*

To be comfortable regulating children you must be secure in the role of an authority figure. Authority means the power or right to give commands, enforce obedience, take action, and make final decisions. Effective authority is based on superior knowledge or expertise and is administered within an atmosphere of love and respect. The aim of parental authority is not to curtail freedom but to give a child freedom of judgment and action within manageable limits. As an authority, you should be both permissive and restrictive and strive to achieve a balance between the two.

To be in charge requires that you deny, demand, and delegate. It means saying "no" to inappropriate requests, saying "Do this" when something needs to be done, and saying "It's your decision" when a child is ready for more autonomy.

Since Vietnam and Watergate the authority of American adults has seriously eroded. As a result, there is less structure for children. Many parents seem hesitant to act with firmness and conviction. It is little wonder then that a major dilemma facing parents today is how to define and apply a relevant policy on discipline. Children want and need guidelines as to what *is* and *is not* socially acceptable behavior. They need to learn that freedom does not mean license to do whatever you please, that individual freedom is limited by the responsibility to respect the rights of others. Contrary to the philosophy of Rousseau, I do not believe that children are noble savages who should be left alone to unfold naturally as flowers. They need parental guidance and limit-setting to curb their tendencies toward hedonistic self-interest.

The foundations of parental authority are threefold:

1. *Legal.* By law you are given authority and responsibility to supervise your child so that he or she behaves in a socially acceptable way.
2. *Power.* You control most of the resources in the home (money, food) and you possess superior strength—at least during the child's early formative years.
3. *Expertise.* You have superior knowledge, experience, and competency which gives you natural authority. Just as children naturally look up to athletic coaches, they should respect your expertise on how to live in a society. Children learn respect for authority from the superior wisdom and strength of character they see exhibited by their parents. Children must see that you are not only wiser, but tougher, braver, and more strong-willed than they are.

Although no parent consistently uses a single approach, psychologists have found that parents can be classified into one of four styles of exercising authority.

1. *Dictators.* Parents who tend to espouse a dictatorial approach and stress authority and blind obedience. They follow a strict authoritarian philosophy and tend to say no a lot. They attempt to rule out of fear so that stringent punishments for transgressions are typical. Valuing obedience as a virtue, authoritarian parents do not encourage verbal give and take, believing that the child should not question authority. Their children tend to be inhibited, fearful, and conforming.
2. *Appeasers.* Parents who tend to be predominantly conciliatory and who give in to the child at crucial times. They seem to be afraid to enforce limits so that their children often get what they want. In an effort to avoid trouble, these parents tend to avoid issues and try to circumvent problems and confrontations. Some, like A. S. Neill, founder of Summerhill, a child-centered school in England, believe that to impose anything by authority is wrong. The child, they maintain, should not do anything until he comes to the opinion that it should be done.
3. *Temporizers.* Parents who tend to vary their approach in accord

with the situation. If the situation is pleasant they tend to be pleasant. If a situation tends to get out of control these parents become confused and uncertain. Lacking a firm philosophy of childrearing, they follow no consistent pattern of parenting.

4. *Cooperators.* Parents who are mostly friendly and interact with children on a basis of mutual respect. They will say yes or no to a child depending on the child's stage of development and what can reasonably be expected of the child. They try to give as much freedom of choice as possible but are comfortable setting limits when necessary. Other terms for this approach include "informed permissive," "democratic," and "authoritative."

Authoritative, according to the psychologist Baumrind,[17] means parents who present clear goals and standards of behavior for their children, and who guide their children as loving and reasoning experts while at the same time allowing their children much leeway in behavior and choices. Authoritative parents balance reasoning with firm control. They exercise their very considerable power over the lives of young children with warmth, support, encouragement, and adequate explanations. They try to treat their children with respect by valuing their opinions and feelings.

Research conducted to date suggests that the middle-of-the-road, authoritative approach is the one most likely to produce children who are both autonomous and socially responsible. Children of authoritative parents tend to be more self-controlled, friendly, and assertive than children of authoritarian or permissive parents.

In conclusion, the American philosopher Thoreau once aptly defined the most important lesson you, as the authority figure, can teach your child:

> Raise your child so that he will make himself do what he knows has to be done, when it should be done, whether he likes it or not. It is the first lesson that ought to be learned, and however early a man's training begins, it is probably the last lesson he learns thoroughly.

How do you know if you have been successful in teaching this lesson? Ask yourself the following questions: "Am I clearly the boss in this family?" "Are my rules really followed by action?" "Do my kids know I'll back up what I say?"

GIVE YOUR CHILD A WARNING, NOT A THREAT

Sometimes children have engaged in a misbehavior so long that it is difficult for them to behave appropriately. So a warning is needed to remind them to stop. A warning consists of briefly informing a child of the unpleasant consequences that will befall him if he continues to misbehave. So if your child does not comply with a rule give a warning before imposing a penalty. Often a warning alone will produce the action you desire. The warning should only be given once and should always be followed by a specific unpleasant consequence when ignored. So do not give vague threats ("You'll be sorry if you keep that up."), doomsday statements ("You'll have your head handed to you if you don't stop!"), or idle warnings that you do not intend to enforce. Rather, give a clear, realistic warning which consists of two parts: (1) a statement of the misbehavior, and (2) the consequence that will certainly be administered if the child continues to misbehave:

"This is a warning. If you use that word again, you will have to go to your room for five minutes."

"I've asked you to stop teasing your sister. If you do it once more, you'll have to go to your room."

"Joel, I'm not going to tell you this again. Either stop complaining or we're going to leave the restaurant. It's your choice."

"You have five seconds to stop crying. If you don't stop by then you'll go to your room. One, two, three, four, five."

When you give a warning it is important not to scream, yell, plead, or threaten the child; rather, state the consequences for the child nonemotionally but firmly.

Remarks

Be sure your tone of voice is firm and carries a negative inflection. Your voice quality—like your message—should be both assertive and disapproving. Otherwise, the child will be confused because your words will say one thing and your tone of voice another.

For effective warnings, the negative consequence should be consistently and immediately administered. Don't repeat a warning ten times before you mean business. If the misdeed is a frequent occurrence, omit the warning and immediately impose the penalty.

If you want your child to trust and respect you, then you should give warnings rather than threats. A warning is a realistic statement of an imminent penalty; a threat is an exaggerated statement of possible harm which is designed to intimidate a child, e.g., "You're going to get killed if you keep that up!" Threats have a high likelihood of making the child fearful of you and aggressive towards others.[18]

HOW TO PUNISH YOUR CHILDREN FOR MISBEHAVING

> *Of nineteen out of twenty things in children, take no special notice; but if as to the twentieth, you give a direction or command, see that you are obeyed.*
>
> —*Tryon Edwards*

Rules and regulations have very little meaning unless they are enforced. Punishment defined technically, is doing something to a child immediately following a rule infraction which reduces the likelihood that this misbehavior will be repeated. Generally, punishment involves imposing a penalty for an infraction. The penalty must be unpleasant to be effective and thus involve some type of loss, pain, or suffering. Applying an unpleasant consequence for a child's misdeeds is probably the most controversial topic in childrearing and the one which makes parents feel most uneasy.

The short-range goal of imposing penalties is to stop the misbehavior; the long-range goal is to teach and motivate children to stop misbehaving on their own, i.e., be inner-directed. Children want to be corrected, but they want correction within a general spirit of helping and caring for them. By enforcing a rule, you help children learn their boundaries and thus establish inner controls. Do not feel guilty about imposing penalties on occasion. It is not only a form of love to enforce limits when they are needed, but it is a necessary part of the socialization process for a child.

Penalties are most needed when the misdeed is serious in nature (harmful to self or others; when it involves open defiance of parental authority, i.e., "I won't do it."); or when it is very frequent. The defiant child who throws down the gauntlet and says, "I will not! You can't make me!" particularly needs to lose the power struggle. This is one situation you absolutely must lay down the law if you are to maintain authority and be in charge of your home. Parents who are prone to be permissive and to give in to problem children should read Dr. James Dobson's book, *Dare to Discipline*.[19]

Logical Consequences

Apart from the certainty of penalty, a key to effective discipline is to make your penalties reasonable. In depriving a child of something or in requiring restitution, be sure that the penalty you impose is logically related to the misdeed—both in type and magnitude. The nature of the misconduct should determine the penalty, not your personal preference or whim. This is an important principle since one of the most common questions parents ask about discipline is how do I enforce limits in such a way that my child will accept the penalty and view it as reasonable? Once children see the logic behind the penalty, they can accept it better—it seems more natural, reasonable, and objective. By giving children the freedom to make choices about how to behave, you have the right to expect them to face the logical consequences of their decisions. Rather than assigning penalties or consequences arbitrarily, make them directly related to the misdeed.

A logical penalty should first of all be proportional to the offense in degree of severity. Thus a teenager who misses a curfew should not be grounded for two months. This is overkill which breeds ill will and resentment because of its injustice. Nobody likes to live for two months with a penalty hanging over their head. Strive for a balance between the magnitude of the misdeed and the penalty. Penalties should never be so mild as to be inconsequential nor so strong as to be devastating or immobilizing. If a penalty is excessive, the children will focus on your unfairness rather than on their role in the act. So avoid trying to eliminate a misdeed "once and for all" by overdoing the penalty.

Secondly, the type of penalty should be related to the type of offense. For example, if a child cannot act in a socially acceptable manner with others in the home, he should be socially isolated for a period until he can behave appropriately with others. If a child leaves toys around, he should not be allowed to play with anything else until the toys are picked up. If a child rides his bike without permission, he should lose the privilege of bike riding for one day.

It is clear that penalties must be planned ahead. In the "heat of the moment" it is very difficult if not impossible to determine reasonable penalties. When emotions are high there is a tendency to generate a "lot of heat but not much light" on a problem.

Further examples and a more complete discussion of the concept of logical consequences can be found in Rudolf Dreikurs' book *Logical Consequences*.[20]

PART I. HOW TO PUNISH CHILDREN

Types of Acceptable Penalties

There are a variety of things that parents can do to punish children. Each one has its own advantages and disadvantages. Three main types of appropriate penalties have been used by parents: (1) make the child perform an unpleasant act; (2) deprive the child of something pleasant; and (3) impose psychological or physical discomfort on the child.

1. *Child Performs an Unpleasant Act.*

  Child corrects a mistake. Correction involves making amends for a misdeed. Often it entails requiring a child to restore the loss or damage to others or to property. The rationale behind correction is that whenever a misdeed is followed by work or payment to undo the harm then the misdeed will be avoided in the future. Of course the cost of making amends should substantially outweigh the benefits of performing the misdeed. Correction helps restore the child's sense of self-worth and also the goodwill of others.

  Making amends to the victim of your wrongdoing teaches you the harmful effects of your misdeed on the victim and encourages you to imagine yourself in the other person's place. Penalties which represent concrete acts of reparation help the child learn that when you hurt someone, you should do something to make it right again. Restitution, then, is an altruistic rather than punitive form of discipline. Studies of altruistic discipline have found it to be related to other acts of altruism in children. Rather than just paying a penalty which is unrelated to the misdeed—thus wiping the slate clean in some children's eyes and freeing them up for repeating the offense—making restitution to a victim seems to help develop a feeling and caring about others.

Examples of correction are: making a child apologize after he has teased or insulted a peer; having a child pay to replace a toy he has broken; requiring teenagers to clean up a school building and playground after an act of vandalism; making a child who has just slammed the door on entering the house go outside and come in again quietly; and insisting that a child who has washed a dish poorly go over it again until it is clean.

Child writes a plan for improving behavior.   Tell your misbehaving child that you expect her to think of a way she can prevent the misdeed from occurring again. Rather than a simple promise you want a specific plan for change. Usually a child will need to go to a quiet room for a while to think of a plan of action.[21]

So in order to train your child to think of appropriate ways of handling and preventing future occurrences of a misbehavior, try requiring your child to write a paragraph which contains the following components:

1. A clear statement of the misbehavior and the rule that was broken.
2. The adverse effect on others or self.
3. A way to immediately correct or undo the harm, e.g., apologize, replace a loss.
4. A plan for preventing reoccurrence of the misbehavior.

At first you may have to write this paragraph for the child but gradually the child should be able to do it all herself. This procedure trains a child to think, to plan ahead, and to use words to control behavior. It is more effective than to write 50 times "I will not do it again."

Examples of this approach are:
For name calling:

"Jimmy, I'm sorry I called you names. Name calling hurts people's feelings and makes the problem worse. You're one of the nicest brothers around. Next time we get into an argument, I'll think about what I'm saying. We have all agreed not to call each other names."

For fighting:

"John, I shouldn't have hit you. Hitting can really hurt people. I like you and you're my friend. Next time I think you took my things, I'll ask you about it first. We shouldn't fight."

For interrupting a parent who is talking on the phone:

"I'm sorry Mom. I didn't mean to interrupt and disturb you. Next time, I'll wait till you're off the phone before talking to you, unless it's a really urgent matter. We have to be considerate to each other."

Another way to help a child write a helpful essay is to ask the child to list three questions and their answers. For example,

1. "What did I do wrong?" "I interrupted my father while he was talking to my mother."
2. "Why shouldn't I interrupt a person who is talking?" "Because it makes it difficult for them to have a private conversation and they'll get annoyed at me."
3. "What should I do instead?" I should wait until they are finished talking or if it's really urgent say "Can I interrupt, it's very important!"

2. *Deprivation.* To deprive a child of pleasant experiences you can either take away privileges and possessions or send the child to a "time-out" area.

Loss of privileges or possessions. It is certainly unpleasant for a child to lose a valued object or privilege. Examples of common deprivations are loss of TV watching privileges, no dessert until the meal is eaten, a fine or loss of part of the child's allowance for failure to do a chore, and "grounding" for a period of time which prohibits use of the family car or visiting with certain friends.

Don't go to extremes and deprive a child of a complete meal. Children should be given food as a matter of course. Using food deprivation fosters the development of food disorders such as compulsive overeating and starving oneself (anorexia nervosa).

Time-out (TO). Requiring a young child to go to a quiet, boring area after annoying other family members is often a good strategy to help the child regain control and to allow tempers to cool off. Thus, a time-out means the child leaves the scene of a misdeed and goes to a quiet place elsewhere in the house to do nothing until allowed to return. The TO area should be devoid of interesting things to do or look at, e.g., select a hallway, corner of a room, or bathroom. The TO area should be far enough away to prevent any further occurrence of the misbehavior yet close enough for the child to hear what he is missing.

Some Do's and Don'ts for Time-Out:

1. Remember to give a warning first that TO is imminent unless the annoying misbehavior stops. For example, you might say, "Joan, you will have to take a time-out if your silliness at the table continues. You can either stay here and act appropriately or leave. You decide."

2. Tell the child to go to the TO area if the misbehavior continues. If the child resists leaving, use the minimum physical force necessary to enforce the departure to TO. Ignore protestations on the way and give no further attention while you escort the child.

3. Tell the child that you will say when TO is over. Make the TO periods short, i.e., 5 to 10 minutes. It is better to have frequent, short TO's than a few very long ones. Be sure to give a TO every time a child cannot behave appropriately with others. Consistency in using TO is more important than severity. Make it swift and sure. Give it early enough to prevent misdeeds from escalating in severity. Usually with a child from two to five years of age, it is best to begin by placing him in TO for 5 minutes; with a child over five years of age, 10 minutes is more appropriate. Set a kitchen timer for the allotted time, and when it is up you will be cued by the bell or buzzer.

   Some parents prefer to tell the child to stay in time-out until he decides he is ready to return and act the way he is supposed to do.

4. The usual response of the child to being placed in the time-out area is to protest, whine, cry, or have a tantrum. To these reactions you should say "The longer you cry and whine, the longer you will have to stay in time-out. I am setting the timer back to the beginning." State this once in a firm manner and then ignore further protests. Once the child has stopped crying wait the standard duration (five or ten minutes). When the timer rings you should inform the child that she can leave time-out and rejoin the family.

5. Some children will attempt to leave the time-out area. If this occurs you must immediately escort them back to the room and reset the timer. Be watchful in the beginning of the procedure so the child will learn that she cannot escape from the time-out room. If the child makes a mess in the time-out area she should earn another ten minutes in time-out which will not start until the mess is picked up.

No eating, playing, or reading is allowed in the time-out area.

6. A major effect of seclusion is to allow the child to calm down by reducing sensory stimulation and frustrating social interactions. Time out is most appropriate for the following behaviors: disobedience, destructiveness, swearing, fighting, teasing, loud or disruptive behaviors, and silliness.

7. After TO is over redirect the child to appropriate behaviors and praise the child for being quiet in TO, and praise again when he or she begins behaving well.

8. TO works best with preschool and school age children rather than teenagers.

9. Don't send a child to bed early as a form of time-out. To associate sleep with punishment cannot help but negatively affect the child's attitude toward going to sleep in general. Going to sleep is difficult for many children because of the separation anxiety it evokes. Don't reinforce the notion that there is something bad about going to sleep.

Recommended Reading on Time Out

Patterson, G. R. *Living with Children,* (Revised), Research Press, 1976.

Silent treatment.   A variation of time-out is to give the silent treatment to a rebellious child. This means not talking to or interacting with the child until she conforms to the rule. A more severe form of this silent procedure is called "Stop-the-World." This involves bringing a child's world to a standstill until a job that needs to be done is finished. The following steps are required:

1. No family member is to give any attention to the child.
2. Don't allow the child to participate in any other family activity until the job has been done, e.g., no watching TV; child has to eat meals by himself.

3. Praise the child for all efforts toward getting the job done.
4. Tell the child when he has completed the task he may continue with normal family activities.

3. *Direct Application of Psychological or Physical Discomfort.* Another way to penalize a child for misconduct is to directly apply psychological or physical discomfort.

    Reprimands.   Reprimanding or scolding a child is probably the most frequent form of parental punishment used in our society. A reprimand clearly expresses a parent's disapproval for a particular behavior by the child. In reprimanding you should avoid "character assassination," that is, expressing negative comments about the child's character or personality, e.g., "You dummy," "You're a bad boy." So disapprove the *behavior,* and avoid labeling the child's personality.

    Try using this five-step approach in reprimanding a child:

Step One: In a clear direct manner point out the behavior that must be changed, e.g., "No throwing food at the table!"

Step Two: Explain the reason for the limit: "Throwing food makes a mess." In other words tell why the behavior is unacceptable in terms of the negative effects on self or others.

Step Three: Tell your child what the penalty will be if he continues to misbehave: "If you throw any more food you will have to go right to your room."

Step Four: At this point you should point out an acceptable alternative way to deal with the problem situation: "Food is for eating not for playing with."

Step Five: Ask for feedback on how the child understood your reprimand: "Now what did I just tell you?"

Step Six: Quickly reestablish affectionate bonds with the child: "Thank you for eating your food so nicely."

Guidelines for Reprimanding:

1. Use sparingly since studies indicate that children tend to avoid adults who frequently reprimand them.
2. Use an assertive, stern tone of voice in reprimanding so as to signal the child that you mean business. Raise and project your voice but

don't shout. Avoid a nagging, shrieking or hostile tone of voice which will alienate your child.

3. Before reprimanding a child, try to ignore the misdeed if at all possible. If ignoring fails, use reprimanding; if reprimanding fails to change the misbehavior, then punish the child with other means such as loss of privileges or time out. By backing up reprimands with stiffer penalties you increase the power of a reprimand. A reprimand will then be a cue to a child that more severe punishment will surely follow if the misbehavior continues.

4. Try not to reprimand a child in front of others. A private talk in a quiet spot is best.

5. Keep reprimands short, that is, a minute or two. If your scolding lasts five minutes or more you are probably lecturing to a child who is not listening.

Physical force. Sometimes it is necessary for parents to reaffirm through physical means that they mean what they are saying. Physical coercion or force should generally be the last control method to be used. It should be employed only when all the other techniques of influencing children have failed. Being responsible for children, however, means that you sometimes cannot be tolerant of a child's lack of compliance or cooperation. Legitimate coercion consists of taking children by the arm and leading or carrying them in a desired direction, e.g., to another room.

At times you may need to physically guide a child over to a task and literally force him to follow through. For example, you may need to hold a child's hands while he picks up objects from the floor that must be put away. Physically assisting (by giving only as much help as is needed to complete the task) conveys to the child that you seriously expect your commands to be carried out. So firmly and kindly lead him by the hand and help him hang up the coat he has left on the floor, or to take the bath that is required.

When using physical assistance, you should remain calm but firm. Show determination, but not hostility. Avoid yelling or glaring at the child. In a matter-of-fact manner explain the reason you are using physical force, i.e., how he brought it on himself by deciding to continue to act inappropriately even though you had warned him of the consequences.

Apart from *physical assistance* to perform desired acts, *physical restraint* may also be needed at times. If a child attempts to hit you you should immediately grab his arms and prevent the blow.

Your child may have a temper tantrum so severe that he will have to be physically restrained so as to protect either himself, others, or property. A particularly effective procedure for restraining an out-of-control child is to hold him from behind and securely place your arms around his. When you hold a child from behind you lessen the danger of your being kicked by him. Hold his arms crisscrossed across his chest and try to sit on a carpeted floor with your back against a sofa. While holding an upset child, you should continually express calm, reassuring words, such as "It's going to be all right."; "Just relax."; "I won't let any harm come to you."; "As soon as you have calmed down, I'll let you go." In a time of crisis such as this, a child with poor impulse control needs to feel that he can draw upon the physical strength of an adult. Holding or restraining a child should be done in a firm but nonpainful way. Use only as much force as is actually needed to control the child. Physical restraint and coercion are not intended to be forms of physical punishment!

Remember that physical control should not be confused with corporal punishment which involves the infliction of physical pain on a child by such practices as spanking, paddling, pinching, squeezing, and slapping.

PART II. GUIDELINES FOR ENFORCING LIMITS

The following general guidelines should assist you to improve your effectiveness in imposing penalties for the misbehaviors of children.

1. *Be Consistent.* Perhaps the most common fault of parents who have problems disciplining children is lack of consistency in enforcement. Consistency is important for the following reason. Research has indicated that inconsistent enforcement (sometimes punishing, sometimes not punishing) may actually increase the undesired behavior. Consistency means giving a penalty *every* time the child breaks the rule.

   Adults should strive for both inter- and intrapersonal consistency in imposing penalties. Interpersonal consistency means that all the supervising adults in the home apply essentially the same penalties for a misdeed. Too often a strict father and a permissive mother will try to balance each other out by becoming stricter or more permissive in their punishment, as the case may be. This balancing approach tends to confuse children by confronting them with extremely divergent reactions and a "two wrongs make a right" approach. Husbands and wives must resolve differing philosophies of childrearing and personality conflicts if they want to avoid placing their children in the middle of a power struggle.

Intrapersonal consistency means your child can expect—over time—the same penalty from you for a specific misdeed. Don't set a penalty one day and a completely different type of consequence the next day—depending on your whims or emotional state. Intrapersonal consistency also means that you impose a penalty every time it is warranted, regardless of how tired you feel. If a child repeats the same infraction and you ignore it one day but impose a penalty the next, this uncertainty will undoubtedly result in an argument with the child to justify the punishment. The more confident you are in your authority and the more vigilant you are in applying penalties each time a particular misconduct occurs, the more your child will accept the penalties without protest and argument. Consistency means rules can be bent only in extraordinary occasions or emergencies. The sooner children learn that you mean what you say, that penalties are almost a certainty for specific offenses, the better for all concerned.

2. *Stand Firm Under Pressure.* Children often pressure parents into being inconsistent. When parents start to impose a penalty they can count on their children to attempt to talk them out of it. The fact that a rule makes children unhappy or frustrated does not mean you are a "bad" parent. Stand firm and weather the storm. Only change a rule when it becomes obvious that it is unworkable or unrealistic. Among the strategies children have found effective in the past are:

- Calling you names ("mean Mommy") and saying "I hate you."
- Screaming, throwing things or having a temper tantrum.
- Denying responsibility for the act: "I didn't do it."

- Holding one's breath until blue in the face.
- Crying or sobbing hysterically.
- Whining.
- Procrastination through arguing.
- Complaining about the lack of your love.
- Comparisons with what other children are allowed to do.
- Comparison with what your spouse allows the child to do.
- Defiance and saying "I won't do it."
- Threatening to leave home, drop out of school, or kill oneself.
- Pouting or not talking to you.
- Promising to be good.
- Asking for just one more chance.
- Blaming someone else: "He started it."
- Protesting that you are unfair.
- Offering to bargain.
- Giving excuses: At times children will have valid reasons for breaking a rule. At other times they will give you an excuse (invalid reason) to change your mind about a penalty. Parents must become adept at teaching children the difference between good reasons and poor excuses.

Excuse: "I didn't clean my room because I didn't have time."

Reason: "I was sick in bed so I couldn't clean my room."

Excuse: "I didn't do my homework because I lost the assignment."

Reason: "I didn't do my homework because we had no electrical power last night due to the storm."

The above strategies are children's natural reactions to frustration. If they succeed then it will be clear to the children that you do not have the strength of your convictions and that you are not in charge of the house. Temporary unpopularity with your children is the price you have to pay for being the leader. As Betty Davis once said, "You haven't been a parent unless your children have hated you." Ignore the above maneuvers and kindly but firmly follow through with the penalty.

3. *Be Calm and Matter-of-Fact.*   Explain a punishment to a child in a calm and matter-of-fact manner, much like a judge reading a

decision, or a referee announcing a 15-yard penalty in football. Avoid name-calling, yelling, insults, sarcasm, and other judgmental, critical techniques which only lower a child's self-esteem while increasing his emotional reaction. A punishment should highlight conflict between a child's behavior and a very sensible rule or principle, while minimizing any personal conflict between you and the child. Remember that children pay more attention to the nonverbal communications of the punishing adult than to the verbal ones. If you discipline with an enraged look, a vocal tone five times higher than usual, and hands trembling, they will feel unloved and disliked, no matter what you say verbally. When you punish out of hostility the child will sense this and see it as vengeance rather than justice. So administer punishments as matter-of-factly as possible. When you stay calm and confident, the child will get over his anger much quicker. The means you use to punish are probably secondary to your emotional attitude in giving the penalty. Children will learn you are every bit as serious when speaking calmly as when screaming. Moreover, research has shown that the more emotional you are in punishing, the more severe will be the punishment you impose. Your attitude should be that of a teacher, i.e., wanting to help the child learn.

One way to stay calm is to expect kids to rebel against your authority as part of the normal process of growing up and developing their own identity. We should expect some nonconformity at times, then, and not overreact by taking it personally. On those occasions when you simply cannot keep in your anger or annoyance, simply tell the child exactly how angry you are at the misbehavior. In other words, express your anger by focusing on your feelings and needs rather than trying to hurt the child by insults, threats, or other demeaning comments.

4. *Be Sure you Have a Positive Relationship.*   Children accept punishment best when they have a positive relationship with the adult, e.g., the adult tends to be generally warm, rewarding, accepting, and supportive of the child. You cannot effectively discipline children you dislike. If a child feels only marginally accepted, your use of punishment will tend to solidify his negative view of you. Within a positive relationship, the most painful aspect of punishment for a child tends to be the disapproval or disappointment of the valued adult. In a good relationship, you will be most influential when a

child has found it emotionally satisfying to want to be like you and to care about what you think of his behavior.

5. *Allow the Expression of Feeling.* "I hate doing homework," "All I ever do is clean my room." These are not "I won't" statements. They are statements about the child's emotional reactions to the rule. Children have a right not to like something. Usually a child will comply with the requirement or take his punishment once she has expressed her displeasure. So allow your children the expression of feelings (as long as they do not offend others) and assist them to be in touch with these feelings by recognizing them yourself, e.g., "You really wanted to go to the movies tonight and feel angry that it's against the rule on school nights."

While showing concern for the child's feelings and desires, you should avoid getting into an argument with an emotionally upset child about the necessity of the rule itself. Such arguments are fruitless. Explain the reason for the rule once (or twice for a young child) and then ignore any further protestations from the child.

6. *Respond to the Child's Requests.* Children are more likely to obey you when you have a close relationship with them and they feel that you have been very attentive to their needs and requests, i.e., there is reciprocity in the relationship in that you both readily comply with each other's requests and are tuned in to each other's needs. You can expect considerable rebelliousness in a one-sided relationship wherein children feel they have to comply with many restrictions while no one seems to be sensitive to their needs.

7. *Timing.* Studies have shown that punishment is generally most effective in fostering learning when it immediately follows the misdeed. If more than a few seconds elapse a young child will have difficulty relating the punishment to the misdeed. Punishment is more effective when it is applied as the child is in the act, i.e., as the child reaches for the materials from the supply cabinet, rather than after he already has taken them. Delay can cause a child to forget what he or she did to deserve the penalty.

The adult who experiences or first discovers the problem, should be the one to impose the penalty. In view of this, mothers should avoid saying, "Wait until your father gets home." The timing is not only poor when this is done, but it places the father in the role of villain who must assume an unfair share of rule enforcement.

8. *Disapprove the Behavior, Not the Child.* The message you want

to convey by using punishment is that, while you disapprove of certain of the child's actions, you still strongly approve of the child himself. Thus, you should avoid expressing global disapproval of the whole child, e.g., "I don't like you for that," or "You bad boy." Rather, your reaction should be limited to specific behavior, e.g., "I don't like your loud screaming in the house."

The message you want to get across by enforcing a limit is that the child made a mistake in judgment for which he or she must accept responsibility. You want to avoid the message that the child is a bad or evil person who has terrible faults. Parents should expect children to make mistakes and then to suffer the consequences of these errors. Don't demand perfection from the children and become incensed when they do not live up to your unrealistic expectations. Try to avoid discouraging a child by taking his or her misconduct as a personal affront or terrible failure. Blaming, damning, or threatening to withdraw love after a misdeed only compounds the problem by lowering the child's self-esteem.

9. *Give a Warning.*   Warnings teach a child to think of the negative consequences of a misbehavior and thus to develop greater self control. Often a warning alone will stop the misbehavior. Before imposing a penalty, then, warn the child once that it's imminent; if the child has received repeated warnings in the past, then you can dispense with this advance notice.

10. *Make the Punishment Fit the Crime.*

> *My object all sublime I shall achieve in time—to make the punishment fit the crime.*
>
> *from the "Mikado" by Gilbert and Sullivan*

As stated above, the punishment you give needs to fit the crime. It is to be hoped that it will be logically related to the undesired behavior. For example, if a child mistreats a toy, or other possession, that object should be taken from the child for a reasonable period of time.

11. *Allow Time to Comply.*   Except in an emergency, don't expect "instant" obedience. There is no need to run your home like a drill sergeant. The child may be engrossed in an activity and fully intends to comply with your direction but not immediately. Chil-

dren need time to disengage from one activity (e.g. outdoor play) and begin another (e.g. eat supper).

12. *Don't Expect Perfection of the Child.*   Remember that the psychologically healthy child is not the "perfect" or "model" child; the well-adjusted child is the one who follows most of the rules but has the independence, individuality, and the courage to break them once in a while.

Don't expect perfection of yourself either. Helping children become mature, self-disciplined individuals requires mature, self-disciplined adults. However, no parent can be ideal nor should one expect to be perfect. We all have our angry, impatient, and unfair moments in imposing penalties. These occasional emotional reactions will not impair our relationship with the child.

Of course, we should try to improve our self-control and disciplinary techniques without imposing unrealistically high standards upon ourselves. Raising children gives us a unique opportunity to know ourselves better and to grow in maturity. As Thoreau once said, "There is a child in every parent who needs to learn discipline."

13. *Be Just.*   In the interest of justice, be sure to consider the following in imposing a penalty: first or repeated offence; premeditated or impulsive act; general character and conduct; and any extenuating circumstances.

14. *Be Explicit.*   In order to avoid any possible misunderstanding by the child about why he is being punished, you should do three things: name the misbehavior; state the rule or principle that is being broken by the misdeed; and describe the punishment or unpleasant consequence that the child will receive because of the infraction. An example of a brief, explicit statement is: "John, you decided to go out of the yard today which is against the rules, so now you'll have to miss outdoor play tomorrow."

By clearly and explicitly linking his misbehavior with the penalty, you weaken any efforts by the child to blame you for the punishment he has earned. Be sure to emphasize to the child that he had a choice in the situation and that by deciding to perform the deviant act, he elected to experience the adverse consequences. Your goal should be to promote self-criticism and confession in the child and to prevent him from avoiding responsibility by such tactics as denial (i.e., "I didn't do anything wrong."), rationalization (i.e., "Everybody is doing it."), or projection (i.e., "He started it.").

15. *Use Different Discipline at Different Ages.* Different kinds of discipline seem necessary at different stages of a child's development. Children between 8 and 13 months of age can usually be controlled through distraction tactics. Children 13 to 18 months of age require distraction and physical removal from circumstances at times; and children between 18 and 24 months require distraction, physical removal, and verbal restrictions. Preschool children respond well to time-out and reprimands while loss of privileges is effective with older children.

Remember that adolescents continue to need supervision and enforcement of limits since studies have shown mature impulse control is usually not attained until age 19 and moral development continues through age 25.

16. *Gather All The Facts.* Before punishing the child, you should calmly, deliberately, and objectively gather all the relevant facts. Moreover, it you adopt a causal approach and seek to determine why the child misbehaved, you will be in a better position to not only set a just penalty, but to eliminate the basic cause of the difficulty by understanding the child's motives. Be sure to allow the child to explain his side of the story. Justice demands that everyone has a right to a fair hearing before being punished. In this regard, mothers have been found to listen to children more than fathers, and thus tend to make better disciplinarians. When you find you have acted too hastily and made a mistake in punishing a child, admit your error immediately.

17. *No Double Jeopardy.* Be sure that the child is not punished by two different sources for the same offense, e.g., both teacher and parent punish child for the same behavior.

18. *Privacy.* A cardinal rule in discipline is that almost without exception, warnings and penalties should be administered to a child as privately as possible. No one likes to be criticized in public and we react with open or hidden resentment when this happens. In accord with the golden rule, we should treat children as we would like to be treated.

19. *Combine With Support.* After being punished, a child particularly needs your immediate warmth and understanding. This will not negate the lesson, but will keep your child from feeling unloved.

Young children especially have a tendency to feel rejected and unloved when punished by their parents. By being friendly and warm to a child after disciplining him you demonstrate that it was the misdeed you disapproved of, not the child. Introduce a positive note as soon as possible by praising the child for taking the penalty well; then redirect the child's attention to alternate acceptable behaviors. The period after a child has completed a penalty is often a good time to have a heart-to-heart talk about the problem. By being friendly and supportive after imposing a penalty, you can break the negative emotional climate aroused by the punishment. Show the child by a hug, praise, or other means that you are eager to relate in enjoyable ways again, that the incident is closed and the slate has been wiped clean. Don't hold a grudge!

20. *Be Sure the Punishment is Unpleasant.*   A punishment must be perceived by the child as a painful or unpleasant experience. What is noxious to one child may be positively reinforcing to another. Studies have shown that scolding some children actually increases misbehavior since this is the only form of adult attention they receive. So unless a punishment serves to decrease the occurrence of an undesired behavior it is not effective.

21. *Use Only as Last Resort.*   Since punishment generally indicates failure to a child—and frequent failure experiences can lower self-esteem and confidence—it is best to concentrate more on positive reinforcement of socially acceptable behavior than on suppression of misbehavior by punishment. Of course, there will be times when penalties must be imposed, but positive methods should be used much more frequently so that you establish an approval-disapproval ratio of about 3 or 4 to 1. The social climate in a home seems to a large extent to be influenced by the approval-disapproval ratio employed by the parents. So make greater use of the more positive forms of discipline such as praise, rewards, modeling, reasoning, presuasion, and diversion.

22. *Reward Positive Behavior.*   The carrot and stick approach is certainly more effective than the stick alone. So rather than just punishing a child for a misdeed, try to strengthen by positive reinforcement (praise, rewards) alternate prosocial behaviors that will compete with the misdeed. For example, be sure to praise a child for sharing his possessions with his peers rather than just punishing him when he grabs his toys away from others. Too often adults take

good behaviors for granted, assuming virtue is its own reward. When this happens the child may have to resort to disruptive behavior in order to gain attention.

23. *Monitor Effects on Child.* Children's reactions to punishment are a very individual thing. Some kids have severe emotional reactions to certain forms of punishment. A very insecure, fearful child, for example, may become quite upset if isolated for a period of time in his room. Consider the child's feelings about the punishment since they are as important as the punishment itself. If a child is already feeling remorseful about the mistake, guilty scolding by you may lead to discouragement and depression. In this case, the child needs encouragement rather than criticism.

24. *Child Involvement.* Before externally imposing blame or guilt upon a child for his misdeed, allow him the opportunity to evaluate his own culpability in the situation. Thus, you might ask, "What did you do?" rather than encouraging the child to project all the blame onto others. After several dodges, the child will usually come up with at least a partial description of his involvement. Encourage your child to assess his behavior in terms of its helpfulness to others and to himself. ("Did your actions help others? Help yourself?")

Occasionally, try allowing children to determine their own punishment. This will encourage kids to be more reflective and responsible for their own actions. If a child gives himself an excessive punishment, you can always tone it down. If the punishment is too light, try it once and see if it proves to be effective.

25. *Point out Acceptable Alternatives.* Punishment is designed to teach a child what not to do. A child will be more likely to change his inappropriate behavior, however, when he not only knows what he should not do, but what he should do. When punishing a child, then, take the time to explain what you consider to be acceptable behavior in that particular situation, e.g., "Joan, blocks are for building things, not for throwing around." Good discipline is a positive force that is oriented toward what a child is allowed to do, rather than what he is forbidden to do.

Epilogue

The final goal of imposing penalties is to teach children to develop their own inner controls. The children's reactions to their misdeeds will give you valuable insights into your effectiveness as a disciplinarian. Consider how they typically react when they have misbehaved and caused harm to others. If they usually react with guilt, confession, and constructive efforts to undo the harm, then you know you are on the right track in that they have internalized parental interdictions and formed a conscience. On the other hand, if they tend to react with denials, Watergate-type coverups, projection of blame onto others, avoidance of adults who punish, or with attempts to rationalize away all personal responsibility, then you should probably consider reviewing and/or changing your disciplinary practices. Children who persist in engaging in antisocial acts because of underlying psychological problems or value differences will probably need therapy, not repeated punishment by parents.

PUNISHMENTS YOU SHOULD NEVER (OR RARELY) USE WITH YOUR CHILDREN

The "don'ts" of punishment are even more important than the "do's." Parents tend to invent new and ingenious methods of punishment which all too frequently are improper methods. An unacceptable punishment is one which is psychologically or physically abusive to a child.

Psychological Abuse

1. *Threats.*   Don't try to frighten or intimidate a child by threatening severe harm if she continues to misbehave. Threats of physical abuse are rather common. "I'll break every bone in your body," "You'll be wiping blood off your face if you don't behave." Some parents threaten to withdraw their love: "I won't love you anymore," or to abandon the child for good: "You can just pack your bags and get out of here," "I'm leaving this house and I'm not coming back," "I'll kill myself if you keep this up." Such threats instill extreme anxiety and insecurity in a child and inhibit learning. Children who are afraid of their parents tend to defend themselves by lying (denying the misdeed) and blaming others.
2. *Guilt.*   Excessive guilt lays the groundwork for neurotic problems

in children. So don't attempt to instill excessive guilt in a child by such statements as: "How could you come home so late. After all I've done for you, how can you treat me like this?" "You're driving me crazy," "You're giving me an ulcer," "You'll be the death of me."

3. *Comparisons.* Don't put a child down by comparing and making the child feel inferior to another child. ("Why can't you eat properly like your brother here?") Comparisons often lead to inferiority feelings and resentment/hostility to the other child.

4. *Yelling/Shrieking.* Much as children dislike spanking, they seem to get more upset and anxious about being yelled at by their parents. Yelling tends to last longer than spanking and it frightens children to see their parents so out of control.

5. *Nagging.* Children tend to tune out when their parents nag or repetitively remind them to do something. Once a child understands a rule, punish an infraction rather than repeating the order again and again. Too much nagging can result in the opposite behavior from what is desired.

6. *Verbal Putdowns.* Parents can verbally lower their children's self-worth by a variety of means including:

   Name calling: "You're a bad, bad boy."
   Sarcasm: "Where were you born, in a barn?"
   Shame: Shame is designed to make a child believe there is something wrong with him, that somehow he is not good, defective, bad, or worthless. "Shame on you. I told you not to take that cookie and you did."

7. *Overgeneralizing.* Avoid overgeneralizing from a few instances: "You never mind me," "You'll never amount to anything," "You always lie." Give a child a bad label and he may well believe it and act accordingly.

Physical Abuse

No one loves the man whom he fears.

—*Aristotle*

Corporal punishment can be defined as intentionally inflicting physical harm on a child as a way of correcting misbehavior. Examples of corporal punishment include spanking, slapping, paddling, pinching, kicking, ear pulling, squeezing, arm twisting, shaking, washing the mouth out with soap, and forcing the child to stand for long periods of time.

Parents do not have to hit children to control them. But surveys show that about 85 percent of American parents occasionally use spanking to discipline children. Parents use it because it is quick, familiar, readily available, and effective in temporarily stopping a misbehavior. Moreover, it offers a release for parental anger.

Among the disadvantages of using corporal punishment are the following:

1. It is likely to impair your relationship with the child. Your child may become fearful, resentful, hostile, and withdrawn.
2. It tends to suppress misbehavior only for a short time. The misdeed is likely to occur again later at its original level. Corporal punishment only stops misbehavior; it does not teach an alternate appropriate action.
3. It models a form of violence (however slight) as a means of resolving conflicts. Research indicates that violence nearly always increases violence. Parents who use physical punishment tend to increase the level of violent or aggressive behavior in their children.
4. It often leads to serious physical abuse of children, such as severe abrasions, broken bones, concussions.

Because of the above disadvantages, I feel corporal punishment is a highly questionable practice that should not be used. If you were to hit, slap, or spank a stranger it would be considered a form of assault. So how can we justify the use of corporal punishment on children. Physical punishment is not allowed in our child-care institutions or prisons and should not be practiced in our homes. A number of effective alternate penalties are available for use in lieu of spanking. Time-out and loss of privileges are two highly successful alternatives that are more humane.

"Quick-lick" Spanking

Unfortunately the "spare the rod and spoil the child" philosophy is deeply engraved in American child rearing. Since most parents will continue to spank, it should be done in a manner least likely to result in serious harm. If you must spank a child, the "quick-lick" spanking seems best wherein you quickly swat the child on the bottom with the palm of your hand hard enough to cause discomfort but not so severe as to be abusive. Be sure to quickly reestablish a feeling a closeness with the child so the child does not feel personally rejected. If you use the "quick-lick" spanking *very rarely* and within an overall context of warmth and acceptance, it is unlikely to severely impair the child's welfare or your relationship with him. If you believe spankings should not be used you will at best never use them and, at worst, use them very infrequently. Remember to always avoid the following harmful practices

Never Use Physical Punishment in the Following Ways

1. *Never* give a child a beating. When you are really upset or angry you are likely to give a beating rather than a spanking. Beatings are likely to permanently injure a child—both physically and psychologically. They are a clear form of child abuse!
2. *Never* shake a child to punish. Recent findings by medical doctors have shown that whiplash effects are not uncommon following the shaking of a child. The whiplash can be severe enough to cause damage to the vertebrae of the neck.
3. *Never* slap a child in the face. Older children, in particular, feel more than the physical sting of a slap which is humiliating to them. Historically slapping is the ultimate personal insult.
4. *Never* hit a child with an object such as a paddle or hairbrush.
5. *Never* spank an infant, or a child over the age of 10 to 12.
6. *Never* use excessive or unusual physical punishment.
7. *Never* fall into the habit of hitting too often or too hard. If this is the case, find another way to punish.
8. *Never* allow anyone else to spank your child—not brothers or sisters, not grandparents, uncles or aunts, babysitters, boyfriends.
9. *Never* spank a child in public.
10. *Never* spank a child when your emotions are out of control.

GUIDELINES FOR GIVING CHILDREN REWARDS AND PENALTIES

When to Give

A well-established learning principle is that the sooner young children receive a sanction (reward or penalty) following their behavior, the more effective these sanctions or reinforcers will be in changing the frequency with which the behaviors occur. In other words, the longer the delay between the child's behavior and the parent's response, the less effective the learning will be. Thus, young children should receive immediate feedback from their parents in the form of positive or negative reinforcements.

For example, a parent who gives his child a penalty immediately following a misdeed, or better yet during the execution of the misdeed will be more effective in decreasing the frequency of this misdeed than a parent who says, "I'll talk to you about that later," or "Wait until you daddy gets home!" So if you look out your kitchen window and discover your preschool child is picking flowers from your garden but you are tied up and can't say anything to the child right away, don't try to punish the child several hours later. Rather, it would be better to wait until the child repeats the act and then administer a warning or penalty. You want the child to associate unpleasant consequences with flower picking, not something the child is doing several hours later.

Also, rather than telling a teenager that "You can't go to the party next week," give a more immediate penalty like loss of TV or telephone privileges. Nobody likes to have something hanging over their head for a week.

If you must delay giving an immediate reward or penalty to a young child, give a symbol or token immediately to indicate that the sanction will be conferred.

As a child matures, he will be more able to anticipate future reinforcers and will have less of a need for immediate consequences. Still, you will often find that children will be unable to persevere at long, difficult tasks. Children often drop music lessons, for example, because practicing is hard work and the joys of playing are minimal in the early stages. The solution to this difficulty may lie in finding a more immediate incentive for the child, such as learning to play in school with his or her close friends, or learning to play with the immediate goal of qualifying for the school band.

One of the main advantages of taking short steps in route to a major objective is that success with the initial efforts tends to fuel and sustain longer term efforts. It is very difficult for a teenager to sustain his effort in studying physics or chemistry solely on the basis of his goal of becoming a doctor some day. He needs a more immediate payoff, such as good grades or otherwise taking each course as a challenging task in itself.

How Often to Give

Kids learn slowly and forget quickly. To be effective in changing a child's behavior, you will have to reinforce their behavior more than once. Be patient and repeat the reinforcers on different occasions. In general, children do not learn things once and for all. Slow learners and/or emotionally disturbed children, in particular, will require a large number of learning trials.

Research has shown that children learn a new behavior faster if they are reinforced every time they perform the behavior. However, if you constantly reinforce children after they have learned an act, then they will not maintain it as well as if you reinforce them occasionally. So it seems best for you to reinforce a child 100 percent of the time until he has mastered the behavior, and then give him only occasional reinforcement, e.g., once for every two or three occurrences of the behavior, to be sure the behavior is continued over time. The fact that an *occasional* reward is all that is needed to keep one at something indefinitely has been called the "Las Vegas" principle, since the behavior of the slot machine faithfuls and other gamblers attests to the power of this motivation.

Need to Vary

Sanctions that are effective with one child may not be appropriate for another. Each child has a unique profile of effective sanctions and parents must vary the sanctions until they find the ones most likely to work with a child. Some children love chocolate candy, others hate it. Some children respond to praise from parents, other's don't. Also, children change. What is rewarding one day may have no effect the next.

The only way to tell whether something is rewarding or punishing to a child is by observing its effects (Brer Rabbit principle). You may think your scolding is punishing but it may actually be rewarding to the child because he is getting attention. So if a certain behavior increases in frequency after your response, you are rewarding it; if it decreases after your response, you are punishing it.

Section B
Child Guidance Skills

HOW TO "INOCULATE" YOUR CHILD AGAINST THE STRESSES OF DAILY LIVING

Anticipation of problems is half the battle.

Stress inoculation means to give your children special guidance to prepare them to cope with anticipated new or difficult situations. Stress inoculation has also been called "anticipatory guidance" or foreshadowing. The concept of psychological inoculation is directly analogous to physical inoculation. By exposing a child to a weak dose of stress (or germs) we facilitate the development of constructive responses.

For example, you might forewarn your child of peer pressure to smoke; peers will often call one a "chicken" for refusing to smoke. You might then discuss an assertive response to such pressure, e.g., "I'd really be chicken if I smoked just because you wanted me to. I don't want to."

Unfortunately, the tendency of many people who are facing a difficult situation is either not to think about it, or to worry about all the things that could go wrong. Stress inoculation, on the other hand, involves preparing a child to meet stress with true mastery. So begin early to help your child so he won't be overwhelmed by the stress and will have constructive responses. By thinking and practicing things through in advance, children will be more confident and skillful when new or difficult events actually occur.

Foretelling

Children should be helped to anticipate what to expect in new and potentially fearful situations and to prepare for them. Foretelling what to expect and how to act by detailed explanations, coupled with reassurance, will contribute a great deal towards minimizing the shock of the unknown and unexpected. For example, before giving a child a needle, a doctor should state what is going to happen next: "I'm going to give you a needle which will hurt a little at first. But I know you're going to be brave about it." Or the doctor might say, "I'm going to give you an injection, and it is probably going to hurt; if you want to cry, that's all right, because when something hurts, it may make you cry."

Before going on a new trip, say something like, "Let's talk about our trip to Disneyland. What do you think it will be like? What are your feelings about the trip? Is anybody excited about it? Does anyone feel a little uneasy or lonely when they think about being away from home?" The idea is to talk about what might happen and to help the child figure out what to say and do.

In a similar manner, parents can prepare children for hospital trips, a new baby, a divorce, camping, a sleepout, or a new school. There are many excellent books available to help parents forewarn their children about many of these experiences.

"What if" Game

Another way to prepare a child for possible problem situations is to play the "what if" game. You might ask, for example, "What is the thing to do if a complete stranger comes up to you and asks you to go for a ride in his car?" or "What is the thing to do if one of your balls rolls out into the street?"

Preparatory Experiences

Try to give children some preparatory experiences to introduce them to future change and challenge. Thus, if your son will soon be going away to college, you might help him prepare for this rather drastic change by insisting that he have some prior experience living away from home, perhaps as a summer camp counselor or with a relative. Be sure there is opportunity for supervision and feedback in the preparatory experience. As a further illustration, before sending a child to five-day a week kindergarten, you might enroll the child in a two- or three-day a week nursery school program. Prior to the nursery school program you should arrange for the child to visit the school, meet the teacher, and try some of the games and activities that will be available.

Role Playing

A child who is experiencing interpersonal difficulties can often be helped by your playing the role of the person the child is having difficulty with and acting out the conflict situation with the child. Role playing or behavior rehearsal tends to change a discussion from a strictly intellectual level to a real feeling and experiential level.

If, for instance, your child has become very fearful of a teacher, you might act out the teacher's typical behavior while the child plays herself. The goal of the play acting is to assist the child to respond to the teacher in a more appropriate manner, i.e., less fearful and anxious. Thus, after your child has responded in her typical fearful way, you might suggest that she try responding in a more assertive but still respectful manner. In the event that your child just does not know how to act more assertively, you would assume the role of the child and act out a proper response to the teacher. At this time, you might suggest that your child play the role of the teacher. By this role reversal, you will be encouraging your child to develop a greater degree of empathy, i.e., the ability to experience events from another's perspective.

Young children especially seem to enjoy role playing, although it adapts well to any age. With younger children, you will find it advantageous to use puppets and dolls during the role playing.

In addition to resolving interpersonal conflicts, role playing can be used to prepare children for complex social situations. For example, if your child is afraid to go to the store alone, you might play the game of "going to the store" in which each element of shopping—selecting the desired item, taking it to the counter, paying the cashier, and counting the change—can be rehearsed in a pleasant, relaxed manner with your help.

Similarly, if your child is experiencing difficulty handling teasing from other children, you might have the child tease you while you model a variety of adaptive responses, including:

Ignore the teasing, or say:

"So what."
"Thanks for telling me my fault."
"Why pick on me?"
"That's really a mean thing to say."

Then, you might ask your child to practice saying these responses while you tease him.

Techinques such as role playing may help a child think out and rehearse adaptive responses to frustrating situation and thus develop more thoughtful and flexible responses to everyday problems.

HELPING CHILDREN SET GOALS FOR SELF-IMPROVEMENT

Before you can score, you must first have a goal.

—*Greek Proverb*

Nothing can take the place of an all-absorbing purpose. Education will not, genius will not, talent will not, industry will not, will-power will not. The purposeless life must ever be a failure.

—*O. S. Marden*

To have goals means to have certain ends or objectives that you desire to achieve. Most of us are aware of the importance of setting goals if we are to accomplish anything in life. Indeed, numerous studies have shown that both normal and retarded persons who set goals for themselves achieve higher levels of performance than people who set no goals.[22]

Children often function at a comfortable level, well below their potential, unless challenged to produce. Wise parents, then, will spur children on by helping them set goals for self-improvement.

Goals are effective for two main reasons. First they give direction to a child. Goals channel a child's energy and focus it in one direction, as opposed to the ineptness of a Don Quixote who jumps on his horse and rides off madly in all directions at the same time. Failing to plan, after all, is almost as bad as planning to fail. Secondly, by striving for a goal which is just out of reach, a child is challenged or motivated to expend that extra bit of effort to obtain it. A child with no definite goal in mind doesn't have the same incentive. So goals disrupt children's equilibrium and "unfreeze their customary patterns of behaving."

Guidelines for Setting Goals

The following are some ground rules for helping children establish goals or objectives which point the way towards constructive change.

1. *Be Specific.* Studies show that specific goals improve performance more than nonspecific ones.[23] Specific goals for a child are "Read ten books over summer vacation." "Get nine words right on the next spelling test (past performance has varied between seven and

eight right). Nonspecific goals are: "Read some books this summer," or "Do my best on the next spelling test."

2. *Keep Score.*   If a child has set a goal of reading a certain number of books over the summer, ask her to keep a record of how many books she has read, and of the goal she is striving for. A record helps one see slow progress towards a goal. Golfers who never bother to keep their scores may get a lot of exercise but it's a poor way to improve their game. There's nothing like an accurately kept scorecard to show whether you're playing a better game or just talking it. No amount of words can make up for a lack of results.

3. *Set Reasonable Goals.*   It is best to set moderately difficult goals for chrilden that are just slightly beyond their reach; just a little better than their past performance. Goals should be set high enough to be a challenge but within view so they can be realized quickly.

   Two common pitfalls in setting goals are to either make them too high (a child who tries to act like a genius will quickly become discouraged), or too low (this is a more common mistake—we fail to realize a child's potential or readiness to go much higher).

4. *Break Down Big Goals.*   Break big or complex objectives into smaller ones that can be achieved step-by-step. Children change gradually by making a small step forward rather than a giant leap. Don't expect too much change too quickly. If your child has daily temper tantrums, set a goal of only having five a week. Once this goal is met, set a new goal of one, two, or three a week, and finally, no tantrums.

5. *Watch Your Timing.*   The start of a new year and the beginning of summer are good times to set goals and make resolutions to improve one's behavior over the next six months. Other changes in a child's life can be capitalized on to motivate needed behavior changes. For example, you might say, "Now that you'll be starting nursery school, we'll have to help you learn to go to the potty by yourself," or "Now that you'll be going to first grade soon, don't you think it's time to work on your thumbsucking habit?"

6. *Involve the Child.*   Discuss possible goals with a child and ask him to select ones which are personally meaningful and worth striving for. In this way the child will be motivated to work cooperatively with you.

7. *Establish a Deadline.*   Set a target date for completion of the

objective. Once you know how much time you have to reach your destination you are more likely to start on time and to pace yourself better.

8. *Review Periodically.* At regular intervals it is useful to review with your child progress towards a goal. If you fail to check with your child on a regular basis, a firm resolve is likely to go the way of most New Year's resolutions. At these times it may be necessary to revise certain goals or set new ones.

9. *Reinforce Achievement.* As a child reaches a goal you should take notice of the accomplishment. Praise and concrete rewards are effective ways to reinforce desired behaviors.

10. *Turn Complaints into Specific Goals.* When a child describes his weakness as a general trait or characteristic, such as "I'm too shy," you should listen carefully and try to understand what this weakness means to your child and under what circumstances it occurs. Get as much information as you can; try for facts rather than opinions. By this procedure, you should be able to help the child restate his vague complaint into the form of a specific, concrete goal which states what the child wants to happen. Thus, the "I'm too shy" statement might be translated to "You feel shy because you haven't been able to initiate conversation with your camp counselor, and you want to be able to do this."

A child's complaint, "Nobody likes me. I'm no good," may be converted into "You feel lonely and left out because you have no friends and you want to have at least one friend play with you on a regular basis." This goal then becomes translated, with the child's help, into the first step of an action program: "The first step, then, is for you to invite one or two of your classmates over to play this weekend." In this way, you have stated the problem so it seems soluble (not so big as to seem overwhelming) and you phrased it so that the child owns the problem (what the child can do to solve it) rather than focusing on what others have done or can do about the problem.

HOW TO HELP YOUR CHILDREN DECLARE THEIR INDEPENDENCE

What is the best government?—that which teaches us to govern ourselves.
—Goethe

There are only two lasting bequests we can give our children. One is roots, the other wings.
—Hodding Carter

From leaving our children with their first sitter to dropping them off on their first day of school to allowing them to cross their first street alone, a lot of us find that it's harder than we ever thought it would be to let go of our children. However, as the poet Francis Cornford wrote,

They must go free
Like fishes in the sea
Or starlings in the skies
Whilst you remain
The shore where casually they
Come again.

Self-reliance or autonomy can be defined as the desire to control one's actions and be free of external control. The goal is to be a self-regulating and inner-directed human being. A self-reliant person takes initiative, overcomes obstacles by himself, and wants to do things on his own. One of your tasks as a parent is to make your child autonomous as quickly as possible and thereby work yourself out of a job. This will not be easy, however, since it is more natural for parents to overprotect a child in keeping with the desire to feel important and needed. You have to constantly remind yourself to let go and step back from the center of a child's world into the background.

Children want to direct their own lives. "Don't tell me what to do— I'll choose for myself." From an early age children will declare their desire to be independent. This is a healthy development and should not be construed as a declaration of war. It's important to recognize and encourage the signs of growing self-reliance so that it progresses naturally.

The following are some strategies for promoting autonomy in children: gradually give more freedom and responsibility; encourage decision making; allow exploration and risk taking; help children solve their own problems; and be independent yourself.

Gradually Widen the Circle of Freedom

How much freedom should you give your child? There is no pat answer to this since how much independence a child can handle will depend upon her age, ability, and readiness to grow. However, as a general rule, you should *gradually* increase a child's freedom and responsibility as she grows older.

The ability to function as an autonomous human being should be developed slowly over the course of many years. Granting more and more independence to children to do things for themselves should be a gradual and continuous process as a child grows older and matures. This gradual process for normal children is illustrated in the following diagram.

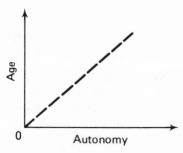

This can also be called the law of diminishing structure, i.e., as a child grows older you impose fewer rules and restrictions. Some parents tend to keep children protected and dependent until they reach the age of 16 and then they expect the children to become mature adults almost overnight. This is like chauffering a child everywhere without letting her touch the steering wheel, then suddenly turning over the keys with, "OK, now *you* drive."

One 24-year-old drug addict I know said that his parents treated him like a child until he was 21, then expected him to be on his own. He couldn't handle the sudden freedom and self-responsibility. His parents had made all his decisions for him until he was an adult and then sent him out completely unprepared to run his own life. In a similar manner, a 17-year-old girl I know recently ran off with a much older married man. Her foster mother said that, in hindsight, she failed to give the girl increasing freedom and autonomy as she matured. For example, she embarrassed the girl by sending a younger sister along with her whenever she went on dates. This led to the rebellious act of living with the married man.

The most reasonable approach is to gradually increase children's self-reliance by steadily giving them more and more freedom and independence. For example, children should normally be given increased freedom with age to manage their own affairs, e.g., care of personal possessions, use of free time, and personal appearance. They should also be given fewer and fewer restrictions in such matters as the hour they retire at night and the distance they can travel away from home.

One noted psychologist, James Sanderson, raised his three children with an "adult at 18" philosophy. Since the law states that one is an adult at age 18, he told his children they would be on their own at age 18. In other words, they had to earn their own money, find their own place to live, and be completely responsible for their own lives at this age. He began talking about this philosophy with his children when they were 13 and preparing them for this eventuality by giving increasing autonomy. While acknowledging that this approach may not appeal to everyone, he states that it worked well for his family.

Encourage Decision Making from an Early Age

Parents should be developing, from an early age, the child's ability to make decisions and accept responsibility for the consequences of those decisions. When you permit children to make decisions, they find out about alternatives and what it is like to make a choice and live with it.

Encourage decision making by saying: "It's your decision."; "It's up to you."; "Whatever you think, it's your choice." Once children make a decision, they must learn to accept responsibility for the consequences of their choices. Thus, if a child decides to spend his allowance the first day he receives it, then he must experience what it is like to do without money for the rest of the week. If he orders a hamburger, he must either eat it or go hungry.

Very young children are capable of making simple decisions (e.g., "Do you want your bread plain or toasted?"; "Do you want to wear your blue or red pants?"; "You have a choice of remaining here and being quiet, or leaving. You decide."; "What would you like for dessert?") I know of one husband who became angry because his wife used to ask their five-year-old which way she wanted her egg—boiled or scrambled. "You're the mother. You decide what's for breakfast. You're the boss," said the husband. The mother answered and carefully stated her beliefs about the child's need to begin to make decisions; decisions that will gradually become more complex and important as she matures.

School-age children should be given freedom to select their own movies, records, clothes, and ways to spend their own money. Their opinion should be sought as to where to spend the family vacation. In general, allow children to make a decision when they can both anticipate and evaluate the probable consequences to alternate courses of action.

Of course, parents must be careful to allow children only those decisions that are appropriate to their age or level of maturity. You would not, for instance, give teenagers complete freedom to choose the high school they will attend when they have insufficient knowledge of basic curriculums or vocational requirements. Nor would you send a child out alone to select his clothes until he had knowledge of quality, styles, and the value of money. Apart from soliciting a child's opinion in these matters, an effective way to encourage them to have a voice, but not the complete say, is to limit their choices. In taking a child shopping, for example, you might show her two articles of clothing preselected by you for quality and price, and then ask her to make the final choice. In regard to choice of high schools, you might say, "Howard, your mother and I have determined that we can afford to send you to either Jefferson or Hamilton High School. Both are high-quality schools that offer the type of curriculum you are interested in. The final choice is up to you." The wisdom of offering limited choices to children is reflected in the saying of the poet Robert Frost: "Freedom moves easily in harness." As they mature, children should be given more and more opportunities to have the complete say in decisions affecting their lives.

Allow Children to Explore and Take Risks

How much risk should you allow your children to take? Roller-skating on sidewalks is risky—but if you do not allow such activities, you can make your child a fragile, fearful child. A basic principle to teach your child is to take only reasonable risks when there is a high probability of success and the reward is worthwhile. Playing Russian Roulette with a loaded revolver to prove your courage is a foolish rather than sensible risk.

The following case illustrates a reasonable risk. Charles Lindbergh's boys once asked his permission to climb an awesomely tall tree. He responded, "How are you going up?" Scott, the 12-year-old, pointed: first this limb, then that. "You're going to get stuck after that, aren't you?" Lindbergh prodded. The boys sadly agreed. Only when they had calculated their chances on various routes up the tree did their father give his consent. Then, to a watching friend he said, "They must learn to take calculated risks. As long as they figure out everything ahead of time and just don't go off half-cocked."

Children who take risks are exposed to accidents—Robert Kennedy's children have incurred a sizable number of broken limbs—but that's a small price to pay for the freedom to venture and grow.

Some families adopt an overprotective approach which is likely to make children feel weak and vulnerable. Charlie Shedd, the newspaper columnist once told about parents who refused to allow their 13-year-old son to try out for catcher on the school baseball team. They immediately said "No. What if you get hurt?" One night at the dinner table the son expressed his pent-up feelings: "You make me so mad. You won't let me do anything. I couldn't go skiing because I might break a leg. Couldn't take jumping lessons at the stable; the horse might fall. And last summer I couldn't even go canoeing on vacation with those kids from Minnesota. What if we tipped over? You've always been like that with everything that's fun. I don't think you're one bit fair. And what I really think is I might as well be dead too." His parents thought over these remarks and admitted their mistake. They had lost their first child shortly after birth and were thus overprotecting their only remaining child. Given the opportunity, he soon excelled at baseball.

Help Your Children Solve Their Own Problems

Avoid the temptation to rush in to solve your children's problems and settle their fights instead of letting them work things out for themselves. Don't tie their shoes or wipe their bottoms when they can do this for themselves. And let them try to figure things out for themselves even if it takes longer and they make mistakes because of trial-and-error learning. Sometimes we make a great effort to spare children pain and frustration but in so doing prevent them from learning from experience. Everytime you intervene to solve a child's problem (with a school bully, with a lack of friends, etc.) you communicate to the child your belief that he isn't capable of solving it himself.

One way to encourage problem-solving is to be question-oriented rather than answer-oriented. When your child asks "How do I do this?" begin by inquiring about his ideas. If, for instance, a 10-year-old about to write a thank-you letter asks you what he should say, you might respond, "What do you think?" You might then correct or add to the child's ideas as needed. This takes longer than telling a child what to do—but it develops skills for future use.

As mentioned in a previous section of this book, another useful technique for developing problem-solving skills is playing "What if?" One person poses a problem (What if you got lost in the woods? What if you found out that your best friend cheated on an important test?) Then encourage your child to figure out a solution.

Be Independent Parents

You can promote autonomy in your children by being independent yourself and being involved in work and activities outside the home that you are excited about and are vitally important to you. By not being always available, you help your children to be less enmeshed with you, less likely to lean on you or to expect you to solve all their problems—to be more self-reliant.

Early, limited periods of separation from parents prepare children for independent living. So don't feel guilty about going out to dinner with your spouse once a week or about sending your preschooler to nursery school for a few hours a day. Separation is also helpful in adolescence. A recent study found that the initial separation of leaving home for college facilitated an adolescent boy's growth toward the developmental goal of becoming independent of his parents while it strengthened emotional ties with them.[24] So leaving home to board at college was found superior to living at home and commuting to college.

Concluding Thoughts

A common mistake of parents is to overprotect their children and allow too little independence. Often we are unaware of a child's readiness for the next higher level of development and we fail to challenge a child to grow. For example, a four-year-old can use a sponge or a dust cloth; the five-year-old can handle a hammer and saw with adult supervision; the six-year-old can operate a simple camera. Apart from lack of knowledge of a child's readiness to grow, we may keep a child dependent for a variety of reasons, including the desire to feel needed and loved.

A crucial test of overdependency is how your children behave when you are not around. Do the kids carry on as usual or does everything grind to a halt? If your teenage children fail to cook or clean when you're absent, it could mean you've let your children become too dependent on you. If your school-age children are good only when you are there to supervise every second, then they haven't developed inner controls.

Some parents go to the other extreme and give a child too much independence too soon. A pseudo-independent child is one who denies his dependency needs because he is forced to be self-reliant too early. So don't tell your 3-year-old that she is "too big to cry" or tell your 10-year-old that he must be "the man of the house" if your husband has departed for some reason. Too much independence or responsibility is as bad as too little. Avoid both extremes if you want a mentally healthy, well-adjusted child.

HOW TO ENCOURAGE CHILDREN TO DO THEIR BEST

They conquer who believe they can. He has not learned the lesson of life who does not each day surmount a fear.
—Ralph Waldo Emerson

There are high spots in all of our lives, and most of them have come about through encouragement from someone else.
—George M. Adams

To help the young soul, to add energy, inspire hope, and blow the coals into a useful flame; to redeem defeat by new thought and firm action, this, though, not easy, is the work of divine men.
—Emerson

The word encourage means to give courage, hope, or confidence; to urge strongly or advise earnestly. All children need words of parental encouragement in order to do their best. Children who are naturally shy or who have become disheartened because of repeated failures particularly need this assistance. Encouragement means giving children the courage, hope, and confidence that they can face and deal with all of life's tasks—especially the ones that are dangerous, difficult, or painful. Parental encouragement serves as an ego-booster when children are confronted with difficult tasks or stressful events. It helps a child develop self-confidence, initiative, and perseverence. Without support your children may find it very difficult to change, to grow, to take risks.

Basically, the encouraging process consists of one or more of the following: (1) Believing in your child's capacity to do something and conveying an expectancy of success ("You can do it."); (2) Showing you understand it is difficult ("I can see this is hard for you."); and being empathic of the child's feelings ("You'll probably be a little nervous and that's okay."); Don't belittle the child's feelings by saying "There's nothing to worry about."; (3) Attributing strength and bravery to the child ("You're a brave person. You've done hard things before"); (4) Being enthusiastic about the value of the desired behavior. When you are enthusiastic you stir up a child's emotions and get the adrenalin flowing. This gives strength and motivation to succeed. So show you are really interested and care by the depth of your feeling and conviction; (5) Offering support as needed. "I'll be here if you need me."

In encouraging children, some of the attitudes that you will want to convey to them are:

1. You are basically a competent, courageous person.
2. You are the type of child who won't give up.
3. I am confident that you can take hurts and setbacks, learn from them, and eventually overcome them.
4. I won't ask you to do anything that is beyond your abilities.
5. A reasonably good effort on your part will please me.
6. You can make of life what you will.

Encouragement must be based on a sincere faith and confidence in humanity, i.e., an inner conviction that your children have the ability to actively shape their own lives rather than being passive victims of fate. It is generally recognized now that we get from children what we expect. If we have little faith in children and expect them to give up easily or fold under extreme pressure or calamity, they will rarely disappoint us. Thus, even though your child may initially fail and be discouraged, you must not lose hope. Rather you should transmit to this child your confidence that he or she will one day learn to overcome the obstacle. Words alone will not give this faith to a child, but somehow the child will understand it if you really believe it. Kids truly need to develop a kind of positive expectancy that they are going to do well in life and not be overcome by adversity or difficulty.

Learning the Language of Encouragement

The following are some specific things to say to encourage children to attempt difficult tasks:

1. *Urgings.* You can urge a child or give the needed push to do something by saying: "Come on, do it! Do it now!" "Keep trying!" "Don't give up!" Be a *cheerleader* for your child.
2. *Express Confidence.* If you really believe that a child can do it, and you fully expect him to, you might say: "You can do it, I know you can!" and "You're going to do it now!" or "Maybe you can't do this today, but I bet you can do it soon."
3. *Coaxing.* Use soothing words, humor, or a pleasant manner to persuade: "It's really very easy once you're used to it," "Everyone's afraid of it at first."
4. *Pleading.* Occasionally, you might give an earnest appeal, e.g., "Please try it! Oh, please, please do it."
5. *Provide Information.* Give relevant facts to dispel irrational beliefs. Research has shown that it is best to give specific facts, e.g., "That bee won't sting you!" rather than general truths, e.g., "Bees won't harm people."
6. *Challenging.* Make it seem like a challenge, e.g., "Don't let life defeat you."
7. *Praise.* Comment upon child's past successes and how persistent or courageous he was in past situations. "Remember last time you were brave and went right in and took the injection." Comment on parts of the task he has already gotten right, minimize his errors, and indicate how the child should proceed to be successful. Also,

praise the times the child gives a good effort but is not successful. You might say, for instance, "I want you to think about this. Sometimes you'll be successful in life and sometimes you won't. The important thing is to try your best. I'm very proud of you today since you did your best in trying out for the cheerleader team even though you didn't win." (When a child fails, you might also recount a time when you failed at something as a child. In this way, the child will not feel unique in suffering adversity.)

8. *Proverbs.* Offer one of your favorite maxims to bolster the child's resolve: e.g., "Nothing ventured, nothing gained," "Practice makes perfect," "No life is so hard that you can't make it easier by the way you take it."

9. *Persuasive Appeals.* Verbally appeal to the child's self-respect or desire for recognition, e.g., "Your teacher is going to love this when you are finished."

10. *Teamwork.* Initially, you and the child might do the task together ("Let's try it together") and then you would gradually fade out.

11. *Support.* Just having a parent there when faced with a severely stressful task can be comforting to a child. You might offer added help by saying, "I'm sure you can straighten this out, but if you need any help, let me know."

12. *Touch.* Sometimes verbal encouragement is insufficient. You have to take the child's hand and lead him to the feared object. Be verbally reassuring as you do this.

13. *Give an Order.* Sometimes an insecure, anxious child needs a direct command to do something she is afraid of. So if your seven-year-old daughter has not responded to your coaxing to take some needed medicine, say in a firm, loud voice: "DRINK IT FAST!" Your child will usually do it even though the look on her face after swallowing the medicine may be "Why did I do that? It tastes awful!"

Discouragement vs. Encouragement

Discouragement is a process that restricts a child's courage to the extent that it prevents him from acting. One who possesses courage tries to act in situations where others would give up or not even make an attempt. The discouraged child is convinced that he is inferior, inadequate, and a failure.[25] Alfred Adler, the noted child psychoanalyst maintained the feelings of inferiority are the one main cause of emotional disturbance and behavior problems in children.

Traps of Discouragement. Be sure to avoid the seven "traps of discouragement":

1. Avoid belittling. Avoid continual criticism.
2. Avoid overindulgence or overprotection (e.g., doing too many things for a child.)
3. Avoid using humiliating punishments.
4. Avoid making disparaging comparisons.
5. Avoid having negative expectations. (e.g., "You'll never amount to anything").
6. Avoid setting unreasonably high standards.
7. Avoid having double standards (one for you, a higher one for the children).

Encouraging Attitude. As previously described, encouragement is a specific technique for helping children over difficult hurdles. In addition to this technique there are a number of things parents can do to develop feelings of worth and competence in children and to promote confidence in their strengths and potentials. The following are components of a general "encouraging attitude" that parents should display toward their children.

1. Value children as they are, not as you hope they will be. Believe in children as good and worthwhile.
2. Show faith in the child. This will help the individual develop a belief in himself.
3. Have confidence in the child's ability. This wins the child's confidence while building self-respect.
4. Give recognition for effort as well as a job done well.
5. Identify and focus on strengths and assets rather than mistakes.
6. Plan for success and assist in the development of skills.
7. Use the child's interests in order to motivate learning.
8. Show appreciation for contributions. For example, don't overlook showing appreciation when your eight-year-old son helps you by reading a book to a younger brother.

A broad "encouraging attitude" such as this will help your children feel accepted and worthwhile. Once a child feels valued and competent he will be less prone to succumb to the feelings of inferiority, low self-esteem, and depression which are so common in children who come to mental health clinics. Various schools of psychotherapy focus primarily on raising people's self-esteem. Among these therapeutic approaches are Adlerian Encouragement Therapy, nondirective or client-centered therapy, and Transactional Analysis, "I'm OK—You're OK" therapy.

HOW PARENTS CAN OFFER GOOD ADVICE TO CHILDREN

> *Advice is like snow; the softer it falls, the longer it dwells upon, and the deeper it sinks into the mind.*
>
> —*Coleridge*

> *There are few things more difficult than the art of making advice agreeable.*

> *Nothing is more confusing than the person who gives good advice but sets a bad example.*

> *The best way to succeed in life is to act on the advice we give to others.*

Sometimes it is wise to seek advice from others. This is illustrated in the following story.

One day a small boy was trying to lift a heavy stone, but he couldn't budge it. His father, passing by, stopped to watch his efforts. Finally he said to his son: "Are you using all your strength?" "Yes, I am," the boy cried, exasperated. "No," the father said calmly, "You're not! You haven't asked me to help you."

To advise a child means to offer tentative suggestions for solving a problem based on your expertise (knowledge, experience, common sense) or objective perspective. For example:

Child: "I can't get my homework done."
Parent: "Why don't you try to keep to a schedule. Perhaps this will help you budget your time more effectively."

Giving advice is particularly appropriate when a child is a rank beginner and you have expert or relevant knowledge to share. Advice is best received when it is in response to a child's request for it. However, most children are reluctant to ask questions about certain topics (sex, drugs) so that you should offer to frankly discuss such taboo topics, or simply raise the question yourself and proceed to talk about it.

To be effective in giving advice or counsel, you have to establish yourself as an expert on the subject in the eyes of the child, i.e., a person with superior knowledge and/or experience. This means functioning as an authoritative parent, that is, a parent who does not make statements or predictions unless he or she is well informed about a topic. So well informed, in fact, that one can readily substantiate personal statements with reference material. Before offering advice about such topics as sex, drugs, or smoking, you should read up on all available information relating to the topics. Federal and state governments offer many excellent pamphlets and books on these subjects, both for parents and for children.

Be sure that you are prepared to offer advice early in a child's development. It has been found, for instance, that it is best to provide children with antismoking information at about the fifth-grade level. This is the age when most youngsters begin to experiment with cigarettes.

In giving advice, you attempt to share with a child information or experiences that you believe will be valuable. You usually only give advice once and then you leave the decision to the child. It is different from preaching wherein you proclaim, often in a tiresome manner, a given course of action as the one and only course to follow. In other words, when you preach, you strongly and persistently urge your child to conform to your recommendations.

Pitfalls in Offering Advice

1. *Manner in Which Given.*   The manner in which you give advice may be more important than the content. Avoid being a "Father knows best" know-it-all who makes authoritarian pronouncements, or being a "Helpful Henry" who is constantly bombarding others with offhand suggestions on how to run their lives. Also avoid trying to live your life over again through your children so that you project your own needs, desires, and goals into the child's situation. Rather, offer advice in a tentative manner so that the child feels free to accept or reject it. Thus, rather than saying, "You certainly must listen to this . . . ," say, "Some people have tried this," or "You might want to consider this approach to your problem."

2. *Positive Relationship.* Advice is most effective when your relationship with the child is characterized by mutual trust and respect.

3. *Expect Noncompliance.* In offering advice, you have to be willing to accept the fact that children will generally not follow it. Moreover, if they happen to take your advice and find it invalid they may blame you.

4. *Draw the Child Out.* Sometimes when children seek advice they know fully well what to do. Rather than promote a dependency relationship, hand the responsibility back to the child ("I think you'll be able to figure this one out by yourself."), or simply reflect the child's dependency feeling ("Sounds like you lost confidence in your own judgment.").

   On other occasions, children will have the answer within themselves and it only needs to be drawn out. The best procedure here is to give indirect advice by using the Socratic method of directive questioning to elicit the solution from the child. By skillful use of questions, you can help a child focus on the relevant aspects of the problem or apply knowledge already posessed that is related to the problem at hand. For example, some questions you might use when a child is afraid of a neighborhood bully are: "Do you think you are strong enough to fight him yourself?"; "How do little birds handle a big bird that is bothering them?"; "What do you think the bully is afraid of?"; or "How do the other kids handle the bully problem?"

5. *Use Sparingly.* Give advice sparingly because even when handled well, there is a danger of making a child feel dumb, inferior, or overly controlled.

6. *Be Brief.* Get right to the point in giving advice. Don't beat around the bush. Be brief and state your thoughts in a few sentences.

7. *Personal Opinions.* When offering your opinions or experiences offer them strictly as such, not facts, law, or the gospel truth. Say, "I wouldn't read that," rather than "Don't read that." Or you might say, "I was once in a similar situation and I just told myself to try harder and not give up."

8. *Try to Understand.* Precede your statements of advice with statements of understanding. Once children feel understood, they are more apt to accept advice.

9. *Promote Independence.*   Teenagers may ask for advice and then accuse you of being "bossy." This is a sign they want to be independent yet still feel dependent and resent this in themselves. You can handle this problem by, (1) giving general rather than specific advice, and (2) suggesting several alternatives and telling the child to make the final decision.

10. *Be Slow to Advise.*   Parents should be available but not help with all the problems. They should have established the kind of relationship where the door is open to the youngster but that solutions are not worked out by the parent before the child has addressed himself to the alternatives.

11. *Some Don'ts.*   If you avoid the following don'ts, you will probably be an effective advice giver[26]:

Don't preach, make windy orations, ramble, over-talk, complicate the simple, talk down, intellectualize, make convoluted interpretations, indulge in jargon, monopolize, keep attempting to convince, give a prolonged lecture, confuse through the multiplication of examples, use sarcasm, mumble, constantly reexplain, make fun of your own utterances or demean their import, hint at but never specify, endlessly contradict yourself or give double messages, never really mean or take responsibility for what you say, hesitate or tremble the words out, think aloud instead of beforehand, fall in love with and repeatedly promote your own causes and favorite themes, insist on the validity of your own interpretations, or communicate one line while living another.

The Power of Proverbs

The great truths are too important to be new.
                                        —*Somerset Maugham*

A proverb is a short sentence based on long experience.
                                        —*Cervantes*

Some people are quick to condemn cliches, but what is a cliche? It is a truth that has retained its validity through time. Mankind would lose half its hardearned wisdom, built up patiently over the ages, if it ever lost its cliches.
                                        —*Marvin G. Gregory*

A quick and simple way to give advice is to use a relevant maxim or proverb. A proverb is a short, concise saying in common use that strikingly expresses an age-old truth, rule of conduct, or familiar experience. Examples of common sayings are:

"If there's a will there's a way."
"If it's worth doing at all, it's worth doing well."
"Easy come, easy go."
"Nothing ventured, nothing gained."

Because common sayings seem so trite, most of us can hardly bring ourselves to say them. Nevertheless, they embody the concentrated experience and wisdom of the human race. If a child was to regulate his life according to their general truths, he would not go far wrong. Ordinary common sense, then, provides an extensive and highly valid understanding of human nature. For this reason, common sayings deserve more attention than they have received of late. They are also an excellent way to teach a child to use deductive reasoning, i.e., application of general principles to guide one's life. Their judicious use in childrearing can inspire, explain, and provide comfort to children.

In offering a maxim to a child, you should clearly state that it is not an original idea of yours. Rather, introduce the adage by saying, "It's been said . . ." or "They say . . ." or "There's an old saying that I like which you might find helpful in your present situation." The more you have found an adage to be helpful in your personal life, the more persuasive you will be in presenting the advice to a child.

Some years ago, the noted research expert, Daniel Starch, asked a sizable sampling of people what were the most valuable guiding principles in living. Several hundred rules, principles, and maxims were submitted. Nine stood out above all the rest. Here they are in the order they were most frequently mentioned:

1. Do unto others as you would that they should do unto you.
2. Know thyself.
3. Life is what you make it.
4. If at first you don't succeed, try, try again.
5. Anything that is worth doing at all is worth doing well.
6. The great essentials of happiness are something to do, something to love, and something to hope for.

7. As a man thinketh in his heart, so is he.
8. Knowledge is power.
9. Be calm and self-possessed, know what you are about, be sure you are right, then go ahead and don't be afraid.

Quotes.   Parents who find it difficult to use the more common maxims might feel more comfortable offering little known but equally meaningful quotes, such as:

> There is nothing so easy but that it becomes difficult when you do it with reluctance.
> —*Terrence Timoroumenos*

> If you are searching for truth, just stop cherishing opinions.
> —*Sixth Patriarch of Zen (700 years ago)*

> Failures, so called, are but fingerposts pointing out the right direction to those who are willing to learn.
> —*Thomas Edison*

> Most folks are about as happy as they make up their minds to be.
> —*Abraham Lincoln*

> When one door closes, another opens; but we often look so long and so regretfully upon the closed door that we do not see the one which has opened for us.
> —*Alexander Graham Bell*

> Humor is an affirmation of dignity, a declaration of Man's superiority to all that befalls him.
> —*Romain Gary*

The following adages point to the positive value of proverbs and quotes:

> We frequently fall into error and folly, not because the true principles of action are not known, but because for a time they are not remembered; he may, therefore, justly be numbered among the benefactors of mankind who contracts the great rules of life into short sentences that may early be impressed on the memory, and taught by frequent recollection to occur habitually to the mind.
> —*Johnson*

The proverbial wisdom of the populace in the street, on the roads, and in the markets, instructs the ear of him who studies man more fully than a thousand rules ostentatiously displayed.

—*Lavater*

I believe in the power of important quotations. I always keep a few in my mind to think about. Whenever I need words to cheer me I want the best that can help me. I am never alone. I can always join the best minds of the centruies. In their great thoughts I can find the courage to believe in the best that I can find in myself.

—*Elmer G. Letterman*

The Ancient Art of Storytelling

Since every child responds to and enjoys storytelling, you can help your children solve their problems by indirectly giving advice via a story. For instance, you might tell a story about your own childhood which pertains to the child's present problem, e.g., "When I was about your age, I had a similar problem with a bully. Do you want to know what happened?" Since children identify so readily with animals, you might also tell a fable, i.e., a story depicting how animals solved a similar problem. You could relate, for instance, how birds solve a difficulty involving bigger birds (or humans) bullying on them. They typically get a large group together and harass the bigger bird by hit-and-run tactics.

Thus, by telling stories or parables that contain healthy adaptations to problems, you aid children to perceive events in a new light and to generate new solutions to difficulties. Such allegorical communications are generally received with less anxiety than messages presented in undisguised form.

In relating stories, cultivate the art of the storyteller, i.e., surprise twists in the story, use gestures, vary your tone of voice, show interest and wonder yourself, use dialogue and humor, and involve the child by stopping to ask questions: "And what do you think happened next?"

A good teaching story should provide the following: It should capture the child's attention; it should be related to the child's problem; and it should provide rewards to the story character who has solved the problem. Try to incorporate these three features when you tell stories to your children. For example, if your five-year-old has recently exhibited fear of dogs you might tell a story about a boy who, while walking in the woods with his mother, discovered a dog who had got stuck in a cave. The small dog was very friendly and the boy, although a little afraid of dogs, crawled into the cave to save the dog. His mother had tied a rope around his waist to pull him out in case he had problems in the small cave. After petting the dog's head to make the dog feel better, the boy freed the dog's leg from between two rocks. The boy held the dog and his mother pulled them both out of the cave. The dog was so happy to be freed that it licked the boy's hand. The next day the boy's picture was in the newspaper and he was a hero to the people in his town, particularly to his parents and the dog's owner.

Reflective Stories.   This technique is for use with preschoolers when you suspect them of a misdeed but you are not certain and need to obtain more information. Try telling them a story about children of the same age, sex, appearance, home environment, and situation. For example, a father seeking to determine why his toddlers are fighting could tell the following story to the older child:

"Joan, you're such a pretty four-year-old girl—with a younger brother. I'm going to tell you a story. Once upon a time, a long, long time ago, across the mountains and over the seas there lived a girl named Maryanne. She had pretty blue eyes and was also four years old. She had a little brother like you. One day Maryanne was playing with her little brother when her mother heard the little brother crying. Why do you think Maryanne's little brother was crying?" Joan: "Because he took Maryanne's toy, and she hit him."

This procedure works remarkably well with young children because they do not have the power to think abstractly. It is extremely difficult for most parents, however, to believe that their children will not see through this procedure.

HOW TO TEACH YOUR CHILDREN RIGHT FROM WRONG

Our weakness in religious-moral education is what is most dangerous in our society.

—*Ralph Wendell Burhol*

In matters of principle, stand like a rock, in matters of taste, swim with the current.

—*Thomas Jefferson*

With the proper type of nurturing, children can emerge from their early childhood years well on their way to the development of true morals—not just mouthings.

—*Sylvia Artmann*

He who merely knows right principles is not equal to him who loves them.
—*Confucius*

Principles last forever; but special rules pass away with the things and conditions to which they refer.

—*Seeley*

—IMPLANT MORAL VALUES

America today is facing an unprecedented moral crisis. We have witnessed a serious decline in moral standards both in public and private life—from Watergate, Abscam, and other scandals in high public offices, to white-collar crimes in American businesses. Children today are confused by the inconsistent and conflicting values of adults and peers. They find it difficult to find a model or hero after whom to pattern their behavior. Consequently, among our youth there is widespread drug use, sexual experimentation, and increasing crime, including the destruction of school property and assaults on teachers. Surveys indicate that most Americans believe that our country is not as honest and moral as it used to be.

Children will not "naturally" grow up possessing correct moral values. They need to be taught by active and purposeful efforts of adults.

Moral principles teach us the difference between right and wrong behavior. Among the core moral values that have been long accepted by our society are honesty as opposed to lying, stealing, and cheating; equality for all men; the need to help the sick, elderly, and disadvantaged; and the desirability of preserving life.

Who Should Implant Moral Values in Children?

Without question, parents have the prime responsibility for teaching children right from wrong and they must be willing to accept this. During their formative years, children need help to make moral choices for which they are unprepared. Since society's values are in transition, it is more important than ever for parents to accept responsibility for helping their children acquire a stable set of values. Children still look to their parents for well-defined values which will help them govern their behavior and live in harmony with others. If children don't get their values and ideals from you, they will obtain them from TV, from their peers, or other sources such as charlatans and radical religious sects.

Unfortunately, many parents today are uncertain of their own values. Others think they know but lack the conviction to impose thier values on their children. Worst of all are those parents who doubt whether they have the right to structure a child's beliefs. As a result, apart from discipline, the aspect of childrearing that parents feel most insecure in and uncertain about is the development of moral principles in children.

How To Teach Children Right From Wrong

To aid your children in developing a lasting set of moral values, I recommend the following:

1. *Be Committed To Moral Values.* You cannot teach morality without being committed to morality yourself; and you cannot be committed to morality yourself without holding that some behaviors are right and others are wrong. So first we must clarify and establish our own guiding beliefs, and then be straightforward in expressing them to our children. In two-parent families, the spouses should reach agreement on important moral values so that the children are not confused by conflicting views. According to Dr. Ben-

jamin Spock, the happiest children are those whose parents present their beliefs unequivocally and expect their children to live up to them.

2. *Teach Moral Principles.* Inculcate morals by teaching and impressing them on your children by frequent repetitions and admonitions. This means to directly teach children right from wrong and to urge them to act in a moral manner. Any specific, well-defined beliefs based upon ethical principles will serve to act as constructive influences.

Perhaps the most important rule of conduct that you should indoctrinate is to be respectful of others and be concerned for their welfare. This principle is the basis for all morality. Other universal values that ought to be taught are the golden rule (do unto others as . . .), equality (equal worth of all men), honesty, justice, charity, and industriousness.

Be enthusiastic in explaining and discussing basic values with a child rather than presenting do's and don'ts in a cold, grim manner. Be positive in your appraoch and teach a child to act morally out of love and caring for others rather than fear of punishment. Show a child that to lead a good life out of heartfelt principles is ennobling and joyful. Apart from just intellectually knowing what is right, a child should be motivated to act morally, so emphasize the joy of giving and caring.

When you teach moral principles be sure to give reasons why certain behaviors are right and others wrong. For example, don't just say, "No cheating!"; include a reason by saying, "No cheating when you play a game. It gives you an unfair advantage over the other players." When you urge a child not to steal, explain that people have a right to have property of their own. By giving reasons you help children develop their own powers of moral reasoning. Research indicates that when parents regularly give reasons for appropriate behaviors, their children are more likely to internalize moral principles and advance to higher levels of moral development.[27] Reasons usually point out the consequences of an act on the welfare of others.

3. *Reinforce Moral Behavior.* Parents should be continually reinforcing moral actions in their children from an early age. Reinforcement means to praise and reward the child for doing good, and to punish the child for doing bad. By applying such appropriate

consequences you will strengthen the desired behaviors in your child and weaken the undesired ones. Often a mother's disapproving look and her tears are the most impelling punishment a child can receive for a wrongdoing. Be sure to reward good behavior more than you punish the bad. Otherwise your child is likely to perceive you as a punitive person, that is, one who freqeuntly punishes. Unfortunately many parents have a tendency to take good behavior for granted. Thus they spend a great deal more time yelling at and hitting their children for bad behaviors than praising them for their good actions.

4. *Set a Good Example.*   In addition to teaching and rewarding moral behavior when it occurs, you should work hard at modeling moral actions by your daily behavior. Morals are more caught than taught, so set a positive example. You can set a high standard by such acts as avoiding cheating on your income taxes or telling "white lies" ("Tell the person on the phone that I'm not in."). Rather, model altruistic behavior, i.e., donate blood and give money or work for local charities. Take every opportunity to allow your children to assist you when you help others in need.

Develop in the child a "cq" (caring quality) by your actions which demonstrate compassion, empathy, concern, and altruism toward people throughout the world. Your caring for others should not be influenced by such factors as their religion, ethnic background, sexual orientation, social class, age, or politics. In this regard moral maturity has been defined as behavior and feeling based on abstract principles in relation to people increasingly removed from our own identification.

5. *Encourage Empathy.*   A moral person tries to consider the implications of his actions on the welfare of others. You can encourage this viewpoint by getting children to put themselves in another person's place. Ask, "How would you like to have that done to you?" Psychopaths are generally incapable of anticipating the reactions of others to their own behavior. Thus, they can manipulate others for their own ends without experiencing guilt or remorse. Various studies have shown that empathy or role-taking ability is positively related to moral development.

6. *Express Love and Affection.*   Children who receive plenty of love and affection from their parents learn to be loving towards others. Also, research indicates that the frequent expression of warmth and

affection toward the child helps promote the child's identification with the parents' values.[28] Fathers' affection, in particular, has been found to be critical for children's acceptance and internalization of the parental value system.[29]

7. *Discuss the Moral Implications of Everyday Events.*   Engage your children in discussions about the moral implications of everyday events such as politicians accepting payoffs for their services, or people starving in refugee camps. Such discussions help children think about and participate in real life moral decisions. Ask questions to get your children thinking: "Do you think it is right for someone to keep a wallet he found if it has someone's name in it?" Listen to the children's reasoning. Expose them to moral reasoning that is slightly higher than their own.

According to Jean Piaget, the noted Swiss psychologist, children's moral reasoning advances in step-by-step fashion from ages 2 to 12. Up to age 8 or so, they cannot understand abstract ideas underlying moral behavior, such as honesty, justice, altruism. Obedience to rules and authority governs their moral decisions. From ages 8 to 12 children seek to understand why rules are necessary.

So discuss moral standards at the highest level you think children can grasp, then rephrase them at a lower level if necessary. In explaining why cheating in school is wrong to a nine-year-old, say "Because your teacher won't be able to trust you," rather than "Because society couldn't survive if everyone cheated."

8. *Provide a Liberal Education.*   The study of the humanities—including classical literature, poetry, drama, and fiction—can teach children the kind feelings, dispositions, and sympathies that are uniquely human. So be sure your children receive an education which requires reading the works of such authors as Homer, Shakespeare, Ibsen, and Plato. Such literature contains a rich source of examples of the moral decisions men make and the consequences thereof. The depth and eloquence of outstanding books can have a lasting effect on the moral development of your children.

—RELIGIOUS BELIEFS

According to a recent survey, the most pervasive trait of Americans is religion. The study, conducted in 1981 by Research and Forecasts, Inc., concluded that religion is the central "core" guiding most Americans' approach to life. A total of 74 percent of the adults surveyed considered themselves religious. A "religious" person is one who prays, attends worship services, feels God loves him, reads the bible, participates in chruch activities, and encourages others to turn to religion.

In a fairly recent survey, more than 2000 adolescents responded to a question asking what they would like changed in their home life.[30] More religion was one of the three most frequent answers. (The other two were better communication and more time together as a family.) Rather than blindly accepting religious beliefs, the teenagers said they wanted to discuss these values with their parents and make the values relevant to their daily lives. A large number of adolescents today clearly have a deep desire to find a transcendental, spiritual meaning to their lives.

How Children Benefit From Religion

Among the many advantages of religious beliefs for people are the following:

1. *Philosophy of Life.*   The religious need appears to be universal, no culture has ever been found where this need does not manifest itself. Man needs to belong to something bigger than himself, to experience himself as part of a higher purpose. Carl Jung, the noted psychoanalyst has observed that there exists in each human being a religious need, a need to believe in a principle beyond and higher than oneself and this need must be satisfied in order for one to be happy. We need faith in something higher, in a creative force such as God. This gives security, humility, compassion, love, and forgiveness. Belief in God answers the fundamental question as to what is the meaning or ultimate goal of life. Religion helps us develop a philosophy of life so that the world seems less confusing and frightening.

   Spiritual questioning is as much a part of childhood as playing and daydreaming because of this universal impulse to seek something to believe in, something that makes sense out of death, suffering, good, and evil. Religion unites the elements of a child's life, and creates an integrated universe for him. The child feels there is someone in charge of the world and that things are happening in a planful, orderly way. In this connection, a recent study[31] found that most young people join fringe religious groups because they are searching for meaning in their lives.

2. *Comfort.* It is historically true that in times of great crises people turn to religion to find comfort and security. Faith gives children security that in time of personal crisis, e.g., dying, death of a parent, God will look after them and help them face the unknown.

3. *Moral Values* Religion gives its adherents a firm notion that there are right and wrong ways of thinking and acting and indicates specifically what these are. As a result, studies show that religious people report less anomie (a feeling that there are no norms or standards for guiding one's behavior).

   The brotherhood of man is the fundamental teaching of religion. One is taught to love others as himself. This concern for the welfare of others is the basis of all morality. Children who possess a set of religious beliefs, as compared with those who don't, have been observed by various sources to be less selfish, less hedonistic, and more aware that they are part of a larger circle and not the center. Studies also indicate that children brought up by families with strong religious beliefs tend to have fewer drug-abuse probelms.

4. *Self-Esteem.* Another aspect of religion is that it teaches a child that she is loved, and is of inestimable worth. Thus it boosts a child's self-esteem and ability to withstand the blows of life.

How to Develop Religious Faith in Your Children

Religious faith is best developed from religious practices:

    going to worship services with your children
    saying daily prayers
    religious ceremonies at home
    taking religious instruction

Religious rituals are concrete activities that appeal to children and faith follows from them. So if you make religious activities an integral part of your life, your children will grow up with a strong foundation of faith. Discussions of religious beliefs should be part of religious practices at home. Teach children of the depth of God's love and forgiveness, and avoid the fearful aspects of religious beliefs. Children will have more inner security this way. So stress the joy, love, and happiness that come from religious beliefs.

In light of the above, many parents who are not themselves particularly devout, intensify their churchgoing and church participation when they become parents. So long as the gap between professed belief and behavior is not too wide, this kind of parental piety is probably beneficial for children because it is an additional stabilizing force in their lives.

Of course, millions of adults have no formal religion and would rightly regard it as hypocritical to adopt one. In these cases, what really matters is that the parents not abdicate their crucial value-setting responsibility. Almost any set of ethical values is better than "you make up your own mind" or "whatever the other kids are doing is OK."

HELPING YOUR TEENAGERS LIVE BY THEIR CHOSEN VALUES

Man, know thyself, all wisdom centers there.
—*Young*

Values clarification is a very useful component of moral education.
—*Lawrence Kohlberg*

What is a Value?

Values are sometimes called the "shoulds" and "oughts" and "have-to's" of the culture. More precisely, "A value is that which every man, consciously or unconsciously prizes and strives for constantly."[31] A value is something more than an attitude, which is merely a predisposition to take in an idea or to do something; it is more than a goal, which is something one now wishes to accomplish; it is more than an opinion or belief. It is characterized by persistence and consistency and by repetition of an established pattern in such a way that it becomes a part of one's philosophy of living.

What is Valued?

Eight universal values have been found to permeate the lives of all peoples, are found in all places, and have been prevalent at all times. These values are given below:

1. Affection, or feeling love and friendship for and from others;
2. Respect, or being looked up to and looking up to others;
3. Skill, or feeling able and being able to do things well;
4. Enlightenment, or understanding meaning and using knowledge to do what one wishes;
5. Influence, or the feeling of power over others;
6. Wealth, or meeting basic needs;
7. Well-being, or experiencing a healthy self-image, contentment, and happiness through good mental and physical health;
8. Responsibility or rectitude, a feeling of being trusted and knowing what is right and wrong in oneself and others.

How Values are Developed

The basic valuing process through which people make a consistent personal commitment to core values consists of three main processes and seven subprocesses:

Choosing one's beliefs and behaviors

1. Choosing freely or making independent choices;
2. Choosing from alternatives after generating all available choices;
3. Choosing after thoughtful consideration of expected circumstances

Prizing one's beliefs and behaviors

4. Prizing and cherishing through determining what is more important and worthy;
5. Publicly affirming through appropriately speaking out about one's beliefs and actions.

Acting on one's beliefs

6. Acting in a manner consistent with choices and prizings;
7. Acting with some pattern which repeatedly demonstrates choices and prizings.

Values Clarification Procedure

Everyday children have to make choices, mostly about little things. The choices they make say a lot about what's important to them. Children do not always act in accord with their basic values because they often do not think of the consequences or implications of their behavior.

You can improve children's decision-making ability, clarify their values, and increase their appropriate behavior by a values clarification procedure.[32,33] This process helps children clarify their own values, explore alternate ways of handling problem situations, examine the consequence of these alternatives, and make decisions about appropriate courses of action based on their own values and the information they have generated.

Values clarification involves asking your teenagers "clarifying" questions to assist them in developing their values by going through the valuing process outlined previously. Among the questions you might ask are:

"Where do you suppose you got the idea?" (choosing freely)

"What else did you consider? (choosing from alternatives)

"What do these terms mean to you?" (choosing thoughtfully and reflectively)

"Are you glad you feel that way?" (prizing and cherishing)

"Are you willing to stand up and be counted?" (affirming)

"Is this very important to you?" (prizing)

"Does it make you feel good when you do that?" (consider consequences)

"How do you know if this is right?" (choosing thoughtfully)

"This seems to mean a lot to you." (prizing)

Another way to help a teenager develop values is to openly and fully discuss moral conflict situations which arise in daily life, e.g., right to life, right to die, mercy killing. In these value clarifying discussions, both sides of a moral issue should be presented to ensure that all moral decisions are based upon informed choice.

In value clarifying, no attempt is made to teach new values, pressure a child to accept your values, or evaluate a child's values. The goal is simply to assist your older children to delineate and clarify for themselves the guiding beliefs in their lives and to consider whether these beliefs are reflected in their actions. If something is indeed a value it will have a significant impact on the adolescent's daily life, including his choice of friends, his career preference, and the way he treats other people.

When You and Your Children "Clash" Over Values

When your teenagers reach late adolescence you have to expect their values to differ somewhat from your own. Adolescents must have the right to dissent and choose their own values. Even if you try to force them to accept your values you probably would not be successful and your relationship with them might be seriously impaired. So be tolerant of diversity as long as your children's values are not destructive to themselves or others. Idealism, long hair, informal clothes, and different music preferences must be accepted with good grace.

Every serious dispute between parents and teenagers is rooted in values. When your values conflict with your children (e.g. choice of friends, value of school) you should openly discuss your differences and the reasons why each of you values what he does. The consequences of each position should be examined and both of you should try to be empathic to the other and endeavor to understand things from the other's perspective. Such discussions, while leaving the final decision to the adolescent for his own life help him see both sides of an issue and make more rational, informed choices.

Too often parents "blow up" when talking to their teenagers who express values different from theirs, e.g., son wants to be a football player or social worker while dad wants him to be a lawyer like himself. Unless the discussion about values is calm, rational, and respectful, little benefit can come from it.

Should You Force Adolescents to Attend Religious Services?

If you do, you can lose sight of one important fact. You can force a child to go through the motions of religious practice, but this will not guarantee—and may even work against—a deeper commitment. Resentment and hostility may build up in your child against religion and against you. When a teenager is mature enough to select his own values, you must grant him freedom to do so.

The best way to handle this situation is to take a firm stand about the importance of religious practices and give the reasons for your convictions, but be prepared to lose. After openly reaffirming your beliefs, tell your child that you respect his right to make up his own mind.

In developing their own identities, some adolescents feel the need to reject, at least temporarily, their parents' religious beliefs. Many of them return to these beliefs as mature adults. Other reasons for abandoning religious practices include boring religious services that are geared more to adults, and a sense of contradiction between what is preached in church and what is practiced at home (parents not living up to the ideal of brotherly love for all men).

Remember that the majority of children in young adulthood do not drastically deviate from parents' values but, by and large, tend to perpetuate parental values. If parents live a moral life, their children will probably live up to their standards. The children may reject the outward observances of religion but the values that have been instilled in them since childhood are likely to remain with them for the rest of their lives.

Rebellion against religion is often a temporary reaction that disappears with time and maturity. But even if it doesn't, parents should try to make it clear that no matter how far their child strays from the family's faith, their love and affection for the child will remain unchanged. Your love for your children should not be "conditional" upon their following your personal beliefs.

HOW TO CRITICIZE YOUR CHILDREN WITHOUT PUTTING THEM DOWN

He has a right to criticize who has a heart to help.

—Lincoln

Criticism, as it was first instituted by Aristotle, was meant as a standard of judging well.

—Johnson

Criticism should not be querulous and wasting, all knife and root-puller, but guiding, instructive, inspiring—a south wind, not an east wind.
—Ralph Waldo Emerson

The rule in carving holds good as to criticism: never cut with a knife what you can cut with a spoon.

—Charles Buxton

A good supervisor they say, is someone who can step on your toes without messing up your shine.

The trouble with most of us is that we would rather be ruined by praise than saved by criticism.

—Norman Vincent Peale

"How am I doing?" That is a question we all need answered every now and then. Children are no exception. Without helpful and compassionate criticism from concerned and loving parents, a child does not learn well. We tend to be too close to ourselves to be able to detect all or even most of the flaws in our personality and behavior that need improvement.

How can a child do better unless he is made aware of what he is neglecting or doing poorly? It is a parent's responsibility to set reasonable standards for social, school, and work achievement and expect them to be met. Correcting and helping our children improve, then, is one of the most important functions of a parent. It can and should be one of the most useful, fruitful things we do.

Unfortunately, many parents tend to postpone, avoid, or neglect criticizing their children. Telling someone that his performance isn't satisfactory and spelling out exactly how to do better, is not a very pleasant task. Criticism is always hard to take, no matter how tactfully presented. By definition it means that somebody is dissatisfied with what you've done. Children, in particular, are very sensitive to criticism because their ego is still weak and vulnerable. Also, a child's self-esteem is greatly influenced by what his parents think of him. Bumbling or harsh criticism by one's parents can devastate a child. Because of the importance and difficulty of giving criticism to children, parents must know how to do it correctly.

What is Constructive Criticism?

Constructive or positive criticism is first of all task oriented, that is, it attempts to focus a child's attention on the task by pointing out in a specific way what needs to be done or what went wrong; negative criticism, on the other hand, is judgmental in nature and is directed towards assigning blame or finding fault with a child's personality. So negative criticism is personality-oriented.

Constructive criticism calls attention to a child's mistakes by describing what went wrong with the task and suggesting ways for improvement. Just pointing out an error without showing the way to improvement can discourage a child.

Examples of Positive and Negative Criticism are:

Negative criticism: "Anne, what's the matter with you, you failed math!"

Constructive criticism: "Anne, I see by your report card that you did well in reading and social studies but that you are having difficulty with math. I know you've been trying hard, so we'll just have to get you a little extra help with this, don't you think?"

Negative criticism: "Marie, stop talking and get to work!"

Constructive criticism: "Marie, you will not finish your reading if you continue to talk."

Negative criticism: "Oh, you clumsy child. You did it again!"

Constructive criticism: "I see the milk is spilled. Here's a sponge to mop it up."

Negative criticism: "You have no friends. It's probably because you tease a lot."

Constructive criticism: "I think you'd be better liked if you said more nice things to others."

In addition to being task-oriented, constructive criticism often begins on a positive note. So before correcting a mistake, you might let the child know you appreciate some positive aspect of their current or past performance. It is always easier to listen to unpleasant things after we have heard some praise for our good points. So try to point to something OK in the child's work or in the effort before offering criticism. Thus, you might say:

"Boy, you worked hard to wipe this table clean. All that needs to be done now is removal of these small spots here."

"You need help in figuring out division problems. All the rest of your answers are right!"

"John, you've got the spoons in the right place and you just need to reverse the knives and forks."

"Karine, you've always kept your room so neat and clean. This past week it hasn't been looking as it usually does."

Guidelines

Your criticism will be more productive if you also adhere to the following pointers:

1. *Be Specific.* Avoid vague or global criticism: "This is sloppily written," "Can't you help out more around the house?" Be specific about exactly what the child has done wrong or neglected to do, and how she can improve. Vague criticism ("You're so careless," or "This is poor.") is always nonconstructive. It generates a climate of dissatisfaction rather than pointing the way to improvement.

2. *Watch Your Timing.* Criticism when someone's down, hassled, tired, or in the midst of an argument with you will seem cruel and heartless. Wait for calmer moments.

3. *Tone of Voice.* Helpful criticism is given in a friendly, matter-of-fact tone of voice, rather than in an irritated, harsh, or accusatory way. Ninety percent of the friction of daily life is caused by the wrong tone of voice. As a wise man once observed: "That criticism is best which sounds like an explanation." Few people are aware of their tone of voice when they give criticism. Try tape recording yourself when you correct children so as to become more aware of the things you say and the way you say them.

4. *Don't Prejudge.* Ask questions first to gather all the facts. Don't prejudge a child or assume he is at fault. So be sure a child has a chance to state his side of a case before you find fault. If a child knows he is at fault he may admit it willingly. This makes the situation easier all the way around.

5. *Criticize in Private.* Don't criticize a child in front of people. Take her aside and talk to her in private. This principle was illustrated in the following incident. New York Yankee baseball player Eric Soderholm was playing poorly for a time in 1980 when the owner of the Yankees publicly criticized him. Soderholm said later that this public rebuke contributed to his "getting down on himself" and subsequently playing even worse.

6. *Prompt Self-Criticism.* Most of the time we can learn from our mistakes. It is best to help the child discover for himself what he did wrong. "Please check your work." If not obvious to him, give constructive criticism. Also, if you rarely compliment a child, don't expect him to remain open to your criticisms.

7. *Be Encouraging.* After you criticize a child's performance, always try to comment on any subsequent improvement.

8. *Assume Some Responsibility.* When you take part of the responsibility for an error your child is apt to do likewise. Ask yourself if the child knew how well he was expected to perform his duties, if he knew the deadline he had to meet. Did the child have the necessary skill and knowledge to do the job well. If some responsibility is yours, admit it immediately: "I should have given you clearer instructions."

9. *Be Understanding.* Rather than blaming a child, be understanding and try to see why the child's performance seemed OK to him.

10. *Examine Your Intent.* If you are upset you may take it out on a child by hurtful rather than helpful criticism. So don't criticize a child when you are tired, irritated or out-of-sorts.

> *When I am angry at myself I criticize others.*
> —*Ed Hoeve*

11. *Close Relationship.* If your child does not respect and like you as a person, she is likely to perceive your criticism as hurtful rather than helpful. So criticism is best given and taken within a close, warm relationship.

12. *Be Thoughtful.* Before you criticize, take time to analyze the cause of the problem and ways the child can improve. For example, instead of saying, "You shouldn't be depressed all the time," work at figuring out some ways the child can get out of the depression.

13. *Be Relevant.* Only give criticism for problems that can be resolved. *Pointless* criticism means to point out some problem a child can't do anything about. A teenager who is in a *deep* depression, for example, cannot get out of it herself and needs professional help rather than your criticisms.

14. *Be Open to Criticism Yourself.* You should welcome criticism and suggestions without taking them personally. Have the attitude that there is a better way to do everything. In this way you will be setting a good example for your children. Too often, people resent criticism. They take it personally and sometimes react like a mule stung by a wasp. Their immediate reaction is to hit back even when the criticism is justified, which it often is. When parents are not open to honest criticism, how can they expect their children to be?

15. *Allow Practice.* Whenever possible, allow your child the opportunity to practice the better way you have pointed out.

Pitfalls to Avoid in Criticizing Children

There are two ways parents can err in criticizing children: in quantity or quality.

Quantity: Criticism should be given in moderation. But don't fail to point out significant mistakes that must be corrected. Children need gentle pushes to succeed. Studies have shown time and again that children who go on to be successful have one thing in common—they came from homes where their parents pushed them to do well.

1. *The "timid" parent.* Some parents soft-pedal or rarely utter a criticism. They let sloppy work from their children slip by and consequently they continue to get it. Sometimes a parent will not directly criticize a child for fear of losing her temper or making a scene. So she simply does not talk to the child or says very little. The child is supposed to guess that she disapproves. This strategy creates too much uncertainty. The best way to let your son know you are unhappy about his coming home two hours after curfew is to tell him so directly. Withholding criticism is not a favor if it reinforces a person's self-defeating behaviors.

2. *The "faultfinder" parent.* At the other extreme is the faultfinder who is never satisfied with what the child does and always finds fault. If a child has worked hard for over an hour cleaning the kitchen, the faultfinder will come in and point out a small smudge on the refrigerator. Don't look for faults as if they were buried treasure. If you have this type of "red pencil mentality," always underscoring errors, it means your standards are too high and/or you are focusing on trivial mistakes. Constant faultfinding makes children anxious, discouraged, and unsure of their abilities.

Children should receive from their parents much more praise and affection than criticism and punishment. Most parents, however, fall into the habit of being too critical of their children. Although they are technically not faultfinders, many parents just do not balance their disapproval with positive feedback. Added together this criticism is a heavy burden.

The following letter from a parent was printed in the *Rhode Island Churchman;* it all too accurately illustrates how prone we are to overdo criticism and "be at" children all the time rather than using moderation. How easy it is to harp and carp and leave everything else unsaid.

SATURDAY WITH A TEENAGE DAUGHTER

Are you going to sleep all day? . . . Who said you could use my hair spray? . . . Clean the dishes off the table . . . Turn down that radio . . . Have you made your bed? . . . That skirt is too short . . . Your closet is a mess . . . Stand up straight . . . Somebody has to go to the store . . . Quit chewing your gum like that . . . Your hair is too bushy . . . I don't care if everybody else does have one . . . Turn down that radio . . . Have you done your homework? . . . Don't slouch . . . You didn't make your bed . . . Quit banging on the piano . . . Why don't you iron it yourself? . . . Your fingernails are too long . . . Look it up in the dictionary . . . Sit up straight . . . Get off that phone . . . Why did you ever buy that record? . . . Take the dog out . . . You forgot to dust that table . . . You've been in the bathroom long enough . . . Turn off that radio and go to sleep.

Similar thoughts are expressed in one of the classics of American Journalism, "Father Forgets." Appearing originally as an editorial in the *People's Home Journal,* it contains a troubled father's sensitive and heartwarming message to his young son.

FATHER FORGETS
By W. Livingston Larned

Listen, son: I am saying this as you lie asleep, one little paw crumpled under your cheek and the blond curls stickily wet on your damp forehead. I have stolen into your room alone. Just a few minutes ago, as I sat reading my paper, a stifling wave of remorse swept over me. Guiltily I came to your bedside.

These are the things I was thinking, son: I had been cross to you. I scolded you as you were dressing for school because you gave your face merely a dab with a towel. I took you to task for not cleaning your shoes. I called out angrily when you threw some of your things on the floor.

At breakfast I found fault, too. You spilled things. You gulped down your food. You put your elbows on the table. You spread butter too thick on your bread. And as you started off to play and I made for my train, you turned and waved a hand and called, "Good-bye, Daddy!" and I frowned, and said in reply, "Hold your shoulders back!"

Then it began all over again in the late afternoon. As I came up the road I spied you, down on your knees, playing marbles. There were holes in your stockings. I humiliated you before your boy friends by marching you ahead of me to the house. Stockings were expensive—and if you had to buy them you would be more careful!

Do you remember, later, when I was reading in the library, how you came in, timidly, with a sort of hurt look in your eyes? When I glanced up over my paper, impatient at the interruption, you hesitated at the door. "What is it you want?" I snapped.

You said nothing, but ran across in one tempestuous plunge, and threw your arms around my neck and kissed me, and your small arms tightened with an affection that God had set blooming in your heart and which even neglect could not wither. And then you were gone, pattering up the stairs.

Well, son, it was shortly afterward that my paper slipped from my hands and a terrible sickening fear came over me. What has habit been doing to me? The habit of finding fault, of reprimanding—this was my reward to you for being a boy. It was not that I did not love you; it was that I expected too much of youth. It was measuring you by the yardstick of my own years.

And there was so much that was good and fine and true in your character. The little heart in you was as big as the dawn itself over the wide hills. This was shown by your spontaneous impulse to rush in and kiss me good-night. Nothing else matters tonight, son. I have come to your bedside in the darkness, and I have knelt there, ashamed.

It is a feeble atonement; I know you would not understand these things if I told them to you during your waking hours. But tomorrow I will be a real daddy! I will play with you, and suffer when you suffer, and laugh when you laugh. I will bite my tongue when impatient words come. I will keep saying as if it were a ritual: "He is nothing but a boy—a little boy!"

I am afraid I have visualized you as a man. Yet as I see you now, son, crumpled and weary in your cot, I see that you are still a baby. Yesterday you were in your mother's arms, you head on her shoulder. I have asked too much, too much.

Quality. Apart from the quantity of criticism (over or underdoing it), the quality of our criticism may be harmful. To be effective, criticism must be perceived as helpful rather than hurtful. Words are like knives—they cut just as deep and as painfully. The following types of criticism are definitely hurtful in nature and should never be used.

1. *Sarcasm—ridicule.* Child: "I'll try to do better next time." Parent: "Sure, sure, I'll bet (in a sarcastic tone)".
2. *Belittling, name-calling, humiliating.* "For God's sake, what's the matter with you. How stupid can you be!"
   "How many times do I have to tell you to be more careful?"
   "You're so clumsy."
3. *Blaming.* We need to overcome our first reaction which is to

blame a child for a mistake: "How could you do it?" "What's the matter with you?"

4. *Exaggerating.* "You always fail," "Your're no good at math," "You don't care about anybody but yourself."

5. *Judging.*   Sometimes instead of evaluating a specific behavior, we judge a child's entire personality. "You *bad boy*. You spilled the milk."

TEACHING CHILDREN TO SOLVE THEIR OWN PROBLEMS

A problem is only opportunity in work clothes.

—Henry Kaiser

Total absence of problems would be the beginning of death for a society or an individual. We aren't constructed to live in that kind of world. We are problem-solvers by nature, problem-seekers, problem-requirers.
—John W. Gardner

Give a man a fish and you feed him for one day. Teach a man to fish and you feed him for a lifetime.
—Chinese proverb

"Mommy, Davey hit me!"
"Terry took my book!"
"Eugene won't play with me!"
"Dad, I don't think you're going to like my report card."
Sound familiar? Most parents hear these statements or variations every day. Children often have difficulty coping with real life problems. How do parents react when their child has a problem? Typically the parental instinct is to produce a quick efficient solution, i.e., solve the problem for the child. A better way is for parents to teach children *how* to think, not *what* to think. Children develop self-confidence, autonomy, and decision-making skills when they learn how to approach and solve problems. Children who cannot cope with life's problems are likely to remain emotional and social cripples. In this regard, research[34] has

shown that delinquents and emotionally disturbed persons are deficient in their day-to-day problem-solving skills.

Problem-Solving Attitude

How do you help a child when he has not engaged in any wrongdoing but has a problem he needs to solve. For example, how do you help a child who has a social problem such as nobody wants to play with him, or a schoolmate is spreading lies about him? First of all you should instill a positive attitude or set towards problems which involves: (a) accepting the fact that problems are normal and inevitable; (b) believing that something can be done to solve most problems; (c) recognizing a problem when it occurs; and (d) inhibiting the tendency to respond either on the first "impulse" or to "do nothing."

Problem-Solving Process

In addition to a positive attitude, children need to learn to take the time to solve problems in a rational and systematic way. Problem solving can be defined as a process which makes available a variety of potentially effective response alternatives for dealing with problematic situations and increases the probability of selecting the most effective response from among these various alternatives.

How does one effectively solve a problem? It is generally agreed that the five-step approach outlined here is the best way to proceed. Remember that the purpose of these steps is to teach children *how* to think when facing a problem, not *what* to think.

STEPS TO FOLLOW IN PROBLEM SOLVING

Step 1. Identify the problem and what is causing it.
Step 2. Generate Solutions
Step 3. Select the Best Solution
Step 4. Implement the Solution
Step 5. Evaluate Results

Step 1. Identify the Problem and What is Causing It.   Begin by asking the child to describe all aspects of the problem in specific, concrete terms. Ask what happened just before the problem (antecedents), what happened after the problem (consequences), and how often the problem has occurred.

Try to determine what is really causing the problem. This teaches a child cause-and-effect thinking. A child who frequently knocks over her milk glass at the table, for example, may not realize that the problem is that the glass is placed so close to her arm, that it is always on-target. In another situation, the problem may not be that the teacher gets angry at the child (effect) but that the child often talks to his neighbor in class (cause).

Finally, help the child phrase the problem in a way leading to a solution, that is, state a specific goal to strive for. A goal is the problem (e.g., no friends) stated in positive (e.g., invite one classmate over to play) rather than negative terms.

Step 2. Generate Solutions.   Thinking up alternate ways to solve a problem is a particularly important skill to teach preschool children since it has been found to be related to social adjustment in children this age.[35] Young children often fail to realize that there is more than one way to solve a problem, and that some solutions will be better than others.

The "brainstorming" technique, first used to generate ideas for advertising, can facilitate idea-finding. The four basic rules of brainstorming are:

1. Criticism of new ideas is not allowed. The judgment of ideas must be withheld until later (i.e., during decision making).
2. "Free-wheeling" is welcome. In other words, the wilder the idea, the better; it is easier to tame down an imaginative idea than to think one up.
3. The more ideas the better. Quantity breeds quality. Research has verified the fact that the more alternate solutions you think up, the greater the likelihood of finding useful ideas.[36] Encourage your child to brainstorm by asking, "What else could you do?" and "Can you think of any other solution?" Often, because of your greater experience and understanding, you can assist in the brainstorming process by suggesting solutions the child has not thought of.
4. Combining and improving ideas are encouraged. So in addition to contributing ideas of their own, the participants in brainstorming

should suggest how the ideas of others can be turned into better ideas, or how two or more ideas can be joined into still another idea.

To illustrate the generation of solutions process, a parent and child might think up (and write down) the following solutions to the problem of a bully in school:

Face up to him
Tell the teacher
Ignore
Avoid the situation
Talk openly to the bully
Offer to be "friends"

In another situation, possible solutions to failing grades by a teenager might be:

Study longer
Don't go out so often
Drop after-school activities
Ask for progress reports from teachers
Drop a few classes
Learn better study habits
Invite a friend over to study
Parents give more freedom in return for improved grades

Remember to involve the child in this brainstorming activity. Children are more likely to accept solutions they have had a hand in generating.

Step 3. Select the Best Solution. After generating possible solutions, the next step in the problem solving process is to make a decision as to the best solution. Critical evaluation is involved here which means weighing the possible consequences (pros and cons) of each solution. So for each solution list the possible good and bad that might happen, the probable costs and risks, the problems and objections that could arise. Try to see immediate, as well as long-term consequences of each course of action. If there are several criteria for evaluating a solution, you might assign each a scale value such as $++$, $+$, O, $-$, or $--$.

For example:

Solution	Evaluation Criteria			Net Total
	A	B	C	
1	+ +	+	−	2
2	+ +	+ +	+	5
3	+	− −	−	−2

The best option (Solution 2) is the one judged to have a high likelihood of success (Criterion A), with the least effort or work (Criterion B), and with a low probability of causing other problems (Criterion C).

Step 4. Implement the Solution.   This step involves spelling out in detail how the solution will be implemented or put into effect. One must spell out who does what and when it is to be done. Adolescents, in particular, seem to profit most from guidance in how to put into action a possible solution to a problem.

Step 5. Evaluate Results.   Allow a trial time period for the solution to work (e.g. three weeks) and then sit down with the child to assess how well the plan is working. Often some revision or modification may be needed to improve the solution. If the solution is clearly ineffective, return to Step 2 of the problem solving process and select an alternate plan.

WHY CHILDREN SHOULD HELP WITH HOUSEHOLD CHORES

Man must work. That is certain as the sun. But he may work grudgingly or he may work gratefully; he may work as a man, or he may work as a machine. There is no work so rude, that he may not exalt it; no work so impassive, that he may not breathe a soul into it; no work so dull that he may not enliven it.

—Henry Giles

I find in life that most affairs that require serious handling are distasteful. For this reason, I have always believed that the successful man has the hardest battle with himself rather than with the other fellow. To bring one's self to a frame of mind and to the proper energy to accomplish things that require plain hard work continuously is the one big battle that everyone has. When this battle is won for all time, then everything is easy.

—Thomas A. Buckner

Every job is a self-portrait of the person who did it. Autograph your work with excellence.

Whatever is worth doing at all is worth doing well.

—*Lord Chesterfield*

A hundred years ago in rural America families really needed every one of their children to help out on the farm. Daily chores gave these children a feeling of personal worth and competence, as well as a sense of belonging and contributing to the needs of others. Children in our electronic age, on the other hand, often have everything done for them and expect to be steadily entertained. Research[37] indicates that children raised in cultures where they have little or no meaningful tasks to perform at home tend to be dependent, self-centered, and attention-seeking. Children of subsistence farmers, in contrast, tend to be generally altruistic. In my experience, children who help out at home are easier to live with. They are less demanding, more appreciative of things done for them, and all-around nicer.

The assignment of chores to children has a twofold purpose: to teach them the concept of family sharing and to introduce them to the world of work. Work has enormous meaning for the development of a sense of competence and self-esteem. Sigmund Freud's famous answer to the question "What is the secret of life?" was "Love and work." We must learn to do both well if we are to enjoy mental health.

Everyone must learn to be responsible, to have challenges, and to experience a feeling of accomplishment through work. Unfortunately it is often easier for parents to do chores themselves than train and supervise their children. To take this seemingly easier route is to deprive children of necessary training in work habits and altruism (concern for others).

Work Habits

Children need to be taught early in life how to succeed in work activities by having a positive attitude towards work, and good work habits. Work habits that you want to instill in your children as they perform chores fall into two main categories:

1. Self-Discipline: finishing tasks, neat and orderly, prompt, dependable, hard working, and high standards.
2. Coping: problem-solving skills, organizing efficiency, foresight or planning ahead, initiative, and alertness.

How to Motivate Your Child

The key to teaching children the necessity of doing chores is to appeal to "fair play." Explain that chores are a part of maintaining a home and that parents shouldn't have to do everything themselves. As part of a team, everyone contributes what he can to the common effort. Everyone has to do his fair share.

Although children will generally recognize the fairness of their doing certain household chores, this does not mean they will enjoy doing them. Certain chores, such as cleaning pots and pans, are just not fun activities. For these "hard-core chores" it is best to take a "This has to be done" attitude. Have a family conference and let each child select a chore from a list. Children usually find a chore they like which becomes their regular task. Eventually only the worst jobs are rotated.

What Chores Can Children Do?

What can you expect from your children in regard to house work? According to Elizabeth Hainstock, author of *Teaching Montessori in the Home,* little children are capable of doing a great deal more than we usually expect them to do. Toddlers can start to dress and undress themselves and put away their clothes and toys. Then, when they reach nursery school age, they can set the table, collect laundry, water plants and do a variety of other tasks. Indeed, children are so enthusiastic about these tasks that "housework" can become their favorite game.

School-age children (ages 5–12) can make their beds, clean their rooms, care for pets, and help in cleaning. They can vacuum, go to the store, dust, set the table, empty wastebaskets, and load the dishwasher. Children tend to be more willing to do chores that benefit themselves directly, such as doing their own laundry and cleaning their own rooms.

According to a recent government survey, parents report that 65 percent of 6-year-old children do some chores at home, and the average amount ot time they spend on chores a day is 30 minutes. By age 11, 90 percent of the children living at home do chores and spend 50 minutes per day completing them. Girls tend to spend a few minutes longer a day on chores than boys. The survey also noted that three out of four children aged 6–11 had one regular home task or more. Moreover, the proportion of children doing three or more tasks regularly more than doubled over this age range, increasing from 20 percent at age 6 to 47 percent among 11-year-olds.

As they enter adolescence, children need to perform more complex and challenging jobs such as cooking family meals, household repairs, or building a storage cabinet. A study by sociologist Ted Johannis, Jr., revealed that three out of four American teenage girls set and clean the table, and also do the dishes. Less than a third of the girls, however, are asked or allowed to prepare the main meal. So enlist the help of your children (boys and girls) as apprentice cooks even though you will have to spend considerable time and energy teaching them this skill. Also, I firmly believe that all children (boys and girls) should have baby-sitting experience. This is an invaluable experience for discovering what parenthood is all about.

Guidelines for Supervising Children's Chores

The following are tips on how to make chores an optimal learning experience for your children.

1. Be crystal clear in assigning a chore, i.e., state precisely what must be done, by whom, and when it has to be completed.
2. Have reasonable expectations of what a young child is capable of doing so that your demands don't seem unreasonable. Overloading a child with work leads to a rigid, compulsive person who is rarely joyful or spontaneous. Be sure chores do not interfere with a child's needs for free time, study time, family interaction time, or rest-relaxation time.
3. Explain your reasons for asking the child to do a chore. Never just say, "Do it because I'm telling you to." That will only make the child feel resentful.

    Rather, as previously mentioned, let him know that in a family whose members care about each other, everyone has to do his share so that no one has too much to do. The child will realize that there is a legitimate reason for doing the chore, and by making him feel like an important part of the family, you give him a sense of self-esteem.

4. Don't approach the child timidly because you fear he won't do what you request. If you do so, you give up all expectations of him doing his share. Kids don't always have to be happy about what you ask of them, but they will chip in if they realize your request is fair.

5. Don't give children too many things to do at once. Start off with one chore at a time, gradually adding more within reason. One job completed is worth six on a list.

6. Provide a wide variety of chores to do and let the children rotate the unpleasant tasks at stated intervals and have a voice in the assignment of tasks.

7. Getting started at a chore is one of the biggest hurdles for a child. You can help by scheduling a regular time for chores (a "family work time" right after breakfast on Saturday often works well), by prompting (school-age children usually respond to impersonal reminders such as notes on their doors, bulletin boards, and posted checklists), by working along side of the child for a while, by rounding up the tools needed, and by showing interest in the task.

8. Preschool children prefer to work with their parents on a task, e.g., picking up toys, while children ages 8–12 often prefer to work independently on a chore. When a child first learns a task it is best to work along with him and show him what to do and how to do it.

9. Be a good role model. Perform your share of chores cheerfully and take pride in your work. Take turns doing the most menial tasks with your children. The most important influence on a child will be your example. Be a model of cheerfully accepting work responsibility, being prompt and efficient in performance of the task, and showing a spirit of cooperation and sharing the work load. Both parents should be active in setting the example. A helpful husband who sets an example of pitching in with household chores, including the traditionally feminine ones, is an invaluable learning experience for appropriate sex roles in today's world.

10. Time periods generally seem longer to a child. To experience work as satisfying a child must be able to complete it in a time frame

that he considers reasonable. One half-hour of adult time may be psychologically equivalent to two hours to a child. So consider a child's concept of time when you assign chores.

11. It is important for parents to accept a certain amount of error as a child learns a chore. Too much pressure on children who are engaged in learning may cause them to develop fear of failure to such an extent that they no longer try to perform tasks or to learn, but withdraw or deceive whenever possible. By overemphasizing error or by blaming the child for mistakes, parents train a child to give up rather than to persist. In offering feedback on a child's performance, take the middle ground between setting unrealistically high standards and tolerating slipshod work. Offer constructive criticism which points out the positive aspects of the performance while showing the way to further improvement. If you are convinced that your child is making a half-hearted effort, you should require him to do the job over again before you accept it as completed.

12. Give praise, appreciation, and recognition for a child's work. Don't just take it for granted. Every time we praise a child's efforts, notice his progress, and show him that we think what he is doing is worthy, we encourage him to take satisfaction in his work and to learn good work habits. Note writing is an impressive way to thank children for a job well done.

13. Children should learn to help because it is their duty to do so. If they fail to perform a specific duty, they should be penalized in some way that is related to their misdeed. Depriving them of something they want to have or do is frequently an effective way of teaching them not to shirk their responsibilities.

14. If a child does a *special* work project at home, e.g. washing the windows, you should pay him for it. This will also involve you in supervising the extra work to be sure it is done reliably and conscientiously. It will provide the child with excellent training for future jobs outside the home where he will also be supervised and paid.

 Don't assign a chore such as washing the kitchen floor, as a way of punishing a child, because this communicates that work is not a positive activity but a punitive one.

15. Most children do not like doing chores, and the most common ploy they use to avoid chores is to plead, "I'm too busy." The best

response to this is to remind the child that chores take priority over other activities during certain periods of the day. If a child says "Why me?" respond, "Why not you?"

SUPERVISE YOUR CHILD'S INITIAL EXPERIENCE WITH DANGEROUS SUBSTANCES

Rather than laying down do's and don'ts for teenagers, parents can help by providing them with information and experiences needed to make rational conclusions. The advantages as well as the dangers and pitfalls of cigarette and alcohol use should be pointed out in advance to prepare the children for it. A one-sided training is to point out the dangers of a behavior and to forbid the child ever to engage in the behavior, e.g., puff a cigarette, sip wine, or light a match. Two-sided training involves describing honestly both the advantages and disadvantages of potentially harmful behaviors. One-sided propaganda—the telling of a one-sided story—has been found to be more vulnerable to counterpropaganda than telling both sides of a story.

After you have described the good and bad aspects of a behavior, you can further help by having the child experience the behavior under your guidance. Children who have held a match under supervision and have felt the heat are less likely to light matches when they are alone than children who have had no direct experience with matches. Children are naturally curious and want to experience new and different things. Once children learn what alcoholic beverages and cigarettes taste like, they won't be as mysterious or glamorous to them.

Wine drinking is taught children by many Italian families as part of the traditional family mealtime gathering. In Italy the per capita consumption of alcohol is the second highest in the world—only the French drink more—yet the rate of alcoholism in Italy is one of the lowest in the world and drunkenness is very rare. Drinking for most Italians is not something you do secretly, quickly, and with mixed feelings of guilt and pleasure. It is also not something you do to get drunk. This attitude towards alcohol is acquired gradually through a long learning process at home.

When parents forbid their children to experience certain behaviors that are potentially harmful, e.g., drinking, smoking, this prohibition often results in the taboo behaviors becoming more appealing to the children so that they are more likely to engage in these behaviors outside the home. It seems wiser, then, for parents to provide a home environment where children can sample these potentially harmful behaviors under careful supervision. In this way, having experienced drinking and smoking under parental guidance, and having learned the facts about the pros and con's of frequent usage of alcohol and cigarettes from his parents, a child will be in a better position to make an informed decision about his future use of both items.

Final Comment

Supervised experimentation can be considered a form of stress innoculation. A person is typically made resistant to some attacking virus if he has had a previous exposure to a weakened dose of the virus. A mild dose stimulates your defenses so that you are in a better position to overcome any massive attack to which you may later be exposed. Having had some experience with alcoholic beverages at home, then, a child should be in a better position to handle the consumption of liquor when he is on his own. Indeed, studies show that an experienced drinker is better able to hold his liquor.

WHEN YOU SHOULD ATTRIBUTE POSITIVE QUALITIES TO YOUR CHILDREN

A person may not be as good as you tell him he is, but he'll try harder thereafter.

—*Crossword Varieties Magazine*

Faith is to believe what we do not see, and its reward is to see and enjoy what we believe.

—*St. Augustine*

Give a man a good name and he will deserve it.

A blend of encouragement, positive suggestion, and persuasion is the act of attributing to children a positive quality or behavior, when there is only the slightest evidence that they actually possess it. In other words, you attempt to inspire children to behave in a positive way by suggesting that they are already behaving that way to some degree. Thus, you might remark to a shy, passive child, "Boy, you really stuck up for your rights last week!" or "You know, the way you just held your ground with your girl friend means that you can't be pushed around so easily anymore. You're really asserting yourself lately!" or "You really were very courageous in getting that shot from the doctor. You stopped crying right away, even though it was still painful." (In reality, there was only very minimal evidence for self-assertive acts at these times.)

To a messy child, you might say the following:

"Our family is clean and does not litter."
"I appreciate your picking up that paper."
"You really lined those books up in a well-ordered row."
"Your room seems cleaner lately."
"I know you want to keep things neat and orderly so that you can find them."
"At heart, you're really an orderly person."
"You really keep your art supplies neat and clean."

If you keep repeating the message that the child is a particular kind of person, it should eventually take hold in the child's mind. As a result, the child should not only begin making self-attributions in the same vein, but gain in self-confidence and positive self-regard.

Concluding Remarks

The average child can be readily led if you have his confidence and if you show him that you respect him for some kind of ability. So you can improve a certain ability or trait in a child by acting as if this behavior was already one of his special skills or characteristics. Give a child a good reputation to live up to and he will work hard rather than disappoint you. In this regard, studies have shown that repeatedly attributing to fifth graders the ability or motivation to be neat proved more effective in improving their performance than trying to persuade them that they should do better and not litter. Attribution seems to be effective because it disguises persuasive intent and does not devalue a child by indicating he should be something he is not.

In using attributions, care should be taken to make them not too discrepant from a child's ability, i.e., don't label a child good in math who is generally a slow learner. You must be able to point to some behaviors which confirm your attributions, or you will lose credibility in your child's eyes. Once you have a positive image of what a child is capable of becoming—despite past behaviors—then treat the child as if he is already what you would like him to be. But you have got to believe that the infrequent good behaviors represent the person the child would like to be and can become. Children see themselves primarily through their parents' eyes and they depend on you for a larger vision of themselves.

HELPING CHILDREN MAKE GOOD USE OF THEIR FREE TIME

People who are busy rowing seldom rock the boat.

Find something worth doing and do it with all your might.
                                        —*Theodore Roosevelt*

Among the best things you can do for your children is to turn them on to something, to get them enthusiastic about some activity. The greatest builder of self-confidence is the ability to do something—almost anything—well. *Channeling* is a process by which a parent directs or channels a child's drives and energies into productive outlets.

It is safe to assume that all normal children are endowed with the ability to function well in some valuable way or ways. A parent's job is to awaken the innate aptitudes by encouraging and assisting (give incentives and materials) children to develop them.

Developmental psychologists maintain that school-age children (ages 6–12) need to develop a sense of industriousness and competence if they are to mature. In other words they need to feel successful, that they can achieve in school and at home. Children need to develop work skills on which they can build their future. So don't let them sit in front of the

TV set at home and become passive, inactive, and uncreative. Surveys indicate that children really do spend more free time watching TV than doing anything else. They sit in front of the tube for three to four hours a day; some rarely turn it off. Rather, encourage and assist a child to be active and do things—both mentally and physically. Children who gain a sense of self-esteem through achievement and accomplishment, find little attraction in the passive "high" of drugs.

How can parents make leisure time more stimulating and more fulfilling for their children? There are three main ways to achieve this goal:

1. *Provide Training and Material.*   Formal lessons outside the home to develop a child's talents and interests are important for the development of an achievement motivation. So music lessons, dance lessons, tennis instructions, and so on, are well worth the cost involved.

2. *Be a Role Model.*   Be sure to set an example of the constructive use of leisure time. Be active outside the home and engage in a variety of outside activities and interests, such as sports, cultural and educational activities, travel and civic affairs. Be a model of initiative, achievement, and self-development for your child.

   It is also a good idea to take a personal interest in an activity your child is interested in. For example, if your child's interest in a hobby, such as stamp collecting, is waning, you might try to rekindle this interest by starting a stamp collection of your own or by reading books about stamps.

3. *Encourage an Active Use of Leisure Time.*   There are a wide variety of leisure time activities that your child can pursue that are active in nature; namely, games, sports, nature, collecting, reading, crafts, arts and music, and social interactions with friends and family. Such activities develop cognitive, social, and physical skills which form the basis for a feeling of competence.

HOW TO HELP YOUR CHILDREN RELEASE PENT-UP EMOTIONS

Never turn your back on tears. Do not stem the flow. Knowing why is not important; weeping sometimes is.

—*Ruth Bell Graham*

I am angry nearly every day of my life, Jo, but I've learned not to show it; and I still hope to learn not to feel it, though it may take me another forty years to do so.

—*Marmee to Jo, in* Little Women

A recent survey of family therapists[38] revealed that they almost all agreed on the prime characteristic of a psychologically healthy family—namely, that each member of the healthy family can communicate fully to the others about both positive and negative feelings. So the family should be an open forum to discuss feelings of love, pride, and appreciation, as well as anger, sadness, and fearfulness.

Prohibitions Against Strong Negative Feelings

However, the dominant American culture does not value open and free expression of feelings and emotions. From an early age children are taught to control, mask, or deny their feelings. Boys are told not to cry; girls are not allowed to get angry. At times every child experiences strong negative emotions such as anger, fear, and sadness. The emotion that children need to express most often is anger . . . occasionally anxiety and sadness.

Most parents disapprove of direct expressions of anger by children of either sex. Typically a parent will respond to a child's angry outbursts with "Don't you ever talk to me like that again or you'll be sorry." By repressing and bottling up their feelings, children tend to become "emotionally constipated." One mother I know reported that when she got angry as a child she got slapped for it so she held in her rage and got sick in the stomach. But anger can be constructive since it is related to self-assertion and active efforts to solve problems.

The ability to experience and express a healthy degree of anger and self-assertion without unrealistic anxiety and guilt is a basic prerequisite to adequate psychological functioning. In females, far more than in males, anger frequently becomes thwarted, inhibited, and misdirected in its expressions.[39] Rather than directly and effectively expressing anger, females tend to express feelings of sadness, being hurt, and anxiety.

Consequences of Stored-Up Tension

Emotions are designed to move certain muscles of the body. When you block your emotions—anger, fear, anxiety, whatever—you block energy. When emotionally aroused your body releases hormones to prepare it for fight or flight. If you do not release this energy it is stored as tension in your body. Tension can be visualized as a clenched fist. It results from holding in—physically, mentally, or emotionally.

If children are not allowed to express and vent emotional tension, the tension will tend to build up and seek release in such destructive forms as:

1. Explosive outbursts of temper which can result in physical injury to others or destruction of property.
2. Depression which can result from anger turned inwards.
3. Passive-aggressive behaviors such as pouting, apathy-withdrawal.

Psychosomatic disorders also tend to result from stored up emotional tension. Research conducted over the past 30 years has confirmed that bottled up emotion comes out in physical disorders, ranging from such obvious things as gnashing teeth to headaches or ulcers or other ailments. Many children with psychosomatic disorders seem to be out of touch with their feelings and thus unable to discharge emotional tension in the body. Alexithymia is a Greek word which means an inability to express one's true feelings. It has been found to be related to psychosomatic illness. A child with alexithymia is unable to describe where or what her body is feeling.

Denying a Child's Feelings

"Crazymaking" is the term that has been applied to the situation where parents deny strong negative feelings in a child even though the child is clearly aware of these feelings.[40] It is a tactic that can only confuse a child, alienate him from his feelings, and serve to make him "crazy." It makes a child doubt his own ability to know how he feels and so the child comes to doubt his sanity and awareness of reality.

Examples of "crazymaking" are the following parental messages to a child:

"It doesn't matter, don't get so upset!" (It may matter very much to the child at that moment.)

"You don't really hate me, you're just over tired." (The child may feel hate at that moment.)

"Shame on you for saying such bad things about your sister. She is such a nice girl." (The child may be experiencing legitimate anger.)

Acknowledge and Accept Negative Feelings

The first step toward encouraging healthy emotional expression in children is to help them become more conscious of their emotional reactions by drawing attention to them ("You seem worried, did something happen today?") and accepting them as normal behaviors. Never ridicule a child's emotions, e.g., "Look at you, crying like a baby," "There are no such things as monsters, what a silly thing to be afraid of."

Recognizing the right and need of children to express negative emotions does not mean that you approve of these feelings. It merely indicates that you expect these feelings to arise in the course of family living and that you believe it is best for children to be in touch with their feelings.

Provide Outlets for Emotional Expression

Any kind of muscle movement can relieve emotional tension in children, including talking, cleaning a floor, taking a walk, and doing push-ups.

Verbal Expression. Encourage children to verbally express their anger. You might say, for example: "Well Eric, I know you are very angry at me right now, and it is all right for you to tell me how angry you feel." So when you make a demand on a child allow him to express feelings of anger or frustration: "I hate doing the dishes," or "I'm tired of cleaning my room." These expressions help relieve body tension and release unpleasant feelings. We can expect children to do what we ask, but they do not necessarily have to be happy about it.

Nonverbal Expression. You can allow an angry child to release tension in the large muscles of the body by lying on a bed and pounding his legs and arms and head—up and down—and even screaming. Or you might give a child an old tennis racquet and allow him to flail away at the top of a bed with it until his anger is spent. One parent I know of saved old china and allowed her child to take it behind the barn when she was angry and "let fly." Other parents suggest that their angry pouting children get out their anger by pounding pillows or clay, punching a Bobo doll, drawing a picture of the person annoyed with and then tearing it up, or going for a walk.

A sad child should be encouraged to cry out her hurt or sense of loss. An effective release for anxiety is to take a deep breath and slowly let it out through pursed lips. An anxious child might also be taught muscle relaxation exercises, that is, systematically tightening and then relaxing different muscle groups of the body, e.g., make a tight fist and then relax your hand.

Limit Unacceptable Emotional Expression

Of course, limits must be placed on children's expressions of anger. For example, you might say to your child, "Karine, it's OK for you to get mad at your brother once in a while and to tell him so. But you are not to hit him."

As a general rule parents should accept all of a child's feelings and try to understand them; they should not accept all of a child's actions but should try to understand them. So angry feelings should be accepted ("I'm really mad at you Mom for keeping me in") but hostile expressions of this anger should not be tolerated. Children should not be allowed to insult, curse, or otherwise attack the personality of another person. Nor should they be permitted to physically harm (hit, kick, spit at) someone else. So teach children to stop and think of another's feelings before expressing anger.

Summary

Feelings are a major driving force in a child's life. Parents need to accept these feelings and help children understand them. This is accomplished by:

1. Accepting all of a child's feelings; don't accept all actions.
2. Avoiding telling a child what she does or does not feel.
3. Provide outlets for the expression of feelings.

It is important to create an atmosphere in the home where the children feel free to talk about their feelings, problems, and worries. If a child can't get mad at home, where can he? When you allow children to openly express and ventilate their negative feelings they will usually dissipate very quickly. You will also be able to offer support and understanding when the child needs it most.

THE IMPORTANCE OF GIVING CHILDREN REASONS TO BEHAVE

Reasoning involves explaining to children why they should do or not do certain behaviors. So in reasoning you give children an explanation, rationale, or justification for the behavior you desire of them. Often we say "no" or "do this" to children without explaining why the action is necessary. Many times the reason is the potential harm that could occur to the child: "If you become angry at your teacher you could be expelled from school," or "If you continue to be late for work you could be fired."

In addition to anticipating the *personal* consequences of a course of action, help your children foresee the consequences of their actions *on other people*: "If I do this, then it will probably have this effect on others." Empathy, or the ability to put yourself in someone else's shoes, is an extremely important aspect of socialization. It is discussed in more detail in another section of this book.

The goal of reasoning is intelligent compliance with your requests, rather than "blind obedience." The latter gives dictators inhuman power and can bring whole nations to ruin.

Importance of Reasoning

Studies[41] have shown that children prefer parents whose disciplinary requests are accompanied by "rationale" explanations. Children whose parents give rationales are more likely to model themselves after their parents and to comply with parental rules in the absence of their parents. The children show more internalization of values, more resistance to temptation, and more autonomy. Evidence also suggests that delinquent youths are apt to lack adequate past exposure to parental reasons.

Moreover, the more you give reasons the more likely you will be respected by children. When you give rationales you communicate respect for children. You show you care about their right to know why they should act in certain ways.

Examples. Some examples of using reasoning with children are:

"Jan, you could get hurt doing that."

"It's important to learn arithmetic because you need it for a lot of jobs you might want to get when you grow up."

"Please finish breakfast. There's not much time to get ready for school."

"I won't play with you since you haven't finished your work."

"If you eat your vegetables you will be stronger and healthier."

"Please shut the refrigerator door. It takes more electricity to keep the food cold when the door is left open a lot."

"Please come inside for dinner. Your food is getting cold."

"I'm afraid I can't let you do what you want because . . . "

By giving reasons for actions, you teach your children to anticipate immediate and long-term consequences of their actions and to see that there is usually a cause-and-effect ("if-then") relationship between what we do and what later happens to us. If I do this, then this will happen to me.

Guidelines for Reasoning with Children

1. State the reason in a clear and concise way. Do not give a long lecture or sermon which will tend to turn the child off.
2. The child has to accept the rationale as a sufficient and legitimate reason for compliance. So you must make a good case why the child should do or not do something.
3. It is often necessary to combine reasoning with other disciplinary procedures, such as withdrawal of privileges.
4. The older the child, the more effective reasoning is because older

children have higher levels of intellectual and moral development. Studies[42] have verified the fact that the use of reasoning is more effective in reducing deviant behavior in adolescents than it is with younger children. Preschoolers, in particular, have a limited capacity to reason.

5. State the reason only once or twice, and do not let the child draw you into a long debate or argument about it. Often when you give an explanation about a rule, the child will try to turn this into an argument by quizzing you, rebutting your reasons, or pointing out exceptions to the rule. Avoid this trap by briefly stating the reason and then cutting off debate by insisting upon compliance to the rule. In other words, exert your authority and do not feel as though children have to always accept the logic of your reasons. Indeed, you do not have to attempt to justify all your directions. At times you should feel free to say, "Do it because I say so!"

Inductive and Deductive Thinking

Apart from promoting the ability to reason by anticipating the consequences of one's acts, you will want to stimulate your children to think inductively and deductively. Induction refers to the ability to draw general principles or conclusions from specific things that have happened to us or to others. To encourage this form of abstract thinking, you might observe how certain truths seem to hold up across different situations, times, and people: "Joan, have you noticed that whenever one of your classmates doesn't want to play by the rules of a game, nobody wants to be their friend anymore?" Or you might say: "It seems to me that whenever one of your friends is with Louise a lot, that friend gets into trouble. I wonder if that could be true?" Another way to encourage inductive thinking is to get into the habit of asking your children what the moral is of a story, movie, or TV show.

Deductive thinking refers to the ability to use general principles or rules to govern one's specific behaviors. One such general principle that would be helpful for a child to learn early is the golden rule, do unto others as you would have them do unto you. Another useful principle for children to apply to their daily lives is that if you want others to like you, you should act in a friendly, helpful, and cooperative way toward them. Also, teaching children to use proverbs, maxims, and adages in governing their behavior is an excellent way to stimulate deductive thinking.

UNDERSTANDING THE HIDDEN REASON YOUR CHILD IS MISBEHAVING

There are two basic approaches to enforcing limits with children: The surface approach focuses primarily on controlling the observable behavior of children; the causal approach seeks not only to control or regulate behavior, but to understand the basic causes of the child's misbehavior. The causal approach looks for the underlying motives and intentions of an act and seeks to ferret out why a child acted as he did. By way of analogy, rather than controlling a dandelion by picking off the top— only to have it regrow in a week—a causal approach would be to try to solve the problem by eliminating the hidden root.

Epitomizing the surface approach would be an "Archie Bunker" type of parent, i.e., one who is rigid, authoritarian, and who expects blind obedience from children. Following this approach one would apply the letter rather than the spirit of the law. This type of person judges the seriousness of an act in accord with its practical consequences, e.g., an accidental spilling of a pitcher of milk might be considered a more serious offense than the intentional spilling of a cupful of milk. Such a parent would not be inclined to take into account the circumstances in which a misdeed occurred or the hidden motives of the child. Moreover, this parent is more inclined to apply moral labels to children, e.g., "John's a bad, mean child," and then respond to the label rather than to the child and the specific situation.

The causal approach, on the other hand, assumes that every behavior of a child is motivated, i.e., the child perceives a good reason or purpose for it. Usually these causes are not apparent at the conscious level. The child does not know why he does the things he does, so there is no sense in asking him why he did it. Yet parents must try to ascertain and understand the child's motives. Among the more common motives for troublesome behavior in children are:

1. *Attention.*   Children want so much for their parents to notice them that they would rather get negative attention (verbal admonishments and criticism) from them than get no attention at all.

2. *Vengeance.* A child who feels hurt or frustrated by you may try to get even or save face by being rebellious or defiant toward you at some later date.
3. *Misappraisals.* A child may simply misunderstand what was expected of him or forget the rules.
4. *Power Struggle.* Children often act in troublesome ways to convince you to give in and let them have their way in a dispute.
5. *Physical Cause.* The child is feeling irritable because he or she is tired, hungry, or sick.
6. *Sibling Rivalry.* The child is jealous of attention or favors granted to a sibling or peer.
7. *Inferiority.* Your child feels inadequate or deficient and tends to give up, withdraw, and act discouraged.
8. *Thrill Seeking.* In adolescence, your child may constantly seek excitement, fun, and pleasure.

Often how parents act toward a child will correspond to and reflect the child's reasons for misbehaving. So if a child is constantly receiving attention from you, his goal may be increased attention. If you are often in a power struggle with a child, her goal may be added power. If you find yourself wanting to retaliate and hurt your child, his goal may be revenge for past hurts by you.

How to Discover Hidden Reasons for Misbehavior

Among the procedures you could employ to discover and verify the underlying causes of a child's misbehavior are the following:

1. *Observation.* Carefully observe the child's typical behavior patterns, e.g., does he misbehave with certain people and not with others? Does he act up at certain times of the day only? Does the child show any physical symptoms of illness?
2. *Listen.* Listen carefully to the child's side of the story. Ask him to explain the events and details leading up to the misdeed. Focus on the thoughts and feelings which prompted the act. Show respect and interest in what he has to say about the situation.
3. *Be Empathic.* Put yourself in the child's shoes and try to see the situation from his perspective. Consider what he must have thought and felt before, during, and after the misbehavior. Carefully ana-

lyze whether you have been overlooking some of his basic needs, e.g., love, attention, competence, acceptance, understanding.
4. *Consultation.*   Consult with others who know the child well, e.g., teachers, siblings, peers, as to their opinion about why the child is misbehaving.

After you have formed a reasonable hypothesis as to the possible reasons for the child's misdeeds, test out the accuracy of these hypotheses by such techniques as:

1. *Interpretation.*   Conjecture to your child the reason you consider to be the main cause of his misdeeds, e.g., "I wonder if you're missing Mommy when she goes to work, so you feel kinda mean and don't want to obey the baby-sitter?"
2. *Experiment.*   Take an experimental, problem-solving approach to discover the root cause. For example, if you suspect that your child is misbehaving because of a felt lack of parental attention, try offering the child more of your individual attention and see if this results in a perceptible improvement in the child's behavior. If no change is apparent after a reasonable period, try testing out an alternate hypothesis. The experimental approach takes a lot of patience, analysis, and careful observation to be effective, but it is often the only way to really discover what is bothering your child.

HOW TO INTERPRET TO CHILDREN THE MEANING OF THEIR BEHAVIOR

The difference between men consists, in great measure, in the intelligence of their observation. It is the close observation of little things which is the secret of success in business, in art, in science, and in every pursuit of life.
—*Samuel Smiles*

It is usually not helpful to ask children why they did something—most often they don't know or will give a rationalization or an excuse. Better to conjecture to a child about the purpose of a behavior: "I wonder if you did that because you enjoy my attention and that's a way of getting me to notice you," "You want your way and hope to be boss" (if suspect child seeks power), "You want to hurt others as much as you feel hurt by them" (if child's motive is revenge). These are examples of interpretation, a technique in which you present to a child an alternate way of looking at a situation. You suggest a different perspective to explain events to a child so that she might be able to see the problem in a new light and perhaps discover new ways of solving it.

When your children fall into the habit of misbehaving, observe them carefully for an extended period. Under what circumstance (persons, times, places) do they usually become upset? If your son acts up when you praise or give attention to another sibling, then you might suspect that his need for attention and approval is unfulfilled.

You would then check the accuracy of this appraisal by making a conjecture to your child rather than giving a direct conclusion. For example, you might say, "I wonder if you get upset like this because you feel bad when Mommy and Daddy don't pay enough attention to you?" Or, "Could it be that you feel bad because you think we like Suzy better than you?"

To further illustrate, if a child has been trying to maintain an over-cheerful attitude after her father's death, the mother might suggest: "Mary, I wonder if thinking about your father is so painful that you just avoid all thoughts and feelings of him and his death?" Or if it is clear that your son has no friends because he is too bossy and bullies others (but the child does not recognize it), you might try to point this out by saying, "John, could it be that the reason the other kids don't play with you much is because when they don't do as you tell them, you throw sand at them and make them cry?" Or you might say to another child, "Jim, do you think Bruce hit you because you wouldn't share your toy?" Note that in the above examples, your interpretations are designed to focus the child's attention on his or her role in causing the problem. This is the kind of insight that can help children find effective solutions by themselves.

Additional examples of the use of interpretation are:

If you suspect the cause of a child's bad dream is a visit to the doctor you might speculate, "Joan, could it be that your going to the doctor yesterday upset you a lot and maybe led to your having a scary dream last night?"

If your teenage son states, "I don't know why but I've been staying away from her," you might respond "You may be afraid to start a relationship with her because you've been hurt before."

Case Study

The following case involves an 8-year-old-boy who was inhibited in expressing his feelings, especially pride and happiness after doing something well.

Father: "I think I know why you don't like to admit that you are proud of your work."

Son: "Why?"

Father: "Your sister Jeannie (age 12) always put you down when you were younger (father reminds son of several such incidents). Can you remember? Think about it."

A few days later the father raised the subject once more.

Father: "Do you remember that talk we had. Have you been able to remember anything about how Jeannie put you down when you felt proud about something?"

Son: "No."

Father: "You would be proud to get a merit badge in cub scouts wouldn't you?"

Son: Slinks down behind the couch, out of his father's view. "Yes" (in a soft voice). The boy then stands up, looks with a red face at his father and smiles broadly.

Subsequently, the boy became more outgoing, open, and exuberant.

Guidelines

Some guidelines for making effective interpretations are:

1. *Interpretation.* Word your interpretation in tentative language and avoid any suggestion of mind reading or intrusiveness. So use the language of hypothesis: "I've wondered if . . . ," "It seems that . . . ," "One possibility might be . . . ," rather than making a direct statement. By being tentative and speculative you avoid communicating to the child the message: "You may think you know why you do certain things, but I know better."

2. *Timing.* Never give an interpretation immediately after a misdeed, when both you and the child are upset. Select a quiet, relaxed time when you feel close to the child, e.g., just before bedtime. Also, be sensitive to a child's ability to handle an insight. Like a good gardener, wait until you recognize something that is struggling to

emerge and then make it easier to surface. Finally, don't be in a hurry to interpret the first time a child misbehaves. You'll have plenty of chances to give an insight.

3. *Common Sense.* Avoid interpretations which require special expertise such as depth psychoanalysis, or insights based on theoretical frameworks such as transactional analysis. Rather limit yourself to matter-of-fact explanations which are employed in everyday life, that is, common sense observations. Common-sense interpretations are a feature of everyday conversation between peoples in all walks of life. Stick to trying to understand the child's present actions, attitudes, and immediate purposes. When the child's feelings or behaviors are clearly related to something that happened before, such as flunking a test at school, then your interpretation is a common sense observation rather than crystal-ball mind-reading.

4. *Know Your Child.* The more you know about your child's value system, motives, past experiences, personality traits, weaknesses, and strengths, the better your interpretations will be. You will also be more effective when you possess wide knowledge about human motivation in general.

5. *Listen With the Third Ear.* A skilled interpreter of human behavior has the ability to listen to the message behind words and to read between the lines of a letter. Become skilled in picking up nonverbal cues and in guessing the underlying psychological meaning of behavior. Like a good detective, you have to develop your powers of accurate observation and inference making. People with such skills are called sagacious, that is, possessing keen discernment and good judgment. Parents readily use these skills with the nonverbal messages of infants, but they tend to become more judging and less understanding of the behavior of older children.

6. *Short and Simple.* Confine your interpretation to one sentence with young children, e.g., "I guess you're afraid you'll make a mistake," or "Oh, maybe you're mad at your father?" Also, use simple, concrete language rather than abstract terms or jargon. In general, the most useful interpretation is the simplest, most economical one which explains the largest number of observations.

7. *Limited Goal.* Don't strive to give the final, complete, once-and-for-all insight that will miraculously change the child. Just strive to

increase the child's self-knowledge a little by focusing on one possible motive for the misdeed.

8. *Sparingly.* Offer interpretations infrequently lest the children feel they are constantly being analyzed or that "big brother" is always observing them.

9. *Open Mind.* Keep an open mind about the possible reasons for a child's misbehavior. Avoid rigid, preconceived notions as to why your child exhibits problems.

10. *Self-interpretation.* Have the child do as much of the interpretive work as possible. People value what they have worked to obtain. "Can we understand the meaning of this sudden drop in grades— what are your ideas?" This emphasis not only shares the responsibility for the interpretive work, but is respectful of the child's capacity to understand the meaning of her own behavior. If the child cannot form any conclusion, you should suggest a hypothesis for consideration.

11. *Seek Verification.* Validity is a problem when it comes to uncovering unconscious motivations. Only the child can really judge the accuracy of your insight, so be sure to seek verification from the child. If you are on the wrong track with an interpretation, you will probably receive a blank stare or a denial from your child. But if you have uncovered the real motive behind a child's misbehavior, you should immediately get a characteristic "recognition reaction" in the child, i.e., a roguish smile and a peculiar twinkle of the eyes, much like the cat who swallowed the canary. This is a child's spontaneous reaction to the sudden feeling of being understood.

If a child resists your interpretation, don't insist that it is true. Seek more evidence before bringing it up again. Sometimes you may not know the actual effect of an interpretation until later when the child has had more time to think about it.

Concluding Comments

We often fail to appreciate how readily young children can begin to behave positively once they understand why they are acting or feeling as they do. Often interpretations correct a child's false assumptions about themselves, e.g., that people don't like them or that they are stupid.

Interpretation is a key technique of many insight-oriented psychotherapists. Their underlying assumption is that if only people see certain connections or understand their situation or behavior in a certain way, they will be able to change it.

By giving interpretations, you are modeling one form of reasoning, namely cause-and-effect thinking. Causal reasoning can be defined as the ability to relate one event to another over time with regard to the "why" that might have precipitated the act. Your ultimate goal in giving interpretations is to stimulate children's ability to do their own causal thinking about their motives.

Apart from verbal speculations, you might offer interpretations in the form of metaphors or stories which may give the child a new insight into current behavior. Of course, the child should feel free to accept or reject these explanations. Leave it to the child to find some similarity in motives between the story characters and himself. To illustrate the use of metaphors, you might say, "Most of the time I see you as a great big stuffed animal that stays in any position placed." Or you might tell a story as follows: "I had a daydream about what you said yesterday. I imagined you were in a sailboat without a rudder and you were being blown about the ocean by the prevailing winds. Finally, you were blown into a strange port and you nonchalantly got out and walked towards the town whistling a happy tune. Does this seem like you?"

ADDITIONAL READING

Dreikurs, R. *The Challenge of Child Training.* Hawthorne Books, 1972. Contains a description of the use of parent interpretation with children.

DO CHILDREN REALLY NEED AN ALLOWANCE?

According to various studies, children who engage in petty thievery tend to have been brought up in a home environment where their parents either ignored their financial needs or gave them large sums of money to spend.

An allowance is money given to a child on a regular basis to cover some of her personal expenses. By providing a regular, modest allowance to children, parents achieve a threefold purpose: they recognize the legimate financial needs of children; they promote a sense of responsibility and decision making; and they teach the value of money. An allowance is not a bribe but an opportunity to give realistic, first-hand experience in planning how money is to be spent and how to get value for it. The principle of saving may also be taught through the use of an allowance. If children do not have the money to purchase something they want immediately, they will learn that it is wise to save for future needs.

When to Start

An allowance typically begins at age five or six. By this age children have an understanding of what money is and what it can do. The best method is to give the same amount on the same day of the week so that the child knows exactly what to expect. With a very young child you may want to give him half the allowance twice a week. An adolescent, on the other hand, can be paid once a month.

How Much?

Each family must decide for themselves how much allowance to give a child, based on such factors as family status, usual practices in the community, and what specific purchases the item is to cover. Apart from incidental treats, the cost of transportation, school supplies, and hobby materials may come out of the allowances of school-age children. Some parents determine the amount required by having their child keep a record of money spent for personal needs over a two- or three-week period. A discretionary sum should always be included no matter how many fixed items the allowance must cover. With the exception of purchases damaging to a child's physical or mental health, let the children spend at least part of their allowance as they please. This promotes learning and a sense of independence. It is a good idea to discuss with your child exactly what items an allowance should cover and reach a clear understanding.

A 1972 survey by *Money* magazine revealed a median allowance of 25¢ for children under seven, 50¢ for 8–9 year olds, a dollar for 10–13 year-olds, and $2.50 for 14- and 15-year-olds. However, the range was wide, depending on regional price differentials and cultures.

The older the child is, of course, the greater his monetary needs will be. For a mature teenager who must use his allowance for dating and clothing expenses, a sum of $20 to $25 a week might not be excessive. Extra money might also be available for special labor around the house.

Should An Allowance Be Earned?

Although professionals disagree on this subject, my firm conviction is that an allowance should never be earned. Like food, shelter, and clothing, it is given to a child because she needs it. It is not a reward for good behavior, nor is it withheld for bad behavior. So keep an allowance separate from chores, good behavior, and grades. Consider the allowance as a learning experience, given so that the child will learn through trial and error how to handle money. You wouldn't deprive a child of books for misbehaving, so don't deprive them of this learning tool.

According to Grace Weinstein, author of *Children and Money: A Guide for Parents,* it is dangerous to give an allowance as payment for chores. By offering money as payment for routine chores, you run the risk of developing what psychologist Lee Salk calls, "a monster, the kind of child who demands payment for taking out the garbage." Children should work for the good of the family because it is their responsibility as a family member.

General Guidelines

The following are some additional guidelines for giving allowances:

1. Expect children to make mistakes and buy unwisely at first. They learn best from such experiential learning.
2. Don't *insist* that your child save something from the allowance. Savings can come from other sources of income, such as gifts or jobs.
3. Don't make a child feel indebted to you for the allowance. Children should see it as their just share of the family income.
4. Don't give too big an allowance. A child should not get everything she wishes.
5. A child should not have to remind a parent that an allowance is due.

6. Docking a child's allowance for misbehaviors is, psychologically speaking, undesirable. Such a penalty teaches a child that certain misdeeds are worth so much money. The underlying message is that unacceptable behavior is O.K. if you can pay for it.
7. Review that amount of an allowance with the child on a regular basis—about every six months with a small child and annually with an older one.

WHY A CHILD NEEDS TO DEVELOP A SPECIAL COMPETENCE

Every man should be able to do something all by himself—something that gives him a sense of mastery: fly, sing, write, bake a good loaf of bread, handle a Bowie knife, tap dance, find a new star, carve in ivory. Man needs to solo.

—Bruce Gould

One of the greatest gifts we can give our children is a sense of mastery, of being able to do something very well. Such a special competence gives a big boost to one's self esteem. The development of a sense of mastery does not come easily. One must devote *considerable* time and effort to the task.

Competency training involves teaching children to practice and acquire skills that are necessary for coping effectively with daily problems and opportunities. In addition to being generally competent, every child likes to feel that he or she has a special area of competence or expertise. This means that the child knows more about a particular topic than anyone else in the family, e.g., rocks and minerals, or that the child can do something better than the rest of the family, e.g., ski, converse, or play tennis. Such an area of distinction is ego-enhancing and provides a continuous source of nourishment to a child's self-esteem. No matter how far removed a child's expertise is from your own areas of interest, you should treat it with interest, respect, and admiration.

Parents can contribute to the development of a special competence by their encouragement and interest, and by providing the child with the required materials and training. Among the variety of hobbies that you might try to interest your child in are: collecting, model building, sewing-knitting, reading, photography, drawing-painting, and magic-tricks. Although there is considerable mess and clutter involved in some hobbies, there is also tremendous satisfaction to be gained by the real enthusiasts. Between the ages of 8–12, you will find that children will blow hot and cold for many different hobbies. By age 12, however, a child may settle on the one that he will stick with for the rest of his life. If your child shows no interest in a hobby despite the fact that he is often bored in his free time, try to share your own special interests and expose him to people who are real hobby enthusiasts. You might also take him to hobby shows and hobby shops.

"At Risk" Children

Hobbies or special areas of competence seem particularly important for children who lack the normal advantages of life, e.g., the middle child, the physically handicapped or unattractive child, the socially isolated child, and the underachieving child. According to Alfred Adler, the late psychoanalyst, we are all born with an innate sense of inferiority which is felt as an inner feeling of inadequacy and a need to demonstrate to oneself and others that we are capable and able to master the environment. Children with special problems or handicaps especially feel the need to be competent since they are more apt to feel inferior to others.

At times, children close in age in a family develop best when their daily activities are channeled into somewhat different directions, according to the interests and talents of each child. One may excel at sports, another may like art. Each may need to join a club or hobby group to cultivate their interests and make their own friends. By arranging for each child to go separate ways you can help them develop most fully.

HOW TO OVERCOME YOUR CHILD'S FEARS

Trying to talk a child out of a fear is useless. So to help your children overcome an atypical fear of a particular object or event, try desensitizing them by gradually increasing their exposure to the feared object while they are otherwise comfortable and secure. The systematic desensitization procedure involves progressively pairing relaxed feelings with the stressful situation until the relaxation displaces the anxiety in these situations.

Often this gradual exposure to a feared object or situation is all that needs to be done. If a child is afraid of dogs, many parents overcome this by buying the child a cute, helpless puppy. In this way, as the puppy grows, the child gradually gets used to being around a bigger pet. Other parents attempt more systematic approaches. If a girl is afraid of dogs, for example, a parent might first read picture books about dogs, buy a toy dog, tell stories about the child and a funny dog having good times together, model dogs in clay, and then buy the child a puppy.

If your daughter is afraid of the dentist, you might have her wait outside his office while you go in for a minute to talk. Then the dentist might come outside to greet the child. Next the child might remain in the waiting room while you go for an appointment. The dentist would be sure to welcome the girl and give her candy or a treat. He would invite her to see his equipment and explain his work. Next the mother might arrange for the girl to accompany a fearless friend to the dentist's office while the friend has work done. Then the child would go for an appointment while the mother stayed nearby.

If your son is afraid of the dark, you might try to overcome this fear by the following steps:

1. Buy him an alarm clock with a luminescent face.
2. Watch TV with him in the dark.
3. Eat dinner with him by very faint candlelight.
4. Play games like hide-and-seek with him in the dark.
5. Sit with him in the dark and discuss pleasant topics.
6. Put a rheostat on the light in his room and slowly make it dimmer until the room is completely dark.

If your child is afraid of school for no apparent reason, explain that you would like to help her get rid of the fear. The first day encourage her to walk with you toward school (halfway). The next day go even further until, after several days, the child is able to enter the schoolyard without fear. Then ask her to enter the school building with you for a short time. Gradually ask the child to stay in school by herself for longer and longer periods of time.

Each step up the ladder of overcoming a fear should be a little more difficult than the previous step, and you should only proceed to a higher step when you are certain the child experiences no fear with the current step. As you progress through the desensitization process, you may have to return to an earlier step if your child shows considerable fear or anxiety at a particular stage. This is a sign that you have moved too quickly. It should be noted that an especially strong fear of long standing will require a greater number of steps and a longer period to overcome. Sometimes, it takes six months to a year to overcome a deeply entrenched fear.

In a similar manner, a physician reduces a child's sensitivity to an allergen (allergy-producing substance). The physician gives the child an injection of a very small amount of the allergen, so that the body builds up a defense against that amount. Progressively larger doses of the allergen are then given, until in time the child no longer has an allergic reaction to natural allergens.

How to Relax Your Child

To be sure your child is relaxed while you gradually present fear-arousing situations, you might have to provide pleasurable objects (candy or other rewards), give continual support ("I'm here. There is nothing here to harm you"), or train the child to relax (deep breathing, muscle relaxation exercises) while thinking pleasant thoughts.

The first step in a desensitization program might be having the child watch a calm, relaxed peer perform the feared behavior several times.

ADDITIONAL READINGS

Schaefer, C. E., and Millman, H. L. *How to Help Children with Common Problems.* Van Nostrand Reinhold, 1981. See section on fears.

Krumboltz, J. D. and Krumboltz, H. B. *Changing Children's Behavior.* Prentice-Hall, 1972. See section on desensitization of fears.

HOW TO BALANCE YOUR CHILDREN'S NEEDS WITH YOUR OWN NEEDS

The goal of the "linking" procedure is to seek a more harmonious balance in a child's life between the opposing forces of freedom and responsibility, and pleasure and pain. By using the following five linking procedures, you should obtain greater harmony between your needs and the needs of your child.

1. *Link Each Parental Restriction with a Freedom.* When you say no to a child you are usually saying yes to something else. Make this explicit when you set limits by stating some of the acceptable options open to the child. For example, you might say, "Jim, you can't use the car on nights before school, but you can use it on Friday or Saturday nights."

2. *Link Each Liberty with a Responsibility.* To teach your child that with increased freedom comes added responsibility, you might say, "Bill, since you're going to be using the family car for your own needs now, you must begin to take some responsibility for the maintenance and care of the car. From now on, washing it will be up to you, and when you start making money from your part-time job, I'll expect you to buy gas for the car on occasion."

3. *Link an Adolescent's Desires to His Earning Capacity.* At times, some of the desired expenditures of an adolescent go beyond the earning capacity of the family. It seems reasonable to link some of the financial desires of an adolescent to his capacity to meet part of the expenses. In this way you avoid turning the child down completely. You might say, "If you want your own private phone, I'll pay for the installation charge if you pay for the monthly maintenance fee."

4. *Link Each Criticism with a Compliment.* When you soften a criticism with a compliment, children resent it less, e.g., "Hey, you're a real good-looking guy and I can't figure out why you don't take better care of your clothes and appearance."

5. *Link Each Punishment with Support and Reward.* When a child has been punished, he or she is in particular need of some understanding and comforting. Unfortunately, most parents tend to combine punishment with emotional distance and coldness towards the child. When punishing children, show them that they are still lovable by listening sympathetically to the pain they are suffering, and offer them both verbal and nonverbal signs of affection.

Also, when you punish a misbehavior, link it with a reward for a positive, incompatible behavior. An example of this combined "carrot and stick" approach is to penalize selfish behavior while praising altruistic acts. The carrot and stick approach has been found to result in very quick behavior change in a child.

Often rewards alone are not strong enough to change a child's misbehavior since there are equally strong rewards for the misdeed, such as stealing appealing objects. So you have to combine punishment for the misbehavior with rewards for appropriate behavior. The carrot and stick approach is also needed to change bad habits of long standing such as nail biting. Such habits are done automatically without thinking so they are difficult to bring under conscious control.

HELPING CHILDREN DEVELOP A REALISTIC BASIS FOR SELF-EVALUATION

Children need feedback from their parents to validate the psychological growth and progress they are making. Rather than taking progress for granted, you should point out to a child that he is able to do certain things that he was not able to do before. For example, you might comment, "John, you know it really wasn't too long ago that you really used to get upset a lot. Remember those times when you would yell and kick and scream? Now you hardly ever get upset like you used to and you seem to have much better control over your emotions."

The purpose of substantiating or validating a child's progress is not so much to impress him with your approval, but to help him realize that there is clear and objective cause for him to be proud of himself. A child's lack of progress should also be noted in a calm, matter-of-fact tone, e.g., "Margaret, you're biting your nails again."

Noteworthy is the fact that studies have shown that children do not naturally develop a basis for realistic self-evaluation. Rather, they tend to be overly harsh in their evaluations and tend to give themselves fewer positive evaluations than adults would judge warranted in the same situation. In giving a child feedback about his task performance, be sure to include positive as well as negative feedback. Some adults take good work for granted and fail to report it to children.

Recording

A useful tool to help you provide feedback is to keep a written account of the frequency of occurrence of a child's behavior. Careful observation and recording by parents of the incidence of a child's misbehavior will not only provide information as to the seriousness of a misdeed, but also will help establish a reference point for evaluating progress. Since a child's behavior change is typically slow and gradual, a systematic frequency count will reveal slow progress that might otherwise be overlooked.

Simple checklists or charts for recording the frequency of a child's behavior can be made by parents. For example, if you wanted to measure how aggressive your child is to his siblings, you would first redefine the problem behavior in more precise, concrete terms, e.g., aggression might be defined as hitting, kicking, or roughly handling a sibling. One parent would then set aside a period each day to record the frequency of the misbehavior. The recording period would be when the misbehavior is usually at its peak, e.g., 4 to 5 P.M. when the children play together in the house. The parent then tallies the frequency of occurrence of the target behavior as follows:

	M	T	W	Th	F	S	S	Total (week one)
Number of times observed:	|||| ||	|||| ||	||||		||||	||||	|||	||	32

You might want to show a child a graph depicting his progress over a series of weeks. A chart or graph can be worth a thousand words.

In lieu of actual counting, you can use a five-point behavior rating scale to measure progress, e.g., Child hits siblings: All the times he is near them ____; Frequently (about 75 percent of the times) ____; Occasionally (about 50% of the times) ____; Seldom (about 25 percent of the times) ____; Never ____. Rating scales are, of course, less accurate than actually counting behaviors.

Concluding Comments

Often just explaining to your child why you are observing (you are disturbed about his hitting, kicking, and pushing his brother) and posting the recording sheet will be enough to reduce the frequency of the misbehavior. In other words, your concern and the daily feedback provided by the recordings will serve to help the child control his behavior.

Your careful observation of a child's behavior will also assist you to determine the circumstances of its occurrence (what triggers off the misbehavior, at whom it is usually directed, what happens after it occurs). This information may aid you in understanding the root causes and/or factors contributing to the disturbance.

ENCOURAGE YOUR CHILDREN TO USE POSITIVE IMAGERY

There is a well-known psychological law which states that images or mental pictures tend to produce the physical conditions and external acts that correspond to them. Thus, if you picture yourself hitting a golf ball well before you actually swing, you are more likely to hit the ball better. As the noted psychologist William James once said, "Every image has in itself a motor element." Therefore, parents should play a role in helping children develop their imaginal abilities. For example, if your children are upset after experiencing a nightmare, you might help them relax by encouraging them to imagine a pleasant scene, e.g., resting on the beach after swimming. You might also help them to picture pleasant images by reading them a favorite story. The pleasant scene will signal a child's muscles to relax.

On another occasion, you might encourage your children to picture in their minds, as vividly as possible, how their life would be different if they developed a strong will to enable them to stop their temper tantrums, or courage to overcome their fear of the dark. You would ask the children to imagine themselves as having attained this courage or willpower. Then ask them to describe in detail the picture they have formed in their minds. A related procedure would be to ask them to draw a picture of this mental scene. Similarly, you might ask children to draw pictures protraying what they want to be when they grow up, or to draw a self-portrait of how they picture their ideal self. In this connection, a child's action-drawing of his conception of an ideal parent might activate your own fantasies in a positive way.

Fantasy as Substitute Gratification

Fantasy can also be used to offer immediate substitute gratification for events. Thus, if your child is hungry and there is no food immediately available, you might suggest that he imagine his favorite food, e.g., a "Big Mac." This substitute pleasure may tide the child over a difficult waiting period. When my son, Eric, was three years old I once helped him obtain in fantasy what could not be given in reality. The day after his sister's sixth birthday party, he kept asking when he could have a similar party. I suggested we have a special "pretend party" right away which he readily agreed to. We thus imagined (and acted out) every detail of a real party, including deciding whom to invite, sending out invitations, blowing up balloons, answering the doorbell, opening the presents, playing party games, blowing out the candles on the cake, and eating the special treats. Eric was very pleased with this imaginary party which seemed to completely satisfy his need for special attention.

It is a well-established psychological principle that fantasy can bring substitute satisfaction to people. In this regard, four types of wish-fulfilling fantasies have been identified:

1. Display—you perform a feat which brings applause.
2. Rescue—you perform a heroic act which brings you the devotion of the rescued person.
3. Grandeur—you are a member of royalty or some deity.
4. Homage—you accomplish some unusual feat for an admirer.

WHEN YOUR CHILDREN DENY RESPONSIBILITY FOR MISDEEDS

It's been said that children have 1000 reasons for failure but not one valid excuse. A common excuse of children is to shift blame onto others, e.g., "He started it!"

Since children are quite skilled at giving excuses and projecting responsibility for their misdeeds onto others, parents must develop an equally effective technique for reversing or shifting the responsibility back when it belongs with the child. Only when a child feels responsible for his actions can he learn from his experiences and resolve his difficulties. A crucial first step for children if they are to change maladaptive behavior is to admit some responsibility or culpability for it.

The following verbal interactions illustrate how you might use the "reversing" technique:

Child: I got into trouble at school today because the teacher is so boring and can't teach.

Parent: You mean that all kids with poor teachers get into trouble?

Child: I hit him because he called me a name!

Parent: I can understand that. I wonder why he called you a name. Could you have done something that annoyed him?

Child: The other kids made me do it.

Parent: You mean to say that you're a puppet on strings and that everybody else pulls your strings but yourself?

Discussion

Effective use of the reversing technique will depend not only on your skills in drawing out of children their role in a conflict, but also your tone of voice, your interest in, and concern for the children, and your attitude (one of wanting to help children by assisting them to see the real source of their difficulty).

ADDITIONAL READING

Vorrath, H. H. and Brendtro, L. K. *Positive Peer Culture.* Aldine, 1974. A discussion of the reversing technique.

RELABELING YOUR CHILD'S MISBEHAVIOR SO AS TO CALL A SPADE A SPADE

No man was ever so much deceived by another, as by himself.

—*Greville*

Children often tend to describe certain antisocial behaviors in a positive light. From watching cowboy and Indian movies on TV, for instance, they may infer that it is heroic to kill Indians; from viewing a number of cartoons, they may come to feel that it is OK to be physically aggressive towards others. Similarly, from associating with their peer group, boys may believe that it is feminine, weak, or stupid to show helpful or considerate behavior. The task of the parent, then, is to constantly reverse their thinking about the positive-negative value of certain behaviors by means of a relabeling procedure. You should refer to any type of helping behaviors as strong, mature, and powerful, while describing or labeling all hurting and dishonest behaviors as weak, immature, or cowardly.

In using this procedure, you should take care not to downgrade a child's motivation to be strong and courageous; rather, redirect this desire into socially desirable channels. By your words, you indicate to children that you believe that a person who is really brave and strong helps others rather than hurts them. Thus, don't let your children get away with whitewashing antisocial, self-defeating behaviors by describing them in exciting or romantic terms. For example, if your child says it's "cool" to "rip off" candy from a store, you would call this being sneaky or stupid, because it's stealing what belongs to another. If a child says he thinks he might give someone a knuckle sandwich, you might relabel by saying, "You mean you're thinking of acting like a hothead or a bully by physically hitting someone with your fist and hurting them?"

By using euphemisms for deviant acts, children and adults try to lessen or eliminate their culpability in the acts. "Ripping off," for example, implies that stealing consists of taking by strength something that is sticking out or extended to you, whereas the word stealing denotes the dishonest and secretive taking of something that belongs to another. Like children, most of us believe we are good and rarely blame ourselves for anything. Instead, we use various strategies to defend our self-esteem and rationalize away the guilt. H. R. Haldeman, for instance, steadfastly proclaimed his innocence in the Watergate affair, despite the overwhelming evidence to the contrary. To be sure, he probably never said to himself, "Bob, you're going to commit a crime now and obstruct justice." Rather, as John Dean stated, Haldeman and others used euphemisms such as "containing" Watergate, keeping the defendents "on the reservation," and coming up with the right public relations "scenario." Don't let your children deceive themselves by whitewashing or romanticizing their deviant acts. Help them to redefine their acts in a realistic, responsibility-accepting manner.

If your teenager attempts to minimize his act of vandalism, for example, by saying he was just fooling around or having a little fun, you might more accurately define it as defacing and seriously marring property that belongs to another. Frequent use of the redefining-relabeling procedure should influence your children to develop appropriate attitudes and values as well as honest, realistic terms for antisocial behaviors.

ADDITIONAL READING

Vorrath, H. H. and Brendtro, L. K. *Positive Peer Culture.* Aldine, 1974. An excellent description of this technique.

CLARIFYING YOUR CHILDREN'S ROLE AT HOME

All parents should examine and discuss the role and function of children in their lives. In delineating the role of children, you should consider why you had children and what your expectations are for them.

One way of accomplishing this is to sit down with your spouse and list what you believe to be the rights and responsibilities of children, as well as your wishes and expectations for them. The more you and your spouse agree on children's rights and your expectations for them, the more consistent will be your childrearing.

One couple listed the following:

Children's Rights

- Freely express their ideas.
- Be loved and wanted.
- Follow own interests.
- Develop own values.
- Be educated (college, then they are on their own).
- Individual attention (one hour with each parent per week).
- High-quality medical and dental care.
- Clean clothing of good quality.
- Privacy (time alone, own phone).
- Right to disagree with parents.
- Have voice in decisions affecting them.

Children's Responsibilities

- Help with housework when able.
- Respect and obey parents.
- Live in accord with society's laws and mores until mature enough to make informed dissent.
- Be considerate of others.
- Develop own talents.
- Work hard and to the best of their ability on tasks.
- Be doers rather than complainers.

Long-term Wishes and Expectations for Children

- Love and be devoted to parents.
- Be source of comfort and security to parents in old age.
- Carry on family name.
- Achieve more than parents.
- Be source of joy and delight.
- Be a companion or confidante to parents.
- Never be source of embarrassment.

In contrast to the above long-term goals, most experts agree that the goal of parents in this country should be to raise children who can function well in a democratic society, who are kind, reasonably altruistic, cooperative and considerate of others, effective problem-solvers, and independent and self-sufficient, yet able to enter into close personal relationships. Once you know your goals, you will find that there are some childrearing practices that are more likely to achieve them than others.

Final Comments

The clearer you are about what you expect from children, the clearer the children will be about their role. Be sure to communicate early and repeatedly to children what you expect. In some homes, you will see displayed a children's "Bill of Responsibilities." Once you have articulated norms which define how children are expected to act in your family, you should consider whether your actual practices belie your beliefs, e.g., do you expect children to be more autonomous as they grow older but refuse to allow them more freedom and continue to offer advice when it is not needed; do you believe children should freely express themselves but you actually practice: "Children should be seen but not heard."

Similarly, you may say that you expect your child to be educated, but you may make no provisions for your child's college expenses and you may make no effort to continue your own education. In regard to academic expectations, research studies have shown that children are more likely to have positive attitudes towards school if they perceive their parents as wanting them to be good students and expecting them to go far in school.

In communicating your expectations to children, be sure you don't keep raising the ante so that as a child meets one standard you raise it higher, and then higher so that it seems nothing will please you. Such perfectionistic and ill-defined standards are likely to discourage children or make them very insecure and anxious. Such an attitude is illustrated by the parent who, when a child brings home a report card with all As and one B, overlooks the As and proceeds to criticize the B. Perfectionist parents are usually too critical in that they expect too much and are always finding fault. They tend to overlook small positive acts and focus too much on children's deficiencies.

HELPING YOUR CHILD THINK IN A RATIONAL, POSITIVE WAY

Rational Thinking

Men are disturbed not by the things which happen, but by their opinions about the things.

—*Epictetus*

Research has indicated that many negative feelings of children, such as anger, anxiety, and apathy, are triggered off by irrational thoughts and beliefs. For example, if a child thinks to himself that he is a bad, worthless person, and that there is no hope, then he will feel sad and depressed. If a child feels he failed an exam because of stupidity rather than poor study habits, then he is also likely to become depressed. Sources of irrational thoughts in children are their tendency to overgeneralize, e.g., one mistake means stupidity, one rejection by a friend means you are not likeable; their proclivity for dichotomous, black-and-white thinking, e.g., "Others are either friends or enemies," and their tendency to overreact and make things worse than they are, e.g., "This is terrible! It's a disaster."

Parents can help children with their irrational beliefs by bringing out into the open and into conscious awareness the thoughts that they are quietly telling themselves. Some of the common irrational beliefs that people have are:

1. The belief that they must be perfectly successful at whatever they do and never fail, or else it would be awful, terrible, and catastrophic.
2. The belief that they must be loved, liked, or admired by everyone they meet.
3. The belief that nothing bad or unpleasant should ever happen to them. If a bike has a flat tire or the weather is bad, the child thinks "Why should this happen to me!"
4. The idea that they must be given whatever they desire, immediately.

Once a child's irrational ideas have been brought to the surface, then you and your child will be in a better position to replace these ideas with more realistic, rational thoughts. Thus, for a child who believes he is bad and worthless, you would point out the things he has done that are good and worthwhile. You would also explain that even if he had never done anything good in his life you would still love him and he would be worthwhile to you.

If a child suffers a minor crisis, e.g., forgets her lines in a play, help her realize this isn't the great calamity that she thinks it is. Assist her to gain perspective on the setback and take it in her stride. Point out that no one expects her to be perfect and that the event in no way diminishes her worth as a person in your eyes. Point out that the important thing is not the mishap, but what the child is saying to herself about the event. It is not the stresses in life that determine your character, but how you react to them. It's not what people think about you that counts, but what you think and know about yourself that matters.

Positive Thinking

Change your thoughts and you change your world. In a very deep sense you are what you think.

—Norman Vincent Peale

Better to light one candle, than to curse the darkness.
                                              —*The Christophers*

The soul becomes dyed with the color of its thoughts.
                                              —*Marcus Aurelius*

Positive thinking is based on the fact that there is more than one way of looking at things. You can look out the window, for example, and see a partly cloudy day (negative view) or look out and see a partly sunny day (positive view). Both are equally correct. One view is life-enhancing, the other is life-defeating. A positive attitude and can do spirit will ensure that good things happen. When Goliath came against the Israelites, the soldiers all thought, "He's so big we can never kill him." David looked at the same giant and thought, "He's so big, I can't miss." Optimism and enthusiasm will spur one on to peak performance.

Apart from optimism, the power of positive suggestion can be used effectively. This technique is reflected in the story, *The Little Engine That Could.* The little engine kept saying "I think I can, I think I can . . ." and was finally able to pull a heavy load. The theory is that if a person repeats positive thoughts often enough ("Day by Day, in every way, I'm getting better and better.") they are going to "seep down" into his unconscious and bury or get rid of the negative thoughts. Positive thoughts awaken one's potential and build self-confidence.

Gary Player, the professional golfer, used to upset people by telling them exactly what he thought of their golf course. "Now," says Gary, "I tell them all they've got the greatest course in the world. And you know something, this has helped me. If I think the course is lousy, I play lousy golf. But if I convince myself it's great, I don't spend my time out there thinking how bad it is." The wise parent, then, will try to convince their children how great life is, including school, work, and the people in the world.

Don't let children start the day by telling themselves that they are going to have a bad day because that is exactly what will happen. Help children replace the negative "vibes" with more positive thinking by telling themselves that they are going to have a good day each morning. Of course, the best way to teach a positive orientation is to model this behavior yourself. Are you cheerful in the morning and do you expect to have a good day?

Positive Self-Talk

We all direct our own behavior by talking to ourselves. Sometimes we do this by talking aloud, other times by talking quietly to ourselves. We usually think in words, and much of thinking is really subvocal self-talk. One way to change what we do or how we react is to modify what we say to ourselves. An impulsive child, for example, could be taught to say to himself short sentences that will make him much more efficient at solving problems. Thus, he might say to himself "Take your time. Work carefully. Check your answer."

So teach your children to say quietly or whisper to themselves "I am a good boy" whenever they feel tempted to hit others; to think "Relax" or "Slow down" when they feel anxious or restless. They can learn to talk themselves out of getting upset over spilt milk by saying "There is nothing I can do to change this. So there is no sense getting bothered about it. I'll just clean it up."

By programming your children's self-sentences you will help them to react more calmly and without making themselves angry, fearful, or anxious. Some useful sentences are:

"One step at a time will get me there."
"It's hard but I can stand it."
"It will be harder if I put it off."
"I don't like this, but it's good for me."

To teach a child to self-talk you should first say the sentences aloud to the child, then ask the child to say them aloud. Only after a child has learned to talk aloud to himself will he learn to talk privately or whisper to himself and use his private conversation to control his behavior. For example, to teach a child to make her bed, a parent might say, "Watch me. I'll show you how. OK, what do I do first? I'll take the pillows off the bed. That will make it easier to pull the sheet and blanket up. Now I'll pull back the blankets and straighten the sheets. Yes, this looks nice and neat. Now I'll . . ." Next you ask the child to make the bed while saying the instructions out loud. Later the child would be told to make the bed while whispering the instructions to herself.

PARENT POWER: BE CONFIDENT OF YOUR ABILITY TO INFLUENCE CHILDREN

Studies[43] of parents who have high achieving children reveal that the parents believed they had the power to shape their children's personalities and futures. All parents need to have a conviction or firm belief that they are right in what they are doing as parents, that it will work out. Every time you make a mistake or your child fails, you've got to admit it and accept the fact that it's going to happen many times, but that you are going to succeed in the long run. When you expect to be successful in something, you are more likely to be so. The expectation of success sets up a "self-fulfilling prophecy" effect.[44]

Parental expectation in the area of discipline is a very important force. The parent who is confident in his own authority expects appropriate self-control in his children and has fewer disciplinary problems. You must be certain that you are right in making the expectations that a child will behave in a certain way. Unless parents are convinced they are right, they will not have the necessary confidence in what they are doing, and this lack of confidence or guilt is easily sensed by children so that the desired results will be more difficult to achieve. The detection of ambivalence or guilt by a child will keep alive the hope that the present set of rules might be changed through stubbornness, sympathy-seeking, or other means. When you are committed to winning and succeeding, then the child will see this and comply more readily.

The simplest and soundest method of deciding on the best course to follow with children is to decide first what the final result is to be, and what kind of person you are trying to produce. What behaviors do you want in a child? Do you want a child who always does what he is told without questioning? Or do you want a self-reliant individual who thinks for himself?

If we think only of the present, we are likely to use techniques which are easiest and produce the quickest results. When we think in terms of the future, we tend to use different methods and stress different values. So plan a philosophy of parenting based on long-term goals. The more you have thought out your approach, the more confident you will be in applying it. The less vague ("I want good children.") and the more specific you are in your goals ("I want my children to be self-directed, empathic, and considerate of others, knowing and valuing their uniqueness, having high standards, happy and fun-loving," and so on), the more effective you will be.

Other ways of gaining confidence in your childrearing ability include reading books, taking courses, attending lectures, conferring and consulting with other parents who have children the same age as yours, and forming parent discussion groups. Family counseling or therapy is still another alternative.

Apart from the above, it is reassuring to know that common sense goes a long way in childrearing. Even more comforting is the fact that kids are remarkably resilient when it comes to psychological bruises so that you can make many mistakes with them and they will still come out OK. What seems of crucial importance is your basic relationship with the child. The more children feel your love and concern, the more your mistakes will roll off their backs.

FAILURE: YOUR CHILDREN CAN'T GET ANYWHERE WITHOUT IT

He only is exempt from failure who makes no efforts.

—Whately

Life is either a daring adventure or nothing.

—Helen Keller

The first time children try to do something they are going to be less than perfect. Allowing a learning leeway means that you expect a child to make mistakes when he is learning a new skill, e.g., learning table manners or how to read, spell, or ride a bike. A calm, accepting attitude by parents as a child learns will create a climate of safety and security. If, for example, your nine-year-old daughter's first cake turns out to be a gooey mess, don't try to give hollow praise. Rather, you might smile and observe, "Well, that cake is pretty sad." This response conveys the message that it is OK to fail, that this is a normal part of learning a new skill.

When children try to discover something for themselves they are also going to make mistakes. Such active trial-and-error learning will be retained longer than learning by rote memory. The wise parent will provide many opportunities for such self-learning. For example, you might let a toddler place different size rings on a spindle in the wrong sequence. Then you would ask if it looks right to him, i.e., encourage task analysis by the child.

High Achievement and Fear of Failure

A most serious threat to a person's success in life comes from his efforts to keep safe in his work, to see to it that he doesn't make mistakes. Eleanor Roosevelt once said,

"The tragedy of our times is that our young people are being taught that they must never make a mistake—that to make a mistake is unforgivable. All great men have made mistakes. If you're afraid of making a mistake, then it means you will stop functioning."

Truly significant success will elude the person who does not flirt with and learn to thumb his nose at failure. Exceptional individuals like Picasso, Einstein, and Mother Teresa were able to sustain themselves in their developing years with few successes, amid, probably, a multitude of failures. Anyone who sets his goals high is bound to have a certain number of failures. Babe Ruth set a record for home runs. He also set a record for strike-outs. But he didn't let that worry him—he just kept on swinging for the fences!

So high achievement is the result of continuous effort and repeated failure. The line between failure and success is so fine that we scarcely realize when we pass it; so fine that we are often on the line and do not know it. Many people throw up their hands at a time when a little more effort, a little more patience would achieve success. Others avoid trying in the first place because of fear of failure. They view failures and mistakes as "castastrophies" rather than as steps on the path to eventual success. Children who learn to set their goals high and persevere at a task despite repeated failures are well on their way to making maximum use of their talents.

Teaching Children How to Fail

Although few individuals are impervious to frustration, children are undoubtedly more likely to react to it in undesirable ways. How can parents help them to respond to failure in constructive ways? First teach children to learn from their mistakes—to analyze why they failed so it will be a step on the way to success. Second, teach children that mistakes are a normal, necessary part of learning for oneself. You should stay calm after failure and avoid the tendency to blame others or oneself. Third, explain to children the necessity to persist longer in the face of difficult tasks. Fourth, encourage them to try to solve problems on their own without outside assistance. Finally, children should expect to be successful in the long run at the highest possible level. Their expectations should be based on their past record of achievements. When you expect to do well you are more likely to try harder after an initial failure.

Part II
Ways to Build Positive Family Relationships

INTRODUCTION

Friendships are fragile things, and require as much care in handling as any other fragile and precious thing.

Randolph S. Bourne

Studies have shown that the disciplinary practices described in the first part of this book are most effective when applied within the context of a close parent-child relationship. It seems that children learn discipline best when they feel that their parents love, understand, and respect them. An open communication between parents and children is essential for real understanding and closeness to develop. Relationships do not just happen, they are the result of much diligence, hard work, and self-sacrifice. A description of the various components of a positive family relationship will be presented in this part of the book. The basic assumption of this book is that the optimal parent-child relationship is not one of master-slave, but a friendship relationship based on equality, respect, common interests, and caring. You cannot purchase a child's friendship by making a child feel indebted to you because of your sacrifices of money or time; you have to earn children's friendships by being a friend—this means mutual loving, liking, understanding, and spending many enjoyable times together.

As Edward Zigler, Professor of Psychology at Yale University recently said: "There is a magic that rests in the relationship between a child and a warm, sensitive, and knowledgeable adult. It is in the fullness of that relationship that we see the child's path to growth and development." The goal of this part of the book is to sketch, in rough outline, some facets of this magic relationship that we all seek with our children.

WHAT DOES IT MEAN TO REALLY LOVE YOUR CHILD?

The greatest happiness of life is the conviction that we are loved, loved for ourselves, or rather loved in spite of ourselves.

—*Victor Hugo*

The most handicapped youth is the child without love.

—*Frank Tyger*

You have a mission to fulfill, a mission of love, but this must begin in your own homes. Let us begin in the place where we are, with the people with whom we are the closest, and then spread out.

—*Mother Teresa of Calcutta*

According to the poet T. S. Eliot, the major cause of anxiety and depression in this century is our inability to love or be loved. Love is also a powerful antidote for alienation, loneliness, narcissism, and drug abuse. Love is to a child what the sun is to the earth. The psychologist Urie Bronfenbrenner states that in order to grow and develop, a child needs at least one specific adult who is "irrationally crazy" about the child in a positive, emotionally involved way. Loving a child seems to have three essential components, namely, unconditional positive regard, cherishing, and caring. A brief description of each component is presented below.

Unconditional Love

Unconditional love means love with no strings attached. It is love with no "ifs"—"I love you if you do this or don't do that." Rather, the child feels 'I am loved because I am me. Unconditional love means that you regard your child as worthwhile and lovable apart from what she does or does not do. It involves recognizing and tolerating children's faults, accepting their right to be different from you and hold different values, trying to understand their moods and negative emotions, standing by them when they are in trouble, and being "up" on your children when they are "down" on themselves. Finally it means loving your children for who they are today, not for what you would like them to become tomorrow.

Signs of this special kind of unmerited love are parental expressions of: "I love you just because you're you," "You're precious," "You're really a special child to me." Another sign would be the absence of parental threats regarding loss of love, e.g., "I won't love you anymore if you continue to do that!" Children need to feel that there is at least one solid, dependable source of security in this world of rapid change and confused values, namely, the unwavering love of their parents. So be careful not to use withdrawal of love or rejection as a punishment for misbehavior. No matter how angry you are at a child's action, the child should feel secure in your basic love and acceptance.

In a close, unconditional relationship, both parent and child know each other well enough to be aware of one another's psychological and interpersonal weaknesses, but these weaknesses are accepted and not exploited. In such a relationship, the parties are free to be themselves and act spontaneously without fear or worry of being rejected for what they do.

As opposed to unconditional love, there is love based on merit ("I'll love you because of what you have done.") or expectations ("I'll love you because you have fulfilled my expectations, because you do your duty, because you are like me.") Such love is given as a reward for good behavior. The negative aspect of this kind of love (some call it "fatherly" love) is that when you feel loved because you have earned it then there is always doubt and insecurity that the love will disappear one day because you may do something to displease the parent. Deserved love tends to leave an uneasy feeling that one is not loved for oneself; that one is loved only because one pleases; that one is, in the last analysis, not loved at all but used.

A story of this kind of love was carried in the newspapers a few years ago. Amy, 15, had always gotten straight As in school, and her parents were extremely upset when she got a B on her report card. "If I fail in what I do," Amy told her parents, "I fail in what I am." This message was part of Amy's suicide note. Such stories are not rare since teenage suicide has now grown to the proportion of a national epidemic (and disgrace!).

Cherishing

Cherishing is valuing the uniqueness of an individual, that is, loving a child for the special qualities that make him the individual he is. Cherishing gives a child a sense, "You're something special," "You're very important," "You're unique." Cherishing involves sensing a child's special qualities and finding them precious. It is appreciating children for what they are, not for what they have done or what you would like them to be. When you cherish a child, you are open to the wonder of his developing self. It is a special kind of engrossment and absorption in the miracle of his existence and individuality. Apart from this awe, cherishing consists of efforts to foster the child's individuality. Implied in this is the recognition of a child's need to differentiate and separate himself from you and become an autonomous human being. If a parent prizes his own uniqueness, this separation will be much easier to accomplish.

Caring

Another pillar of love is caring, which means having an intense interest in everything about the child—his thoughts, feelings, activities—and being concerned about what happens to him. It also means placing the welfare of the child on at least a par with your own welfare. With this kind of love, a child is inclined to think that if someone cares so much about me maybe I ought to care about myself also. Moreover, when a child feels that a parent has his welfare at heart, he is more likely to accept the rules and regulations of the parent.

What Love Is Not

After considering what love is, it is wise to indicate what I believe love is not. Too common pitfalls in loving children are excessive sacrifice or martyrdom and "smother" love.

Excessive Sacrifice. Loving a child means being willing to make some sacrifices for a child as long as they are not excessive. Some parents believe that their role in life is to almost completely sacrifice themselves and their personal pleasures for the sake of the children. In return, they expect their children to give them a great deal of love, devotion, and gratitude.

Parental love, in these instances, is not made a joy but rather a profound duty and unending obligation. By their sacrifices and grim existence, some parents try to put their children in psychological bondage for the rest of their lives. Being obliged to love someone is a difficult burden to carry. To bind your child by guilt, be sure to remind him at every opportunity how much you have done for him, and at what sacrifice to yourself. Never become a self-reliant person. Look to your children for the main source of your happiness, rather than to self or spouse.

Suffering and making sacrifices for children are part of the role of being a parent. In compensation, there are many joys to be found in raising children. Weighing the good and the bad, most parents admit that it's worth it to have children. One could speak of parents being indebted to children for adding joy and fulfillment to the parents' lives. Rather than speaking of debts and obligations, it seems best to speak of a balanced ledger wherein the needs of both parties have been met and all concerned are the better for it. The enduring bonds between parent and child should be those of love and affection rather than guilt or indebtedness.

Mothers, in particular, should be on guard to avoid the "Portnoy's Complaint syndrome" of attempting to vicariously, obsessively, and possessively live their lives through their children. In general, you avoid this by actively pursuing procedures that enhance self-awareness, self-development, and self-liking, i.e., becoming a fully actualized person, and by cultivating your relationship with your spouse, relatives, and friends.

"Smother" Love. Rather than offering "smother" love to a child ("We try to give our child everything she wants.") in which you over-indulge, dominate, or overprotect the child, make your love tough in the sense that you hold your children responsible for their actions. Don't place the children at the center of your universe, rather teach them from an early age that they not only can't have everything they want but they must do certain things whether they want to or not. So parental love should be both unconditional (which provides basic security to a child) and tough (which teaches a child to be independent and responsible).

Final Comment

Two basic human needs are to love and be loved. Hopefully, between ages 8½ to 12, your child will begin to return your love and you will have a reciprocal relationship in which you both have the same goal—the happiness of the other person. In a mutual love relationship, the needs of the other person are as important as your own. To give is as satisfying as to receive. Of course, it takes many years before a child is able to fully leave the typical self-centered orientation of youth and be capable of mature love. By the end of adolescence, however, your children should be exhibiting altruistic love and be able to handle close, intimate relationships with others.

HAVE YOU PUT YOUR CHILD IN AN "EMOTIONAL REFRIGERATOR"?

In the man whose childhood has known caresses and kindness, there is always a fibre of memory that can be touched to gentle issues.

—George Eliot

Better is open rebuke than hidden love.

—The Bible

If people aren't cuddled, they curdle.

—Bob Hope

Many parents love their children yet their children do not feel loved. Why? Because the parents fail to openly communicate their love. It sounds strange but a lot of people are embarrassed to tell members of their family that they love and care about them. Affection means to express your feelings of love and liking for a child either verbally, such as terms of endearment, or nonverbally by smiles, positive facial expressions, and touching.

An affectionate person is direct and explicit rather than subtle about showing his love. A subtle person shows his caring by indirect means, e.g., hard work, gifts, of self-sacrifice. Subtle expressions tend to lack the power, punch, and directness of explicit statements. So don't leave any doubt in your child's mind that he is liked and loved, be open and overt in expressing it. Feeling the love of his parents, a child develops a sense of security, belonging, and self-worth. Like praise, affection helps expand a child's self-esteem. It lifts the spirit and promotes a close parent-child relationship. It tells a child that you not only love him but like him as well. Consequently, affection increases the odds a child will identify with you and your values. Also, a child who experiences warmth and liking from his parents will be more apt to accept their discipline. In this regard it has been said that:

Love makes obedience lighter than liberty.

—R. W. Alger

The challenge in giving affection is to avoid the extremes of too much and too little. In the connection, the philosopher Schopenhauer once told the following fable:

> One wintry day, a couple of chilled porcupines huddled together for warmth. They found that they pricked each other with their quills, moved apart and were again cold. After much experimentation, the porcupines found the distance at which they gave each other some warmth without too much sting.

The moral of this story is that every family has to solve this dilemma— how to be close enough for emotional warmth and support, and yet not so close as to hurt each other by "smother love," overwhelming affection, and other means.

Too much affection or "smothering" occurs when a parent indulges in exaggerated verbal or physical expressions of fondness for the child or singles one child out for special attention. Some adults engage in sickly sweet sentimentality towards everyone they know, as manifest in calling all their acquaintances "darling" or "sweetheart." Deprivation of affection, on the other hand, occurs when a parent never communicates warmth or affection for a child and maintains a cool, aloof attitude.

When confronted about their lack of demonstrativeness, some parents will respond, "Why should I say 'I love you', you know it and that should be enough." An "emotionally retarded" parent is one who is insensitive to the affectional needs and emotions of children. One adolescent I know remarked, "Not once did my father ever put his arms around me and tell me he cared about me."

Physical Affection

All of us need to touch and be touched. Physical affection is an excellent way to express love. It is direct, immediate, and warm. However, our Puritan heritage has kept most Americans from feeling comfortable touching. The noted anthropologist Ashley Montagu has pointed out that Americans tend to touch one another less than people of most other cultures. Compared to mothers in other countries, American mothers tend to soothe and hold their babies less.

There are also sex differences in the ability to express physical affection. Studies have shown that fathers not only interact less with children, but as compared to mothers, are less affectionate with the children. Henry Fonda said recently, "It is only in the last two years that I have been able to say 'I love you' to my children. Of course I have loved them since they were born."

Research has indicated that touching babies is just as important as feeding them. Frederick Leboyer, the French doctor who wrote *Loving Hands* and *Birth Without Violence* says that touching and caressing an infant are crucial to a child's development. It seems we are all born with intense skin hunger. Our need to be touched, caressed, and cuddled is as basic as our need for food. Touch-starved babies often die from a disease called marasmus, a Greek word meaning "wasting away." Denied stimulation for sensory nerves, infant spines literally shrivel up.

Touching is needed by children of all ages. How we express physical affection should vary with the age of the child. Some children respond best to a playful hug while others like a warm pat on the arm or a soothing back rub.

Children raised by parents who rarely or never touched them may have problems in accepting closeness and intimacy as adolescents and adults. They may have other problems as well, including difficulty controlling violent impulses, delinquency, apathy, decline in intelligence, and failure to thrive physically.

Guidelines for Showing Affection

1. Every day in some way resolve to let each of your children know: I love you. Remember that the adolescent's need for parental affection continues throughout his teen years although his need for control diminishes.
2. Children should feel affection from both parents. Some men tend to shy away from expressing their feelings and emotions which are considered unmanly. This "flight from tenderness" as it has been called, tends to lead to a closer mother-child rather than father-child relationship.
3. The principle of reciprocal affect states that it is a rare human being who does not respond to warmth with warmth and to hostility

with hostility. Accordingly, the more you express liking for a child, the more you can expect to be liked in return. You can be pretty sure your children return your liking if the following three behaviors are present: (1) the children want you to understand them and are very open about their thoughts and feelings; (2) the children imitate your behaviors; and (3) what you think really matters to the children so that they will change their behavior to please you.

4. To assess how warm and positive you are to your children, consider the following questions: Are you absolutely crazy about each of your children? Do you smile and joke around a lot with each child? Do you frequently tell the children how much you like and love them? Do you call each child by special pet names? Do you hug, touch, and kiss your children often? Do you praise them more often than criticize them? Do you share confidences and mutual expressions of tender warmth? Do you take home surprise gifts for your children? Do you give them loving greetings and goodbyes? At bedtime do you reassure your child of your love?

5. Avoid inconsistent affection, that is, being loving one moment and cold and rejecting the next. Also, don't give your child a double message by saying "I love you" but recoiling when the child gets too close.

ADDITIONAL READING

Simon, S. B. *Caring, Feeling, Touching.* Argus Press, 1976.

TAKE PLEASURE IN YOUR CHILD'S COMPANY

It is given to many to have children, but to comparatively few to know and understand them and to be companions to them.
—D. A. Thom

"I'm too busy now to play with you—wait until later." Children are regularly told this by their parents not because of a lack of love but because of a lack of commitment to spending time with children. Companionship, more than love, is the key to good parenting. The most important thing a parent can do to ensure the development of a competent, well-adjusted child is to spend time with the child.

However, many parents have little interest in spending a lot of time in close interaction with their children. Psychologist David Elkind recently stated that American parents can't wait until their children grow up. Feeling children are always in the way, parents send them to camp, to baby-sitters, to schools, and to sit in front of the TV sets.

How Much Time is Your Child Worth?

Surveys indicate that parent involvement with children is decreasing in America. Parents in America now spend less time with their children than parents in almost any other country in the world. In this regard, psychologist Daniel Brown reports a study of 300 seventh- and eighth-grade boys who kept a diary of the time that their fathers spent with them. He noted that during an average week the typical father and son were alone together a total of only seven minutes! On the other hand, fathers spend an average of 6.1 waking hours per day at home, a substantial amount of time.

The situation for infants is even worse. A recent study of middle-class men shows that, on the average, a father spends 20 minutes a day with his one-year-old baby, but only 38 seconds actually interacting in any meaningful way with the child. It is difficult to see, then, how many fathers can establish an attachment with their infants or have any real impact on their young children. Fathering as personal involvement does not seem to interest many men these days.

There is nothing you can give your children that will make them happier or feel more important than your time and undivided attention. When you ask a child why another child is causing trouble, he will most likely respond, "He's trying to get attention," or "He just wants to be noticed." People need each other and are the greatest source of satisfaction for one another.

A national survey of school-age children conducted in 1976 under the auspices of the Foundation for Child Development revealed that nearly half the children wished that their fathers would spend more time with them, and more than a third wished that their mothers would spend more time with them. To give a child time is a more meaningful gift than praise or expensive presents. The gift of time requires an investment of yourself; no such investment is required in momentary praise or tangible gifts. The gift of your time and yourself is in the fullest sense the gift of your love.

To illustrate, the wealthy parents of a young boy were extremely hard working and had little time for their son. On his seventh birthday they bought him a pony, a large dog, and gold jewelry. At the birthday party the parents' friends greatly admired the expensive gifts. The boy, however, was found crying because "My father and mother did not even buy me a toy." In an indirect way he was saying that his parents had bought him gifts which represented money but they had not given of themselves.

It is important, then, for parents to make a concerted effort to keep in touch with their children's lives, especially now that both Mom and Dad work in over half of all the families with kids under 18. Don't live for tomorrow and fail to enjoy your children today. Tomorrow is often too late. As Kahlil Gibran said, "Your friend is your needs answered." Your child needs you today. Are you willing to be his friend?

Quality Time

In addition to a certain minimum amount of time being home with the family, it is important to set aside "quality time" with each of your children every week—time along together without distraction or interruption where you participate in mutually enjoyable activities. This is the simplest technique I know of for maintaining and strengthening your relationship with a child. Every child should have his own weekly time, from one-half to two hours, from which other family members are excluded, and this special time should be cancelled only under unusual circumstances.

Activities during these times should be ones you *both genuinely enjoy*. Children of all ages need warm companionship times of playing or working together on things of mutual interest and enjoyment. An essential prerequisite, for example, for adolescent sons to feel understood by their fathers is the issue of time spent with and interests shared with their fathers. A recent study[45] found that for adolescent males who felt understood by their fathers, the time spent with the father was experienced as being pleasurable and as being shared in common interests with the father whether they were sports or intellectual pursuits; whereas for the misunderstood sons, the time spent with father was conflictful and experienced as being coerced into unwanted activities with the father.

The rules for quality time are simple: no criticizing, lecturing, or trying to get your child to do something; you should initiate the interaction so your child feels you really want to spend time with her; and both of you should actively try to think of activities you will enjoy. By following these few rules you will be most apt to achieve the goal of quality time which is companionship, that is, to sincerely enjoy each other's company and to experience true intimacy or closeness. Like touching, time spent in close company with another person tends to intensify relationships. One has a heightened feeling of intimacy.

Some additional guidelines for establishing quality time with your children are:

1. Some of your children need more of your time and energy than others. Children have differing needs and we must respond to them on an individual basis in accord with their needs.
2. There are times when it is absolutely valid to pull your child out of school for a day, and you stay home from work for a day, and the two of you go off and have fun. Pack a lunch and go off alone together to the beach or an amusement park.
3. Have your children spend one day with you at work. They're undoubtedly curious about what you do.
4. Share your hobbies with your children.
5. Substitute fun times with you for TV watching.

Case Illustration

The importance of spending an enjoyable time alone with each of your children is illustrated in the following quote from a professor of psychology.[46]

"Many years ago, when my boy was in second or third grade, I was on a very hectic schedule lecturing on "How to be good parents and teachers." I began to notice that I was not getting the same results with my boy that I used to. I finally decided to take a day off and spend it alone with the boy on the beach. We did. We played with balls and kelp and did all the things one does on the beach. At the end of the day I was completely exhausted and even my boy was kind of tired—but extremely happy. On the way home, he said quite suddenly, 'Didn't we have a good time?' After I agreed, he said, 'You know, I am going to do everything you ask me to do from now on.'

ADDITIONAL READINGS

Millman, J. and Behrmann, P. *Parents as Playmates. A Game Approach to the Pre-School Years.* Human Services Press, 1979.

Sutton-Smith, B. and Sutton-Smith S. *How to Play with Your Children and When Not To.* Hawthorn Books, 1974.

HOW TO COMFORT YOUR CHILD IN TIME OF NEED

Words of comfort, skillfully administered, are the oldest therapy known to man.
                                                        —Louis Nizer

When a friend is in trouble, don't annoy him by asking if there is anything you can do. Think up something appropriate and do it.
                                                        —E. W. Howe

One of the most important jobs of a parent is to be the safe harbor in the storm, the refuge when the going is rough. Everyone is basically insecure and frightened and needs comforting when in distress. Comforting means to soothe and console a person who is hurting either emotionally or physically. In psychologically healthy families, a child's pain, hurt, sadness, tears, and disappointments can be openly and immediately shared with her parents. The child has the feeling that her parents will be there when she needs them.

Children have relatively few sources of support so they often feel overwhelmed by psychological wounds, such as when a person dies they were very close to. Loss of a pet or favorite possession can also trigger intense feelings of abandonment, loss, and anger. At such times they experience increased dependency needs and long to be protected by nurturing persons. If children are unable to share their hurt it tends to remain unresolved like a festering wound. To relieve the pain of such wounds, children may turn to sexual promiscuity, self-destructive behavior, drug abuse, or violence.

Ways to Comfort Children

Among the specific techniques that one can use to soothe and ease the distress of a child are the following:

1. *Be calm and reassuring.* Remain calm yourself and create an atmosphere of safety and optimism that the child can handle the situation. Give reassuring remarks such as:
   "Many people feel very upset but get through it."
   "Sometimes it seems that nothing will help, but the feeling passes and things are fine again."
2. *Actively Listen.* Encourage the child to talk out his hurt. A problem shared is a problem halved in most cases. Try to listen for the feelings underlying the words.
3. *Establish Body Contact.* There is a marked reduction of psychological tension when one is being held by another person. Touching provides a calming effect and a sensation of warmth and well-being. So don't hesitate to soothe with your hands, shelter with your arms, and console by holding a child on your lap.
   Almost everyone likes to be touched when they're grief-stricken. The warmth of another's body is especially comforting then. Author Theodore White, who was on the premises when Robert Kennedy was shot in a Los Angeles hotel, immediately went to the room of the senator's son, David Kennedy, then thirteen, and gave him "bodily comfort" by holding him close.
4. *Allow Dependency.* Let your child symbolically return to the womb at times and be cuddled and smothered with reassuring words. The desire to return to the safe position of infantile passivity and dependence is present in us all. The safety and quiet of a temporary "regression" offers the child the opportunity to experience a safe haven, and to recuperate and become revitalized. So indulge your child with comfort at times and don't let the child feel this need is a sign of weakness. For instance, if your child's dog just got run over by a car, be sure to cradle the child in your arms, while expressing how sorry you are over the mishap and encouraging the

child to cry it out. Let the child be emotionally dependent on you for a time until he regains composure and strength.

Even adults feel little and vulnerable at times and have to lean on others for support and comfort. The freer your children feel to come to you when they have psychic pain, the less need they will have to turn to psychotherapists or to alcohol. So don't emphasize self-reliance so much that your children feel ashamed and guilty whenever they long to become dependent and rely on you for psychological sustenance.

5. *Be Empathic.* Try to see things from a child's perspective and express that understanding. For example, you might say, "I know you are very disappointed because you tried so hard and still came in nearly last in the race."

A little sympathy or compassion is also helpful at times as expressed in comments as, "I'm very sorry this happened to you."

6. *Be Loving.* When a child is down on himself, assure him that no matter what he thinks of himself, you are *up* on him. Express your love by such comments as "I love you for yourself, not for what you do or fail to do."

7. *Promote Emotional Release.* At times you should help lower a child's crying threshold and encourage the release of tension through tears. One often feels better after crying out or screaming out the hurt.

8. *Be There in Person.* Sometimes you don't have to do anything to console a child except be there. Studies have shown that the simple physical presence of another person can be sufficient to decrease feelings of anxiety.

9. *Be Responsive.* Be sensitive to your child's need for assistance. Often a child does not give you clear signals as to the kind of support he needs, or how much, or when to offer it. Since a child will usually not ask for support you have to sense when he needs it. So try to be alert to subtle clues that your child is hurting. With some children this can mean irritability, unexplained silence, physical withdrawal, even a sudden eating, drinking, or spending splurge.

10. *Give Aid.* When your child requests it, be generous in giving specific aid such as information, money, advice, time, and so on.

11. *Show the Problem is Normal.* Let your child know that others have had the same problem. One way to demonstrate that the situation is not unusual is to have the child read books about the sim-

ilar experiences of others. Or you might relate a personal experience that is similar to the one the child is experiencing. For example, a father might tell of the time in junior high school when he dropped what would have been the winning touchdown pass in a championship game.

Pitfalls to Avoid

Some pitfalls to avoid in helping a troubled child are:

Don't minimize the event ("It's nothing to get upset about.").
Don't shame or fault find ("You're acting like a baby.").
Don't punish ("Go to your room if you want to cry.").
Don't threaten ("If you don't cheer up you'll really have something to cry about.").

Unless asked, don't try to solve the child's problem for him. Often the child can handle the situation himself with just a little sympathetic listening.

TRUST: THE MAGIC INGREDIENT OF SUCCESSFUL PARENTING

To be trusted is a greater compliment than to be loved.

—*J. MacDonald*

What do people value most in a leader? Most of us want someone who is honest, truthful and straightforward, someone we know really has our interests at heart, someone we can trust. Of late, however, our country seems to be in a "trust recession"; there are few prominent individuals we are willing to trust, with the possible exception of Walter Cronkite. Trustworthiness, then, is a precious personal trait, well worth whatever effort it requires to increase its presence in the home.

The development of trust in children can pay rich dividends. Studies[47] have shown that people who trust more are less likely to lie and are possibly less likely to cheat or steal. They are more likely to give others a second chance and to respect the rights of others. Moreover people high in trust of others are less likely to be unhappy, conflicted, or mal-adjusted; they are liked more and sought out as a friend more.

What can parents do to be perceived as trustworthy by their children? Three basic facets of trustworthiness are honesty, reliability, and altruism.

Honesty

Trust is based on honesty. Children of all ages want honest answers to their questions. If we tell them something will not hurt when we know that it will, we have deceived them. If we shield them from family problems by saying everything is all right and then children are faced with the loss of a loved one, or a divorce, they learn not to trust us. It is important to give truthful answers to difficult questions such as divorce, sex, and death.

If we tend to exaggerate, we undermine a child's ability to correctly assess reality. So don't boast and build yourself up excessively and unrealistically. Few parents admit personal faults to their children. As a result, the children never learn to own up to personal faults either. So admitting you are human and not perfect is very important if your child is to learn to get along with people and to be honest with himself.

Also, parents should never make promises to a child unless they intend to keep them. Children tend to equate an adult promise with an oath. As a result, they find it difficult to trust someone who breaks a solemn pledge. Rather than making a vague promise and then reneging, it is better to be straightforward and say, "I can't promise to go to the game tomorrow, but I'll make every effort to do so."

In addition to truthfulness, honesty means to be genuine. Genuineness basically means to be oneself, without trying to play a role or hide behind a facade. It means an absence of phoniness, superficiality, or any kind of pretense in relating and communicating with children. By being straightforward, you generate trust and confidence in your children.

Authenticity first of all requires that you be objectively aware of what you are thinking, feeling, and doing. If you are angry you are aware of it. You would not shout at a child while saying, "I'm not angry!" If you are doing well at a task, you know it. Apart from self-awareness, being genuine means being open with the children about your thoughts and feelings. When you are not doing well you can say you are discouraged. When you are angry at a child, you can directly confront a child with your feelings rather than taking it out on the child in subtle ways. When you don't know something, you can be honest and say "I don't know." You'll be surprised how an admission of ignorance increases your credibility with children and sparks their desire to find out things for themselves.

Honesty also means to admit your mistakes. Parents invariably make a lot of mistakes in raising kids. If these errors occur within a context of a reasonable, kind, and loving relationship with children, they can be admitted and quickly corrected with no irreparable harm having been done. The kind of person you are and your relationship with the kids is more important than occasional errors.

For example, if you yelled at your child for a minor infraction of the rules when the real reason was your tiredness, irritability, and crankiness, honestly admit the true cause to your child. You might say, for example, "Amy, I got mad and shouted at you before, but I can see now that you didn't do anything that was really that bad. I was feeling tired and out-of-sorts and I took it out on you. There's no excuse for that, I'm sorry!"

The more you quickly, frankly, and emphatically admit your mistakes, without excuses, the more likely the following consequences will occur:

1. Your children will admit their own errors without excuses or deception. This honest acceptance of responsibility for one's actions will form the basis for mutual trust between you and your children.
2. Your children will view mistakes as a normal part of living and they will be more tolerant of their own shortcomings. This means they will be less likely to experience a sense of defeat from their mistakes.
3. Your children will feel reassured that perfection is not really expected of them, nor is it the price they must pay for your approval, acceptance, or love.
4. Your children will see you as more human, and thus feel closer to you.
5. The quicker you admit mistakes with absolutely no excuses, the more likely it will be that your children will forgive you and try to take your side.

6. Your children will not only trust you more but will also become less dependent on you and more self-confident.

Reliability

Apart from honesty, you establish trust by being reliable in your behaviors and how you treat a child.

Reliability means that you have the same attitude towards the children day after day. In other words, you would generally not fluctuate from being loving, cheerful, and appreciative toward the children one day, and being an angry Scrooge or sad recluse the next. If you do find yourself regularly vacillating like this for no apparent reason, then you should seek professional counseling.

Altruism

The final component of trustworthiness is altruism. An altruistic person is unselfishly concerned for and devoted to the welfare of others. In contrast, manipulative, egotistical parents will use children to satisfy their own selfish needs. They really do not have the child's best interests at heart and the child senses this and does not trust adults.

RESPECTING CHILDREN AS PEOPLE TOO!

Without feelings of respect, what is there to distinguish men from beasts?
—Confucius

If you have some respect for people as they are, you can be more effective in helping them to become better than they are.
—John W. Gardner

When we respect someone we hold in high regard the worth of that person. It has been said that the true measure of a human being is how one treats his fellow man. Too often adults treat children with less respect than they treat fellow adults. Parents are saying and doing things to their children that they'd never say and do to friends. A mother will scream at her child for nicking up the Wedgewood, but she wouldn't yell at a guest for the same offense. For a child, respect means the rights to the complete dignity of a whole person, not just the embryonic dignity of a half-pint. Good manners and honoring a child's need for privacy are crucial aspects of showing respect for children.

Good Manners

Manners make you and everyone around you feel better. Being polite and courteous with children conveys the message that you hold them in high esteem. So develop the habit of saying "Thank you," "You're welcome," and "Please" to children. Children deserve the common courtesies which adults use with each other. If your lateness has inconvenienced a child, say "I'm sorry."

Courtesy also involves not interrupting or contradicting a child during a conversation. Verbal abuse or rude ways of talking should be avoided, such as: "That's enough from you," "Get out of here," "You talk too much," "Shut up."

Tactfulness is another aspect of good manners. This means showing respect for a child's feelings and taking care not to hurt them unnecessarily.

Right to Privacy

Nothing is more upsetting to children and teenagers than to have their privacy invaded by parental prying—listening in on phone conversations, reading mail, inspecting desks and drawers, and entering a child's room without knocking. A child whose privacy is invaded feels insulted, outraged and denigrated. So let your children know that their privacy is as important to you as it is to them.

Private Thoughts

One aspect of the right to privacy is the right of the individual to decide for himself how much he will share with others his thoughts, his feelings, and the facts of his personal life. Some parents show an overriding and too often exaggerated emphasis on knowing everything about their child's life, including explicit details of their dating experiences. So personal matters should be shared by family members but boundary lines must be set beyond which such matters do not extend.

Private Space

Every person needs a private retreat, a place in the home to call her own, where she can retreat when she feels a strong need to be alone. This must be a place where other family members won't intrude. This space may be a bedroom or a desk in the corner of a room. Just how much private territory a child needs is an individual matter, but certainly no one can do without a safe, secure refuge where he can be free from the attention and influence of others, and in which he can refresh his spirit, order his thoughts, and plan his future.

According to the anthropologist Margaret Mead, recognition of the right to privacy is a recognition of "the fact that each individual is in some sense unique and must have freedom to be herself for herself alone. Privacy protects the inner core of the individual's being."[47]

Guidelines for Respecting Children

Some general guidelines for respecting the dignity of children are:

1. Don't be authoritarian. Children are usually more willing to listen to adults outside the family because they talk with them more as equals. Parents tend to talk down to or "at" children and emphasize their superiority. The more parents do this, the less children are apt to respect them or listen to their advice. Also, the less likely the children are to respect themselves which is so necessary for self-control.

   Most of your interactions with children should be democratic rather than authoritarian in nature, i.e., you should treat them as people equal in worth and dignity, rather than treating them as inferiors. Avoid a master-slave relationship in the home with the children acting as slaves or servants.

2. Don't embarrass your children by criticizing them in front of their friends or arguing with your spouse when your children have friends in the house.

3. Don't publicly discuss things your children have told you in private.
4. Don't throw away a child's old clothes or toys without first asking the child's permission.
5. Don't talk down to your child, and don't talk baby talk. Rather, let children know you are talking to them as equals.
6. Do ask for your child's opinions about important things.
7. Do try to imitate a child's behavior since this is the highest form of praise. For example, you might say, "Let me see if I can do that puzzle as quickly as you did." You might also repeat or write down what a child has said . . . , e.g., "I like the way you said that. Let me write it down before I forget it!"
8. Do respect a child's views even when you disagree with them and convey this respect to the child.
9. Do tell your child you believe his needs are as important as yours and thus you will search for a solution which meets everybody's needs when a conflict arises.
10. Do respect an older child's desire not to be seen nude.

Children's Rights

It is a good idea to post and respect a "Children's Bill of Rights" in your home. A sample Bill of Rights[48] follows:

1. Each child should have full privileges in the house. The living room should not be a holy ground where kids and toys are not permitted.
2. Each child should be answered when he has a question or a point to make.
3. Each child should be able to have his friends in the house.
4. Children should be able to entertain their friends in private.
5. Parents should not open children's mail or get into children's private places unless there is a very serious reason for doing so.
6. Children should be given the use of the TV set for their kids' shows, with the understanding that adults have the right to watch their shows, too.
7. Children should be able to choose their clothes at an early age. They shouldn't be forced to wear something they hate.
8. Children should have some say in the decorating of their rooms.

9. Children should not be talked about by adults as if they were not there.
10. Children should be able to expect adults to keep their promises.

How to Develop a Real "Family Spirit"

How to Develop a Real "Family Spirit"

Family spirit is the potent and invigorating tonic that enables families to overcome the inevitable conflicts and tensions that plague them all. Family spirit occurs when the family members identify with each other and the family as a whole. Parental efforts directed at developing a real family orientation in their children can pay rich dividends. Children need to feel part of a larger social unit and to feel responsible for it. They need to think in terms of a we/us/our point of view rather than an I/me/mine. A close family does not just happen, you have to promote it by stressing the importance of human relations within the family, of mutual acceptance, protection, enjoyment, support, and consideration.

In this age of individualism, declining moral values, and a "do-your-own-thing" attitude, it seems particularly important to instill in your children a concern for a common good, such as a family. Most families will tend to come closer together in times of crisis or adversity, i.e., wars, economic misfortunes, sickness, and natural disasters. This same close family spirit can be deliberately fostered by parents during normal times. The willingness of your children to modify their personal goals when these goals conflict with the more pressing needs of the family will indicate to you the general strength of your children's commitment.

Three main aspects of family spirit are shared activities, a sense of kinship, and family values.

Shared Activities

When a family spends considerable time together in common activities a sense of cohesiveness develops. So do things together as a family; establish family traditions, celebrations, and rituals. Activities that a family can share include family discussion meetings and family projects such as designing a family coat-of-arms or family flag. Family game-time for a half-hour after dinner is another good custom. Each family member should have the opportunity of choosing the family game, e.g., scrabble, monopoly. Family mealtimes, which stress mutual sharing of experiences and enjoyment are also important. In other words, you want to have a family life that has as many shared and mutually enjoyable experiences as possible.

Don't let family members always go off in different directions. Go for walks together, play musical instruments together, go to the zoo, museums, sporting events. Keep the family spirit. Some families deliberately set aside a specific time each week for family activity. One father said, "We keep Sundays free for family visiting, outings, day-trips, a dinner out, and the like. It brings us together."

Researchers once asked[49] over two thousand adolescents what they would like changed in their home life. The two most frequent answers were "More time together as a family" and "Better communication." Clearly, a close family involvement is what most children are asking for.

A Sense of Kinship

How can you bring your children closer to all their relatives and help them have a feeling of family pride? One way is by having regular family reunions which encourage interaction among members of the extended family and thus build family ties. Family reunions are mostly a summertime event, planned around vacations or holidays. Typically there will be a cookout and each family will bring their specialty food to the feast. Some families schedule a reunion of the clan around special events such as a wedding or golden anniversary celebration.

Pride in the family history and ancestors should also be encouraged. Children need to touch base with their origins. To know one's roots is to fulfill a need that has been in humans from the beginning and will be within us to the end. To bring a family's heritage to the surface, Alex Haley, the author of *Roots,* recommends that the children in a family go to the oldest members with a tape recorder and get as much oral history as possible. Many grandparents carry three or four generations of history in their heads but don't talk about it because they have been ignored. Next, Haley advises that the history of the family should be written and a copy sent to every member. Included in one's family history should be family letters and other memorabilia.

A child's self-esteem is nourished by pride in her ancestors, history and family. Belonging to an extended family whose members respect, support, and enjoy one another gives a child an ego boost and minimizes feelings of alienation and loneliness.

Family Values

A family should strive towards some kind of consensus of beliefs, values, and goals that members will share. This consensus creates a family image which each member can draw upon to affirm his personal worth and identity.

So parents should attempt to directly teach children values that will promote a family feeling, i.e., cooperation, friendliness, sharing, and family loyalty. For example, you might make comments such as:

"In this family, we all help one another."
"We're the Andersons, and we don't do things like that."
"We have our own way of doing things in this family."
"I'm really proud to be a member of this family."
"We may not have much money, but we all like and enjoy each other in this family."

Appeals to common values, customs, and routines can help minimize personal conflicts between parent and child. Thus, you might say, "In this family everyone is expected to make his own bed."

HOW TO MAKE YOUR HOME AN ENJOYABLE PLACE TO BE

Happiness in a family is unique, the product of endless labor, never ending struggle.
—*Time Magazine, March 28, 1977*

The less you can enjoy, the poorer and scantier yourself; the more you can enjoy, the richer and more vigorous.
—*Lavater*

Puritanism is the haunting fear that someone, somewhere, may be happy.
—*H. L. Mencken*

Enjoyment has to do with the quality of life in your home, which means much more than a rich material standard of living, good conduct, or high achievement levels. It has to do with valuing happy, giving, and cooperative children more than the successful, nearly perfect, better-than-others, smarter-than-others type of child. Making your home a pleasure and joy to be in does not come easily, it takes a lot of soul-searching and hard work for most of us to create this type of environment. We have to decide such basic questions as whether we are living to work and achieve or whether we are working and achieving in order to really live and enjoy ourselves and our family. The rewards of an enjoyable home life are many; first, through humor and fun activities parents establish a "pleasure bond" with their children, and second, children learn how to relax and savor life.

If you can answer yes to most of the following questions, the chances are good that you have the type of friendly, fun-filled home atmosphere which produces happy children.

- Do family members assign a higher priority to the enjoyment of each other and of daily living, than to achievement or success?
- Can the general mood of the parents be described as happy, agreeable, and pleasant? If your home is less than harmonious because of constant squabbles among family members, it's probably an unpleasant place to be and your children are likely to spend more and more time away from home or escaping to their bedrooms.
- Do parents often play with children where the sole object of playing is mutual fun and delight?
- Are family members friendly to one another?
- Do the parents make the children feel that their friends are welcome at home?
- Do the parents spend more time listening to the children than criticizing them?
- Are any hobbies or arts-and-crafts projects a joint venture between parent and child?
- Do the parents avoid arguing in front of the children?

- Are parents confident enough to act like a child at times, e.g., have pillow fights or play peek-a-boo?
- Are the parents primarily interested in seeing their children happy rather than perfect?
- Do parents and children enjoy a quiet relaxing time together each day?
- Are the facial expressions of the parents generally ones of pleasure and approval?
- Do the parents smile or laugh a lot while interacting with the children?
- Are parents and children affectionate with each other, i.e., kiss, touch each other?
- Do the parents regularly go out alone for their own enjoyment?
- Are the parents consistently and predictably cheerful?
- Do the parents enjoy watching their children grow up—are they filled with wonder?
- Do the parents regularly bring home surprises and treats for the children?
- Do parents know how to use a light, humorous touch to relieve tension and/or motivate kids?

Concluding Remarks

One of the most important lessons you can teach your children is to take the time to relax, to do what they like and enjoy themselves. Usually a happy child is a good child. The best way to teach, of course, is to model this attitude of not taking life so seriously all the time. If many parents were to take the time to record how they typically spend their time during the week, they would discover that almost all their time is spent taking care of chores, duties, and obligations and almost no time doing what they like. Enjoying self and family just does not seem to be as important as learning, achieving, and acquiring things.

A recent study of family background of fifty highly successful Americans[50] revealed that most of them came from families in which "harmonious relations were present." There was a positive mood in their homes which was described by one mother as "noisy, bustling, cheerful and full of music."

WHY YOU MUST PUT YOUR MARRIAGE BEFORE YOUR CHILDREN

Love is strongest in pursuit; friendship in possession.

—Emerson

The best thing a father can do for his children is to love their mother.

The marriage relationship should be the axis around which all other family relationships revolve. When husband and wife make their marriage the No. 1 priority, they automatically place all other family relationships in the proper perspective. Unfortunately, once children come, parents complain, "We don't do things together anymore," "We don't seem to have much to say to each other."

Studies have shown that children tend to detract from, rather than enhance, the closeness between a husband and wife. In fact, a couple's satisfaction with marriage and with each other drops sharply soon after their first child is born. With minor variations, it tends to stay at a lower level throughout the years of child raising, increasing again only after the youngest child leaves home.

Childrearing demands a heavy expenditure of parents' time, energy, and commitment. Consequently, the relational aspects of marriage may be easily relegated to a position of low priority and show a gradual deterioration over time. When a wife works outside the home, the likelihood of a deterioration in the marriage is increased. For example, husbands of working wives indicate that they are less likely to reveal their problems and tensions to their wives and tend to be less satisfied with their wives as confidantes.[51]

About half of all marriages end in divorces. For those who are still married a recent survey indicated that about half of the couples are emotionally divorced, that is, they do not feel a real closeness with their spouse. Troubled marriages tend to produce troubled children. Numerous studies have shown that when children live in homes where there is chronic stress or conflict, they are at serious risk to develop psychological problems. So the best thing that parents can do for their children is to love their spouse.

A major long-term goal of the parents, then, should be to maintain the closeness and primacy of their relationship. This doesn't just happen, both husband and wife have to work hard at keeping their relationship warm, considerate, and close.

Research on Healthy Marriages

Successful marriages do exist. A recent survey[52] focussed on couples with a close relationship, that is, couples who found their prime joy in life in each other, while still maintaining separate identities. The results of this study revealed the following keys to a "vital" marriage:

1. *People in Vital Marriages are Giving People.* They seek to help each other and give each other pleasure. They offer one another help, sympathy, and kindness.
2. *They Have a Strong Sense of Commitment to Their Marriages.* They stated that they are willing to fight as hard to preserve their marriages as they are to save their own lives. They do not take marital happiness for granted, they work at it.
3. *They are Strong-Minded.* Although they list marital harmony as a top priority, these couples do not lose themselves in the relationship. They value their independence—the right to form their own opinions, make their own decisions, pursue their own goals.
4. *They Have Vigorous Sexual Drives.* The majority of vital partners reported moderately high to very high sexual needs, with levels similar to their spouses.
5. *They Like to Talk.* These couples spend a lot of time sharing thoughts about all sorts of topics—from serious to trivial.
6. *They are Interested in Each Other.* The spouses take a very active interest in each other's work and hobbies.

The Importance of Intimacy

In virtually every survey of what people want from marriage, friendship ranks at the top of the list. Friendship has been defined as the feeling of being safe with a person, having neither to weigh thoughts nor measure words. Intimacy or a feeling of closeness to another is a crucial aspect of friendship. Intimacy develops from confiding in another, from revealing our private thoughts and feelings, from sharing with another our sorrows as well as joys. Intimacy, then, involves both openness and trust. Many spouses do not achieve a deep level of intimacy with one another.

To maintain an intimate relationship you first of all need time alone together to talk and enjoy each other's company without extraneous demands or expectations. Many couples achieve this by scheduling regular "dates" with each other where just the two of them go out to dinner, to a show, or away for a weekend. But beyond time alone, intimacy requires honest revelation of the inner self; that is, getting beyond the light reporting of small talk to deeper thoughts, feelings, and desires. Private time creates the context for intimacy, but only good straight talk can bind couples together.

Guidelines for Loving Your Spouse

The following are some do's and don'ts for maintaining a close relationship with your spouse:

Do look to your spouse to comfort you when you are troubled, rather than to your children.

Do confide in your spouse about your dreams and wishes.

Do keep your marriage strong by doing thoughtful, romantic things for each other.

Do realize you are entitled to marital fulfillment even if it means doing a bit less for and with your children.

Do insist on marital privacy and forbid your children to invade it.

Do openly express your affection for your spouse by words and actions. Let your children see the warmth in your relationship.

Do helpful things for your spouse which show that you care.

Do treat your spouse as you did just before your marriage.

Do share many interests with your spouse since this has a bonding effect.

Don't expect your children to be your main source of comfort and care as you grow older.

Don't look to your children for solace after arguing with your spouse.

Don't be afraid to leave your children with a qualified sitter.

Don't depend on your children to provide the main source of your happiness.

THE IMPORTANCE OF COMMUNICATING WITH YOUR CHILDREN

We all know that communication is important. There must be communication if there is to be understanding and closeness between parents and children. Nearly all the troubles that plague family life grow out of, or are aggravated by ineffective communication.

Whenever two people are together, some communication is going on. A communication is any behavior (verbal or nonverbal) that carries a message which is perceived by someone else. But it is more. It is sharing. It is the opening up of two people to each other. To communicate effectively with your children, you need to accurately express your own ideas and feelings to them, as well as listen to and understand their thoughts and feelings. Although this may sound simple and easy, it is in fact quite difficult and complex. You must, for example, acquire the skills of understanding children who are not very good at explaining, and at explaining things to children who are not very adept at listening and understanding.

Communication is inadequate when there are forbidden or closed-off topics between parents and children, such as death or sex; and when there is any hiding, pretending, distrust, or attempt to manipulate the other person.

Communication skills, like those of any art, require thought and practice, but they can be learned. In the next two sections, I will discuss the skills needed to *listen* so children will talk, and to *talk* so children will listen.

HOW TO LISTEN SO CHILDREN WILL TALK

A good listener is not only popular everywhere, but after awhile he gets to know something.
—Wilson Mizner

Men are born with two ears and one tongue in order that they listen twice as much as they talk.

—*Old Rumanian Proverb*

A major complaint family members make of one another is "No one really listens to me." Being listened to and understood is a fundamental human need. At times we all seek someone to use as a sounding board; someone to help us ventilate and get things off our chests; someone with whom we can talk out our problems. When this need is unmet, many people go to psychotherapists for the healing effect of a warm and understanding relationship.

The art of listening to children is possibly the most important of all our parenting skills. Among the many benefits of listening to your children are:

1. It builds a close parent-child relationship.
2. It fosters self-esteem in the child. The child reasons that since my parents believe I am worth listening to, I must be a person of value and importance.
3. It helps the child release pent-up emotions.
4. It strengthens the child's ability to solve his own problems.

Yet most parents readily admit that it is very difficult to listen to their children. Accustomed to the roles of teacher and disciplinarian, parents find it hard to keep quiet and just listen. When we do listen, it is usually with only one ear. We may "tune out" the child because we think we know what the child is going to say. More likely, we try to take over the conversation by employing one or more of following strategies:

evaluating—judging
lecturing—preaching
blaming—scolding
directing—criticizing
offering solutions—relating personal experiences

In short, we wind up talking *at* children, rather than talking *with* them.

General Guidelines for Listening

The following 10 Do's and Don'ts should be kept in mind when listening to children. They will be followed by a discussion of specific listening skills.

1. *Hold Conversations in Private.*   The best communications between you and the child will occur when others are not around.
2. *Encourage your Children to Talk.*   Give your child praise and appreciation for his efforts to communicate.
3. *Keep an Open Mind.*   Don't hear only what you want to hear or expect to hear. Don't immediately evaluate what a child has said, e.g. "That's not a nice thing to say. Don't talk about your teacher that way."
4. *Listen with Respect.*   Listen to a child as you would to a friend. Be courteous and don't interrupt or dominate the conversation.
5. *Maintain Confidentiality.*   Demonstrate to your child that you can keep a secret and respect confidences.
6. *Keep it Brief.*   Watch your child for cues that it is time to end a conversation. When a child begins to fidget, to stare into space, or to act silly, she is probably signaling you that it is time to end the discussion.
7. *Make Listening a Priority.*   Set aside some time each day—even if only 5 to 10 minutes—to spend alone with each of your children. They need the security of knowing that they have their parents' complete attention every day.
8. *Be Available at Critical Periods.*   There seem to be certain critical periods in a child's life when he or she needs a parent to be there to listen. When they experience intense emotion because of severe stress children particularly need a parent to be available to listen and supply whatever comfort or support is needed. Children also need to feel that their parents are readily available to share good news or joyful experiences.

   The period right after school seems to be an especially important time to be available to a child. If both parents work, then one parent should reserve this time to be available to talk with the child on the phone. A substitute parent, e.g., mother's helper, should also be available to a child at this time. In this connection, a growing problem in our society is the increasing number of "latchkey" children, i.e., kids who return home from school to an empty house. Such children are particularly prone to a variety of problems (school, drug, and behavior).

Another period when children seem to feel keenly a parent's unavailability is when a parent is on the phone for long time periods. I know of one father who solved this problem by devising a signal that the children could use when he was on the phone to indicate that they really needed him. At these times they were to come up to the father with both hands on their heads. This unusual procedure worked very well because it allowed everybody's needs to be met.

Is it important that both parents be available to listen to children? A study[53] of well-adjusted college men sheds some light on this question. The study reports that the psychologically healthy college students had experienced a high degree of father availability as well as father nurturance. There is growing recognition of late that fathering is as important a parenting process as mothering.

9. *Be Accepting.* Show your children that you accept and love them no matter what their weaknesses, faults, or mistakes. We all have the basic fear that others will not like us if they knew who we really are. This fear is highlighted in the following poem:

THE REAL ME

Don't be fooled by me. Don't be fooled by the face I wear.
For I wear a thousand masks and none of them are me.
I give the impression that I'm secure, that all is sunny and unruffled
    with me, within as well as without.
That confidence is my name and coolness my game,
That the water's calm and I'm in command.
But don't believe me. Please.
Beneath dwells the real me in confusion, in fear, and aloneness.
But I hide this. I don't want anybody to know it.
I panic at the thought of my weakness and fear of being exposed.
That's why I frantically create a mask to hide behind,
To help me pretend, to shield me from the glance that knows.

But such a glance is precisely my salvation. My only salvation. And
I know it.
That is if it's followed by acceptance, if it's followed by love.
But I don't tell you this. I don't dare. I'm afraid to.
I'm afraid that your glance will not be followed by acceptance and
love.
And so begins the parade of masks. And my life becomes a front.
I idly chatter to you in the suave tones of surface talk.
I tell you everything that is really nothing and nothing of what's
everything.
Of what's crying within me;
So when I'm going through my routine do not be fooled.
Please listen carefully and try to hear what I'm not saying.
I dislike hiding. Honestly!
I'd really like to be genuine and spontaneous, and me, but you've got
to help me.
You've got to hold out your hand, even when that's the last thing I
seem to want.
Each time you're kind and gentle, and encouraging, my heart begins
to grow wings, very small wings, very feeble wings.
With your sensitivity and sympathy and your power of understanding
you can breathe life into me. I want you to know that.
I want you to know how important you are to me, how you can be
the creator of the person that is me if you choose to.
Please choose me. You alone can break down the wall behind which
I tremble, you alone can remove my mask.
Please . . . do not pass me by.
I fight against the very thing I cry out for, but I am told that love is
stronger than walls, and in this lies my hope.
Please try to beat down those walls with firm hands, but with gentle
hands—for a child is very sensitive.
Who am I, you may wonder. I am someone you know very well.
For I am every man you meet and I am every woman you meet.

ANON.

10. *Show Genuine Interest.* We tend to open up more to people who
are sincerely interested in us. Be curious about each of your children and try to learn all you can about their preferences, opinions,

beliefs, and experiences. The "How Well Do You Know Your Child" questionnaire that follows will help you gauge the current level of your knowledge about each of your children. After you have completed the form, ask your child for the correct responses. If you get more than half the items wrong, you probably need to pay more attention to this child.

HOW WELL DO YOU KNOW YOUR CHILD?

	Parent's Response	Child's Response
1. What is your child's favorite color?		
2. What is your child most afraid of?	___	___
3. What is your child's favorite holiday?	___	___
4. Which teacher (past and present) has your child liked the most?		
5. What is your child's favorite TV show?	___	___
6. Who is your child's favorite friend?	___	___
7. What is your child's favorite food?	___	___
8. What does your child want to be when he/she grows up?		
9. What does your child daydream about the most?	___	___
10. What does your child worry about the most?	___	___
11. What was the happiest time in your child's life?		
12. With Mommy, what is this child's favorite activity?	___	___
13. With Daddy, what is this child's favorite activity?	___	___
14. What movie has your child enjoyed the most?	___	___
15. Who is your child's favorite relative (outside immediate family)?		
16. What book has your child enjoyed reading the most?	___	___
17. What is your child's favorite game or toy?	___	___
18. If your child could change one thing about himself/herself, what would it be?		
19. What is your child's favorite part of his/her body?	___	___
20. What is your child's earliest memory?	___	___
21. What one thing does your child hate to do the most?	___	___

	Parent's Response	Child's Response
22. If your child could have one wish, what would it be for?	_____	_____
23. What is your child's favorite number from 1 to 10?	_____	_____
24. If your child could change anything about Daddy, what would it be?	_____	_____
25. If your child could change anything about Mommy, what would it be?	_____	_____

Listening Skills

Communication research has identified the following six skills as being important for effective listening: give undivided attention, encourage the child to talk, question appropriately, repeat key ideas, listen with the third ear, and be empathic. It is the rare person who is born with these skills well developed. Indeed, studies show that most of us listen at only about a 25 percent level of efficiency. With hard work and practice, however, parents can master the art of listening.

I. Give Undivided Attention

The first step in listening so children will talk is to show that you really want to attend to what they have to say. To pay attention you must give complete concentration and be in a position to listen.

Complete Concentration. Our attention is restless—it tends to be distracted by things around us and by our inner preoccupations. Often busy parents listen to their children with "half an ear" while continuing to do other activities, such as reading the newspaper or preparing the evening meal. If you cannot stop what you are doing to listen when a child is ready to talk, let her know when you will be finished, preferably in only a few minutes. Then give the child your full attention. Also, since we can listen at a much faster rate than people can talk, our minds tend to wander when we listen. We have to work hard to train ourselves to turn off our personal thoughts and to fully focus on the child's words. Five minutes of giving full concentration is better than fifty minutes of half listening, saying "Uh hum" now and then while thinking of something else, or interrupting a conversation to take numerous phone calls. So set aside at least 5–10 minutes a day to give each of your children your full attention.

Remember to listen not only to the child's words but to carefully observe the child as well. The difference in information gathered from seeing and hearing as opposed to hearing alone is illustrated vividly by contrasting television with radio. Young children tend to communicate more nonverbally than they do with words. Often they will say nothing is wrong when their dejected facial expression and lack of eye contact tell you differently.

Be in a Position to Listen. By effective use of your body position you can show a child that you really want to listen and that he is being heard. Body language includes the following four elements.

1. *Eye Contact.* Be sure to initiate and maintain eye contact with the child. Spontaneous glances are best, rather than a fixed stare or an intense gaze. Eye contact tells the child that you are interested in what he is saying and provides you with valuable visual information about the child.

2. *Body Posture.* By your body position you can communicate to the child that you are interested in what she has to say. An upright seated position with your upper body leaning slightly forward is generally considered to convey a desire to listen. Keep your arms open to signal a receptive orientation since arms folded across the chest and legs tightly crossed indicate an attitude of self-protectiveness and defensiveness.

3. *Comfortable Distance.* How close should you sit to a child when you want to have a personal conversation? Studies suggest that most people are comfortable about two to three feet away from another when having a conversation. Of course, this is a matter of individual preference and you will have to experiment to determine the interpersonal distance at which your child is most comfortable. A shy child, for example, tends to prefer to sit slightly further away from other people.

Should you have your chair directly facing the child's chair? This is also a matter of personal preference but research indicates that

an angle of about 60 degrees between the fronts of the chairs is best for a relaxed conversation. In this position you can easily see and hear one another while avoiding a confrontative (face-to-face) position.
4. *Facial Expression.* When your facial expression is alert and animated you will find children more willing to talk with you. So vary your facial expression in accord with the topic of conversation. In this way you will avoid a fixed expression which seems chiseled in stone.

II. Encourage the Child to Talk

To encourage children to start talking you might use "door-openers," that is, specific invitations to discuss something, such as "I'd like to hear about school today."

Once the child has started to talk, he may need only short responses from you to keep talking. Minimal responses that let the child know that you are listening include silence (just maintain eye contact, and smile or nod your head at times), and simple acknowledgments such as "un-hum," "I see," "yes." These minimal responses convey to the child that "I'm with you" and ensure that you do not take over the conversation, change the subject, or interrupt the child's train of thought. Although they show understanding, they do not necessarily mean that you agree with what the child is saying.

III. Question Appropriately

The ancient Greek philosopher Socrates frequently used questions to draw out the wisdom in other people. Questions are particularly useful to you as a listener when you wish to gather information about a certain topic, focus on a particular idea, or help the child consider a point. When you want to assist a child to explore a particular subject, it is often useful to ask an open-ended question which begins with what, where, when, or how. Examples include, "What are some of the things you like about your teacher?" "When do you feel that way?"

It is generally best to avoid starting a conversation by asking questions beginning with "are," "is," "do," or "why." The first three words ask for a specific fact and tend to elicit one-word "yes" or "no" answers. These are called closed-end questions. "Why" questions are very diffi-cult for children since they often do not know the underlying motives for their actions. As a result, the child may feel defensive and avoid further discussion of the subject. Instead of asking why questions ("Why were you angry?"), ask what questions ("What made you angry?"). The what question requests descriptive information and is less difficult and threatening for a child.

In regard to the effectiveness of your questions, you can gauge it from the child's response. If your question encourages the child to talk in greater detail about the topic, then the question has probably been help-ful. If the child tends to "clam up" or become annoyed after your ques-tions then you need to examine if you are asking too many "why" or closed-end questions, or falling into one or more of the following pitfalls.

Pitfalls to Avoid in Asking Questions

1. Avoid asking "leading" questions such as "You would never take something that belonged to Mrs. Jones, would you?" Leading ques-tions only put your words into a child's mouth.
2. Be friendly and sincere in asking questions. Don't put your child on the defensive by asking a string of accusing questions.
3. Questions asked of a child should be brief and easy to understand. If a child doesn't understand the question, rephrase it or approach it from another angle. Don't become annoyed and just repeat the question louder.
4. Each question should contain only a single thought. Avoid lumping several questions together ("Why are you upset and how come you don't go to your mother with this problem?").
5. Avoid negative questions which are used to snoop, lead, interrogate, or trap a child. Remember that constructive questions are those that are used to understand, clarify, or direct a child's attention to an important area.

IV. Repeat Key Ideas

Paraphrasing or repeating back the thoughts and feelings that another person has just expressed is a particularly effective listening technique when used in moderation. This method, which first emerged from client-centered psychotherapy,[54] has been associated with favorable outcomes in psychotherapy. Paraphrasing consists of restating in your own words what a child has just said, returning it to him for confirmation of your understanding.

This technique has several advantages. Perhaps the most important being that it lets the child know you are making the effort to really understand him. Also it sharpens a child's meaning to have his words rephrased more concisely and often leads the child to expand his discussion of the topic.

An effective paraphrase has four characteristics. First, it must *contain the key thoughts* of the child. Since you cannot repeat back everything a child has just said, you must select the most important and relevant ideas to feedback, rather than minor details. Be sure to feedback repeated themes and strong feelings since these are clearly very important to the child. Don't be a "wipe-out artist" who unravels minor threads of a story and never allows a child's main theme to develop.

Your paraphrase must also be *concise,* that is, contain fewer words than the child's verbalization. Thirdly, a paraphrase should be *accurate* so that your understanding reflects exactly what the child meant to communicate. Finally, when you repeat key ideas you should do it in a *tentative* or questioning way: "It sounds like . . . " "What I hear you saying is . . . " "In other words you . . . Am I right?" By so doing you make it clear that you want the child to verify the accuracy of your understanding.

The following examples illustrate the use of the paraphrase technique by a parent.

Example 1:
  Child   (in angry tone): "You never let me do anything and you always let Joey do whatever he wants!"
  Parent: "Sometimes you feel that I'm unfair to you. It seems to you that I let your brother do things that you'd like to do. This makes you angry."

Example 2:
  Child   (age five, kicking the blocks on the floor): "I hate these blocks, I can't pile them up right."
  Parent: "You're really mad because you can't build what you want."

When does one use this active listening technique? Generally, it is most useful with thoughts that are hard for the child to express, either because she does not clearly know what she is trying to express or because the topic is emotionally laden. Only with experience is one able to use this feedback technique appropriately and skillfully.

A variation of paraphrasing is summarizing—tying together the main points expressed by a child. Summarizing is most appropriate after a particularly lengthy discussion with a child. A summary should be brief, to the point (include key thoughts and feelings), and should not contain new or added meanings.

Pitfalls to Avoid in Repeating Key Ideas.

1. Don't use paraphrasing when a child is asking you for specific information, advice, or assistance.
2. Parroting or repeating back word for word what a child just said can become extremely annoying.
3. Since negative emotions (anger, fear, anxiety) tend to make us feel uncomfortable, we often fail to reflect back these important feelings to the child.
4. Overuse of paraphrasing can make a conversation sound like a broken record. As with all listening techniques, moderation is the key to success.

V. Listen With the Third Ear

Listening with the third or inner ear means tuning in to the message the child expresses nonverbally. It has been called "global listening" and "listening in context." Often what a child does not say is as important as what is said, such as when a child suddenly remains silent about a topic she had been eager to talk about. Sometimes you have to listen "between the lines" when a child talks. Ask yourself what is the child trying to tell me.

A child's nonverbal behavior can also speak volumes. Studies have indicated that when we talk, about 90 percent of our meaning is transmitted by nonverbal signals such as tone of voice and facial expressions. So a shrug, a nervous laugh, gestures, tone of voice, facial expressions, and body positions contain important messages that we need to decode accurately. A child who is feeling depressed, for example, will tend to avoid eye contact, be "down-in-the-mouth," and show a lack of energy. Sometimes a child may convey conflicting messages with her verbal and nonverbal behavior. She may say, "I'm not upset," when her hands are shaking and her face is red. Remember that actions speak louder than words! So always believe a child's nonverbal messages over the verbal ones.

Parents should be particularly sensitive to the absence of usual nonverbal behavior for this will often give valuable cues to a child's inner feelings. An obvious example is when a child does not eat, sleep, play, or concentrate as well as usual. A more subtle example is the failure of a child to give the customary goodnight kiss or welcome home smile.

Examples of "Listening With the Third Ear."

1. A child comes home from school, does not say hello as usual and slams the door. Picking up these nonverbal signals, his mother asks, "Did something happen in school today?" Child grumbles, "No." Mother says, "Well, your behavior tells me different. If there is anything you would like to talk about later, I'm here and would like to hear it."
2. A child has been acting irritable all day. She is apathetic and listless. Father says, "Joan, you seem 'down in the dumps' today." Joan does not respond. Father says, "Well, you know I'm available if you want to talk about anything."

Advantages of "Listening With the Third Ear." The benefits of bringing a child's nonverbal behavior to his attention include:

1. You create a bond by letting the child know you understand.
2. You often crystallize a child's feelings and thus help him become more aware of his emotions.
3. You promote better communication between you and the child. More lines of communication are opened.
4. You teach a child that he communicates not only by what he says, but also, and especially, by what he does and does not do.

VI. Empathy

Instead of putting others in their place, put yourself in their place.
                                                            —*Baptist Trumpet*

"Great Spirit, help me never to judge another until I have walked in his moccasins."

—*Sioux Indian Prayer*

A. How To Be Empathic Toward Children. The noted psychologist William James once remarked that the major problem in life was the fact that one cannot feel another's toothache. Empathy affords us the nearest thing to the actual experience. Empathy simply means putting oneself in the other person's shoes. Empathy requires us to temporarily suspend our way of looking at things so we can understand the way another person views them. First, it involves a parent attempting to perceive the world through the child's frame of reference by imaginatively projecting oneself into the child's situation. Then the parent must accurately convey this understanding to the child.

Research, in general, indicates that empathy is likely to have a positive effect on the child's personal, social, and moral development. Training in empathy has been found to reduce aggressiveness in children and to facilitate more constructive forms of social interactions such as altruism, generosity, and conflict resolution.[55] Thus, it seems well worth parents' efforts to be empathic toward their children and to encourage the children to empathize with others.

Empathy can be either cognitive, emotional, or some combination of the two. Cognitive empathy refers to an intellectual understanding of another's thoughts and feelings so that you could actually play the role of the other. In emotional empathy, you actually experience an emotional response which is similar to that of the child. Tuning in to these emotional reverberations in us has been termed "listening with the fourth ear".[56] An example of emotional empathy is for you to spontaneously cry "Ouch" on seeing your son hammer his thumb instead of the nail.

Empathy is a particularly effective skill when you wish to understand a child's misbehavior or soften the effect of punishment. By being empathic you can often get behind a child's defenses to understand the real meaning of a child's troublesome behavior. One parent reported, for instance, that the vicious bullying of an older boy towards a younger sibling seemed to be the act of a heartless monster until she realized that the older child was acting meanly because he felt his mother favored the younger boy. The only way the older child knew to express his feelings of rejection and jealousy was to lash out aggressively. The first step in resolving this problem was for the mother to coexperience the hurt thoughts and feelings of the older boy and communicate this understanding to him. Nearly all problem children have as a part of their life history the fact that they have not been fully understood by those whom they need to have know them best—their parents.

In punishing a child you can often soften the blow by showing empathy for the good motives or intentions underlying the misdeed. For example, you might say, "You're yelling because you have strong feelings about this." Or, "I know you are late for dinner because you were having so much fun playing and it was hard to break away." Or, "You don't want to go to school because you're bored there and you get restless." Children tend to take criticism and punishment better *after* you have shown empathic understanding of their point of view. When parents see the good intention behind a misdeed, then children think that perhaps they are not so bad or abnormal as they might have thought. Rather, they will more likely think, "Perhaps I don't have to judge myself so harshly."

Examples of empathy. Some illustrative empathic remarks by parents to children are:

1. "No wonder you were frightened."
2. "That must have come as a real shock."
3. "If it happened to me I would feel just as upset."
4. "Gee, you must be worried sick."
5. "It must feel real bad not to be invited to that party."
6. Father: (to a child watching a baseball game on TV) "It's time for dinner."

    Child: "Can't I watch a little longer? It's the eighth inning and the score is tied."

    Father: "I know it's hard to leave an exciting game. I'd probably want to stay and watch it if I liked baseball as much as you, but this is the time for dinner. The food has to be eaten now or it will get cold."

7. Son comes home from school crying. His teacher had yelled at him and belittled him in front of the class.

    Typical parental response: "What did you do to make the teacher mad?"

Empathic parental response: "It must have hurt your feelings to be yelled at like that."

8. Child comes in after hitting his first home run in a Little League game. Parent: "Wow, you must be bursting with joy. I bet it feels great to have done what you've been dreaming about!"

Guidelines for Expressing Empathy

1. Be as concrete and specific as you can in describing your understanding of the child. Avoid abstract or complex terms.
2. When being empathic, suspend your own judgments about the goodness or badness of a child's behavior.
3. Focus on underlying feelings that the child may have difficulty expressing.
4. Use observation, inference, and your own experience to gain a reasonable picture of what the child must be thinking and feeling. Then communicate this understanding so the child can correct any misperceptions.
5. Another way to enter into the world of the child is to ask yourself, "If I were doing _____ and saying _____, what would I probably be thinking and feeling?"
6. Empathy should not be confused with sympathy. Sympathy is *feeling sorry for* another, while empathy is *feeling with* another so that your feelings match those of the other's.

Discussion

By listening empathicly to the thoughts and feelings of a child, you not only promote self-understanding in that you encourage more accurate self-listening, but you develop self-acceptance since you validate the child's inner experience, i.e., you show it makes sense from another person's point of view. As long as our reactions seem reasonable to others, then we are less likely to feel strange, isolated, or confused, and fewer problems are likely to emerge since the child feels, "Well, at least my parents understand me."

Studies have shown that empathy is a reaction that we can seldom expect from our parents or even our friends. On the other hand, it is a skill that one can learn, and professional therapists and counselors rate

it as the most important personal characteristic of a helping professional. Also noteworthy is the research finding that people who experience the strongest degree of empathic reactions towards others are the
ones most willing to help others, even though it means jeopardizing their
own welfare.

Finally, it is important to note that there are two basic types of
understanding, only one of which is empathy. Nonempathic understanding means knowing why a child has misbehaved, rather than
experiencing what it is the child is thinking and feeling at the time.
Empathy, on the other hand, does not try to determine why a child is
behaving in a certain way, but to understand the child from his or her
point of view. Thus empathy may involve understanding how it may
have seemed OK to the child to steal, and actually feeling the emptiness
inside which motivated the act. Of course, it is particularly difficult to
be empathic when we disagree or morally comdemn the act of a child.
Rather than being empathic, our first inclination when a child misbehaves is to impose penalties on the child. After a child sees that you
first understand the situation from his point of view, however, then the
child will be better able to look at the situation from other perspectives
and accept penalties.

B. How to Develop Empathy in Children.   In addition to modeling
empathy in interacting with your children, you should take every opportunity to directly teach them this reaction. Some ways of encouraging
your children to be empathic towards others are:

1. Point out to them the effect of their behavior on others—especially
   on the feelings of others. You might say, for example, "Pulling the
   cat's hair can hurt the cat and cause him pain," or "If you don't
   call your aunt and thank her for the present, she may feel disappointed and think you are ungrateful," or "I feel very annoyed and
   frustrated when you tie up the phone for hours."
2. Story telling and story reading are excellent ways to help children
   step into the shoes of others. In reading a book you tend to be drawn
   out of yourself so that you actually feel some of the feelings and
   think some of the thoughts of the main characters. Like a tuning
   fork, you emotionally vibrate in accord with the feelings of the
   characters.
3. Encourage your children to role play, that is, to speak and act as if

they were a certain character. To this end, provide preschoolers with plenty of puppets and costumes for pretend play. Try switching roles with your child wherein you act like the child for awhile and he behaves like you.

4. In explaining the consequences of your child's actions on others, you should include a description of the needs, vulnerabilities, or feelings of others whenever it seems appropriate. Thus, you might say, "She's afraid of the water, so please don't splash her," or "I know he's very lonely and would appreciate a visit from you." A suggestion by you about the possible motives underlying the behavior of others will also contribute towards the development of empathy in your child. You might say, for example, "I think that dog bit you because you frightened him by suddenly running at him."

Discussion

By developing children's capacity for empathy, you provide them with a powerful emotional and cognitive support for the development of moral controls. An empathic person is more likely to apply self-praise after helping another and self-condemnation after hurting someone. This internal locus of evaluation forms the basis for conscience development and self-discipline.

HOW TO TALK SO CHILDREN WILL LISTEN

> *Most of us will never speak that succinctly or concretely. We may, however, aspire to. For direct and precise language, if people could be persuaded to try it, would make conversation more interesting, which is no small thing; it would help to substitute facts for bluster, also no small thing; and it would promote the practice of organized thought and even of occasional silence, which would be an immeasurable blessing.*
>
> *—Edwin Newman*

Studies have indicated that over 90 percent of the times parents speak to children they correct, admonish, criticize, or order that something be done. Little wonder, then, that children do not want to listen—it's usually bad news! Not all of our talk should be designed to direct the child's behavior. Talking should be fun and enjoyable for both parent and child. Parents and children should talk frequently and about many things, not just problems. Daily experiences should be discussed as well as personal thoughts and feelings. Politics, literature, and art, are also important topics of conversation, especially if you want to assist your child toward high achievement.

Daily experiences will result in greater learning for children if they have regular opportunities to share them with you, discuss them, and examine their implications. So be sure your priorities are such that you have scheduled time each day to have informal discussions with your children. These should be open discussions in which various points of view are expressed and everyone both talks and listens. Not only will these talks promote close bonds between you and your child, but you will find that they are one of the most powerful character-building skills you possess. Ideally, informal talks with your children will be a continuous, ongoing process in your home, not an infrequent occurrence.

Talking to children is different than talking to adults. You need a radical change in your attitude and approach. Since factual information is not a child's strong point, you have to relinquish some of your propensity for data-gathering. Also, to develop the necessary empathy for this task, you need to reactivate to some degree your own childhood experiences and recollections. Finally, you must respect the child as a person with ideas, opinions, and experiences worth listening to.

Since the ability to talk to children is just as important as listening to them, the following principles of effective talking are offered to assist you in improving this skill.

Principles of Effective Talking to Children

1. *Be Brief.* The time to stop talking is *before* children stop listening. So if you want children to listen to your message, you have to put it before them briefly. As a rough guide, when describing or explaining we should keep each remark under 30 seconds, and ask the child to comment after each remark. So we should feed a little information, get a reaction, and feed in a little more if we are understood.

"Brevity is not only the soul of wit," said Samuel Butler, "but the soul of making oneself agreeable, and of getting on with people, and indeed of everything that makes life worth living." In a similar vein, Jonathan Swift once said, "Take as many half minutes as you can get, but never talk more than a half minute without pausing and giving others an opportunity to strike in."

2. *Be Simple.*

> *The American penchant for using big words is deplorable. If an American had uttered Winston Churchill's famous line, "Give us the tools and we will finish the job," it would have come out, "Donate the implements and we will finalize the solution of the matter."*
>
> *—Lord Cornford*

Young children, in particular, should be spoken to with simple, concrete words rather than with big complex ones or in long sentences. Speak slowly (close to the child's rate of speech), and with exaggerated intonation. Studies show that children comprehend better with this approach. If you find the child does not quickly understand you, rephrase your message in a simpler manner.

As children grow into adolescence, they still need to be spoken to in a simple, concrete manner. Sometimes the grammatically correct speech of an educated person in our society is so filled with stilted bureaucratic phrases that it sounds worse than the ungrammatical speech of an illiterate. Examples of bureaucratic jargon known as doublespeak are such phrases as "at this point in time" used during the Watergate hearings in Washington. Other examples are:

Jargon	*Clear*
"We participated in the game."	"We played."
"We arrived at our victory."	"We won."
"How are your offspring fareing?"	"How are your kids?"
"I overresponded in a very emotional manner."	"I panicked."
"Our previous decision is inoperative."	"We changed our minds."

Another name for doublespeak is "Gobbledygook," i.e., the inflated, involved, obscure verbiage characteristic of the pronouncements of officialdom.

3. *Be Specific.*   Clear communication depends upon speaking in specific, descriptive terms, rather than in a vague, general way. In trying to explain something to others, it's wise to remember this fundamental rule of communication: one specific is worth a hundred generalities.
Examples of specific messages to children are:

Vague: "I wish you would eat better."
Specific: "I want you to eat foods that are healthy for you, like eggs, cheese, fruit, vegetables, and unsweetened drinks."
Vague: "Lately you seem unfriendly. What's wrong?"
Specific: "Lately you have a frown on your face or you look away when we talk to you."
Vague: "I'll take you to a movie soon."
Specific: "I'll take you to a movie in a week or two."
Vague: "Don't be a baby."
Specific: "I'd like you to do what I say and not cry about it."
Vague: "The hotel has recreational facilities."
Specific: "The hotel has tennis courts and a swimming pool."
Vague: "Do you have any hobbies?"
Specific: "What do you like to do after school?"

PRACTICE EXERCISE

Change the following general statements to make them more specific. Use your own experiences to help you create the details.

1. "I would like you to behave in the house."

_____

2. "I want you and your brother to get along better."

_____

3. "I'd like you to try harder today."

_____

4. "Please clean up the mess in your room."

_____

_____

4. *Don't Dominate the Conversation.*   Adults tend to do most of the talking when conversing with children. Avoid dominating the discussion by giving equal time for the child to talk. Listen as much as you talk. Seek reciprocal, rather than one-sided communication, i.e., a dialogue rather than monologue. Dialogue can be defined as a talking together or a conversation. The art of conversation depends heavily on your ability to shut up and listen to your child. Children, like most people, generally prefer talking to listening. So give them the opportunity to talk too. After talking for 30 seconds, pause to give the child a chance to respond or get her point across.

So often we talk *at* our children instead of *with* them. According to Haim Ginott, the late child psychologist, the main reason that few real dialogues exist between parents and children is because kids resent being preached to, talked at, and criticized. Ginott maintained that conversations between adults and children typically sound like two monologues, one consisting of criticism and instructions, the other of denials and pleadings. The tragedy of such interactions, he stated, lies not in the lack of love but in the lack of parental respect; not in the lack of intelligence, but in the lack of parental communication skill.

5. *Spend Time Talking to Children.*   To develop a close personal relationship with your children you must spend time talking with them. Take time to converse with your children on a regular basis. This is the only way you will know what is going on in the childrens' lives and what they are thinking and feeling. Frequent talks will also help you spot problems before they become crises.

Dinner can be a good time to share events of the day and have a general family discussion. It is important for parents to create a nurturant, friendly climate at the dinner table and to avoid using this time to lecture or criticize the children. The goal at dinner should be a free-floating dialogue among all family members.

Apart from making family dinnertimes an enjoyable experience, parents need to have one-to-one intimate conversations with each child. In many families the children rarely have an opportunity to spend time alone with each parent. When other family members are present one is not likely to share private thoughts and feelings.

I have found it a good idea for a parent to have periodic "dates" with each child in the family. On a date, the parent and child go somewhere by themselves (out to dinner, out for a hike), away from the rest of the family. This is a time for relaxed enjoyment of each other's company when both are not tired or preoccupied with other things. It is a time for talking and getting to know each other better.

6. *Be Responsive to the Child's Language Skills.*   Parent-child communication should change over time, i.e., how one communicates with a 5-year-old should be different from how one communicates with a 16-year-old. However, this does not always occur. Often, the way parents communicate to young children or even to a young adolescent, does not change when that individual becomes a young adult. The tendency is for many parents to talk down to their children rather than across.

   A. *Talking to children under seven.*   In talking to children under the age of seven, be sure to be animated, be specific, be simple, and be graphic. Being animated involves the use of such techniques as lively facial expressions, exaggerated gestures, humor, dialogue, and rhetorical questions ("What do you think happened next?"). Conversations with young children should be brisk and vigorous; like an animated cartoon they should move right along.

   Being graphic means using concrete words which stimulate children to picture the thought in their minds. Young children are visually minded—they see and understand pictures better than abstract concepts. Thus, when explaining something to a child it is best to make your point by vividly painting a picture with words. This is done by using plenty of concrete examples that draw upon their experiences. For example, you might relate the abstract concept of death to something the child has directly experienced ("Like when your dog Tora died, he didn't move."). Also, make frequent use of figurative language (simile, metaphor, symbol) which stirs a child's imagination. It is a picturesque, vivid, and colorful form of expression that appeals directly to the emotion, e.g., "The boy felt lonely, like a football lying on a basketball court."

   B. *Talking to children age seven and older.*   In talking to older children you can be less graphic but still be simple and specific.

Talking to adolescents is an art in itself. Some guidelines are:

1. Be informal.
2. Be authentic and sincere. Don't try to act like an adolescent again. Be yourself.
3. Talk about things they are interested in.
4. Use background activity if necessary while talking, e.g. talk while eating, walking.
5. Adolescents tend to be prolific complainers, so let them complain and get things off their chests.
6. Don't push a topic the adolescent is reluctant to discuss.
7. Avoid questions which are difficult for the adolescent to answer, e.g., "Now why haven't you cleaned up your room?"
8. Expect some testing behavior. The adolescent, for example, may needle you with provocative questions to see if you really care and want to listen.

7. *Tune in to your Nonverbal Messages.* In talking with others it's not so much what you say as how you say it that conveys your message. So be aware of how you "talk between the lines."

Albert Mehrabian, a well-known researcher on communication, has stated that when we talk to others, over 90 percent of our meaning comes across nonverbally, such as through our facial expression (55 percent of meaning) and our tone of voice (38 percent).

A. *Vocal communication.* The components of vocal communication or intonation include volume, pitch, tempo, or rate of speech, and emotional tone (enthusiastic, angry, sad).

1. *Volume.* Speaking louder than necessary can make children feel intimidated or frightened. Yelling is unpleasant to listen to and should be used infrequently and only as a form of punishment. Speaking too softly, on the other hand, may lead to your child disregarding an important message. When you give an order, speak with a firm, resonant, and strong tone of voice.

2. *Pitch.* Avoid speaking in a monotone; change your pitch frequently for interest. Listen to your natural tone of voice. If you tend to speak in a whiney or high pitch, practice lowering your tone of voice.

In general, speak with feeling, with conviction, with interest. When feeling is added almost anything said will be interesting. Peo-

ple who have heard Richard Burton read the phone book have said that they have rarely heard anything so fascinating in their lives.
3. *Tempo.* With young children, adults need to slow down the tempo of their speech. Also, remember to talk faster for unimportant topics, and slow down for important ones.

   B. *Facial communication.* Eye contact is one of the most important ways of communicating interest, firmness, anger, and other emotions. Children are very sensitive to our facial expressions. How we look at them when we talk will largely determine how our message is received.

   C. *Physical distance.* Adults in our society generally stand about eighteen to twenty-four inches apart when they converse with each other. They generally stand even closer to children. During times of confrontation or affectionate expression, it is important to stand close to the child.

8. *Be Authentic and Disclose Some of Your Inner Self.* Self-disclosure is defined as the art of revealing personal information about oneself to another.[57] It involves talking about your inner self to a child, i.e., some of your personal thoughts, feelings, and experiences. Talking directly of personal experiences promotes reciprocity—a similar sharing of self by the child. Most parents find it hard to talk to children about personal matters; it is easier to talk about external events and factual data. Moreover, we must have considerable trust in another person to reveal our inner feelings and thoughts. Sometimes this basic trust is missing between parent and child.

   Some types of self disclosure are: (1) "Me-too" disclosures wherein you describe an experience you had that was similar to the child's. (2) "Existential disclosure" where you state, "That last remark of yours made me feel ... " (3) "Historical disclosure" when you say, "That reminds me of the time when I was a child ... "

   Dialogue can be described as an active ongoing process whereby two people reveal themselves to each other and listen to the disclosures of the other in order to "understand and make oneself understood." Such a dialogue process is contrasted to interaction where the goal of one or both is to negate, change, or in some other way manipulate the perspective of the other person. Persons engaged in dialogue are revealing and discovering their authentic, "real" selves, whereas interaction not involving dialogue is designed to reveal only the "public" selves of the participants. There is some evidence now that authentic self-disclosure is related to healthy personality functioning, while neurosis is related to an inability to know one's real self and make it known to others.

Self-disclosure does not mean that you should reveal everything about yourself, including weaknesses that will make the child feel very upset, resentful, or insecure.

A State University of New York study on the effect of self-disclosure on friendship indicates that revealing too much of an intimate nature about oneself can have an adverse effect in establishing close relationships. Disclosing too little about oneself, it was found, is also likely to prevent the establishment of close friendship ties because low disclosers—individuals who refuse to reveal personal thoughts, feelings, and experiences—tend to be viewed as social stand-offs. Evidence strongly suggests that the moderate discloser is the most successful—not only in making friends but in keeping them. A guiding principle as to how personal to get with your children lies in the answers to two questions: Will it benefit the child and will you feel comfortable in revealing the information.

9. *Talk With Respect.* Talk to children with as much courtesy, respect, and interest as you show to your adult friends. So don't be patronizing, dogmatic, or talk down to a child. Don't monopolize the conversation. Be courteous and polite, e.g., don't interrupt when the child is speaking. Maintain a friendly, respectful tone of voice and nonbossy manner.

10. *Be Genuine.* Being genuine means that there is a congruity between your verbal and nonverbal signals to children. Sometimes we say one thing but communicate something else with our nonverbal behavior. For example, a parent might say, "Let's talk" while continuing to cook and failing to give undivided attention to the child. Saying "I love you" in a flat, off-hand manner may confuse the child as to your true feelings.

Other examples of "double messages" include saying "Oh, take your time," when your nonverbal signals (sitting on the edge of your chair and keeping your coat on) say "Hurry up,"; saying

"How interesting" in a dull monotone; Saying "I love you" but then cringing when the child hugs you.

Frequent use of this doubletalk will make children suspicious, confused, and always on the lookout for hidden messages. So don't try to deceive a child by saying one thing, but looking and sounding another way.

Additional Guidelines

To supplement the basic principles just described, the following guidelines are briefly noted.

1. Don't start talking until the message is absolutely clear in your own mind.
2. Avoid introductory material—get to the point quickly, immediately if possible.
3. Avoid stereotyped, long-winded monologues. Whatever is wholly predictable interests nobody. To hold a child's attention, you must make what you say somewhat unexpected.
4. Minimize filler words. Frequent use of the same filler words or phrases gets boring and distracting. Examples include: "You know ..." " Right?" "Don't you think ... " "Well ... ah ... "
5. Be patient. When you ask a question, give the child more than a second or two to respond. Children will talk more if allowed time to think.
6. Ask for feedback. It is often advisable to check to see whether a child has understood you. Ask, "Could you tell me what I just said so that I know you got it?" "Do you understand?" "Do you have any questions?"
7. Enjoy talking to children. If you really enjoy talking to a child, chances are that she will enjoy speaking with you. Enjoyment of children is based upon a sincere interest in them and their reactions to life. A sense of humor is also helpful. If you have fun interacting with children, they will too, and it will be equally rewarding for everyone.
8. Be relevant. Stay on the topic of conversation. Don't try to control or lead an informal conversation around to your hidden agenda or pet topics. Let the direction of the discussion flow naturally.

9. Select the right time and place. Don't try to have a discussion when someone's hurried, tense, tired, or upset. Find a time when you are both in the mood to talk and can give each other undivided attention. A good time for a talk is right after school when the child is having a snack. Don't try to talk when the child is more interested in something else, like going outside to play.

   In regard to the right place, some families have established a special talking place where a parent and child can discuss things of important in privacy and without interruptions. Examples include a porch swing, a bench in the laundry room, and a couch in the den.

10. Avoid arguments. If parents and children can respectfully disagree and avoid raising their voices, then they can probably avoid letting a discussion deteriorate into an argument. Remember that the goal of a conversation is companionship, not one-upmanship; pleasantness, not animosity. Try to avoid sensitive topics which either you or the child cannot discuss calmly. Be alert to the early warning signs of emotional upset in either you or the child, and quickly change the topic when these signs are present. Hopefully there will be few sensitive topics between you and your children and you will be able to freely discuss differing values and such taboo topics as death, religion, sex, money, and growing old.

HOW TO CONDUCT A FAMILY COUNCIL MEETING

A family council is a formal family meeting, usually held once a month, designed to promote an open discussion of family concerns and problems. It is a time for getting things off your chest, clearing up the inevitable misunderstandings that arise in group living, settling small disputes before they build up, and planning joint family ventures. Topics might include allowances, leisure-time activities, job and house changes, and use of family possessions such as TVs and phones.

At a family council meeting, parents have the opportunity to ask the children's advice and opinions and show children that their ideas are listened to and respected. It is also a time to teach children the principles of group decision making. These family meetings help everyone in the family learn to listen, to negotiate, and be concerned about the welfare of the entire group. Since everyone has a voice in solving problems, they are more willing to accept the final solutions.

Guidelines

1. At this meeting, everyone is encouraged to express themselves freely, and everyone has a vote in the final decision. As heads of the household, parents could retain veto powers on important issues relating to the general welfare. Some parents prefer to conduct these meetings in a completely democratic manner by letting the majority rule.
2. Rules of order for these meetings should be spelled out in advance, e.g., no talking out of turn; no lecturing, preaching, or insulting others; if disruptive, a person has to leave the meeting; everyone is expected to contribute to solutions, not just gripe. The problem-solving efficiency of this meeting is facilitated by appointing a chairperson (typically a parent in the beginning) who sends and receives messages from all group members and coordinates the activity of the group. Often the chairperson has to encourage the younger children to speak.
3. It is best to announce well in advance a definite time for the meeting (e.g., Sunday or Wednesday evening from 6–7 P.M.) and a definite place (the dining room table). Children age four and up can participate.

ADDITIONAL READING

Dreikurs, R., Gould, S., and Corsini, R. J. *Family Council: The Dreikurs Technique for Putting an End to War Between Parents and Children (and Between Children and Children).* Henry Regnery, 1974. Complete details for setting up a family council.

TREAT YOUR CHILD AS AN INDIVIDUAL

We live too much in platoons; we march by sections; we do not live in our individuality enough.

—*E. H. Chapin*

Variety is the spice of life, that gives it all its flavor.

—*William Cowper*

Every child wants to be special and feel unique. In school, a child tends to be treated as one of a group with similar characteristics. There is considerable pressure towards group conformity. One of the prime tasks of a parent, then, is to see each child as unique, different, and separate from all others. The development of individuality begins at the end of the second year of life when the child attempts to emotionally separate from the parents. This process intensifies in adolescence since the teenager's responsibility is to achieve a separate individual identity.

Too often parents have a way of determining a child's life for her, as they were conditioned by their parents. So don't try to mold a child in your image or ideal image. Let it be understood that each family member has the right to act in a unique, creative, and separate manner in the family. Encourage each child to pursue his own unique interests, talents, and life goals, even if these interests differ from yours. It is parental respect for differences that fosters a sense of individuality and positive self-concept in a child.

Tell Your Children How They Are Special

Each day communicate your excitement and delight at something special about your child. You might comment: "Your smile is really beautiful!" "I love your quiet confidence," "Only you could get him to do it," "You make us all laugh."

Encourage Self-Expressions

Do you allow your children to speak up at home, to express a differing opinion, to question your position on an issue? Such free expression helps form a child's sense of identity. So have a high tolerance for your child's right to disagree and be different from you in taste, values, or behavior as long as it is not destructive to self or others.

Pitfalls to Avoid

A pitfall to avoid in parenting is an unrealistic even-handedness approach to raising children. This leveling approach is evident in such reactions as treating sick children as if they were well, treating young children as if they were older, or treating neighborhood children as if they were your own. It is also seen in treating children as adults, e.g., holding up the evening meal until your husband comes home even though all the family members are extremely hungry.

The even-handedness approach takes no account of crucial individual differences in temperament, in age, in emotional maturity, or in physical strength or dexterity. Be sure to guard against responding in a stereotypic manner, i.e., responding to an adolescent rather than to a unique person who happens to be an adolescent.

Another pitfall to avoid is comparing a child with another sibling or child—either favorably or unfavorably. Thus, you should never say, "Why can't you be as studious as your brother John?" Every child wants to be treated as a unique individual and not in competition with his brothers or sisters for your love and approval.

Finally, don't endeavor to be strictly "fair" in how you treat children. "Measured fairness" is self-defeating. If you can't give a hug to one child for fear of antagonizing the others, life becomes unbearable. Children want to be attended to uniquely not uniformly. Some children need more attention and care than others because of personal characteristics, e.g., hyperactivity, slow learning, physical handicaps.

Fairness in raising children does not mean uniform treatment but that you avoid showing favoritism or special liking or love for one child. Also, don't let your children persuade you that equal treatment must occur at the moment and in kind; rather help them understand that it occurs within a longer time frame and over a wider range of behaviors.

WHAT KIND OF PERSON MAKES THE BEST PARENT?

Some people strengthen the society just by being the kind of people they are.

—*John W. Gardner*

The most significant factor in child caring seems to be the parents' own personality characteristics. It's what we are that gets through to children more than what we try to teach. In the final analysis, then, what makes one parent more successful than another often comes down to the personal qualities of the parent.

The basic assumption of this section is that you must be prepared to develop aspects of your personality to win your children's affection and to encourage them to identify with you. Children tend to find it difficult to care about parental values and ideals unless they have first learned to care about their parents. The following personal traits seem particularly conducive to building a relationship of mutual love and liking with your child.

1. *Be Patient.*   Surveys show parents list patience as the number one characteristic of a good parent. All children can be very irritating at times and without a great deal of patience, a parent is likely to respond in a harmful way. Like most personal traits, patience can be developed if you work at it. What does it mean to be patient with children? The following are some thoughts.

- Letting children learn things for themselves—often the slow or hard way.
- Letting children make many decisions themselves, even if it does take a while for them to decide what kind of treat they want.
- Allowing children considerable time to master new skills. Expect to teach them the same thing over and over again. Expect many mistakes.
- When you find yourself getting mad at the kids for some little thing they did, ask yourself, "What's wrong with me—what personal weakness of mine is causing me to lose control?"
- Recognizing that a child moves at a different pace and tempo than you.
- Listening and concentrating on what your child has to say, even though you have a million other things to do.
- Staying calm when you have to repeat directions a second and third time.
- Allowing your child to fully express herself without your acting bored or annoyed.

2. *Be Well-Adjusted.*   Pediatricians and mental health professionals have known from long experience that calm and emotionally adjusted parents raise calm and emotionally adjusted children. One

study conducted at The University of Nebraska found that mothers rated high in self-esteem, as compared with low-esteem mothers, got along better with their children, showed more affection, made fewer negative remarks; their children were better behaved and paid more attention to the parents' suggestion and admonitions.

According to Honoré De Balzac, "Nothing is a greater impediment to being on good terms with others than being ill at ease with yourself."

3. *Be Cheerful.*   Cheerfulness is one of the most important qualities of a good parent.[58] Cheerfulness tends to make other people in a home feel good and helps them accept minor frustrations much more readily.

Cheerfulness is closely related to humor, joy, and play; it is blocked by criticism, hostility, worry, impatience, and self-pity. According to the theory of "Psychosynthesis," it is one of the signs of a psychologically sound, fully integrated individual. Develop cheerfulness by being optimistic, i.e., looking on the bright side of things; by reflecting on the value of cheerfulness; and by developing the habit of telling yourself positive things, e.g., "Smile," "I'm going to have a good day today." You should also practice living with enthusiasm, i.e., whatever you are doing at a given moment, do it with zest and relish. Don't let parenthood become a grim, joyless, serious endeavor. Also, don't burden or depress those around you by dwelling on your minor aches and pains and small disappointments. Remember that everyone is carrying some kind of load.

Cheerfulness, like Spring, opens all the blossoms of the inward man.
—Jean Paul Richter

4. *Keep a Sense of Humor.*   The amount of laughter in a home is a pretty good barometer of the health of a parent-child relationship. You will find little humor in a family racked with conflict. Conflict and emotional disturbance consist largely of taking life too seriously and exaggerating the significance of things.

Humor is a rare and precious gift that only humans possess. All of our lives would be happier if we could learn to laugh at ourselves more and not take things too seriously. An often overlooked but very effective way of relieving tensions and conflicts between parents and child is humor. The quality of humor should never be lacking in dealing with children. Indeed, many situations can best be handled by a humorous or light-hearted comment from you. Humor can reduce the strain not only in yourself, but in your children. If you make somebody laugh, he cannot possibly remain angry at you. In using humor, the goal is to make your child laugh with you at the situation or at yourself, never to make light of the problem or belittle the child by ridicule, sarcasm, or mockery.

A sense of humor enables us not so much to laugh at the people who provoke us, as to laugh at ourselves for being so easily provoked.
—*Robert Power*

5. *Like Children.* To be a good parent you need to genuinely like children and enjoy being around them. This means you have to be in touch with the childlike spirit that exists in all of us. This spirit is full of wonder, enthusiasm, imagination, curiosity, and spontaneity.

6. *Be Energetic.* Parenting requires more energy and body vigor than many other jobs. Only with physical stamina will you be able to provide a variety of experiences and meet the various needs of children over the day's long hours.

General Principles of Emotional, Social, and Moral Development in Children

General Principles of Emotional, Social, and Moral Development in Children

All parents function as child psychologists whether they know it or not. The more you know about the characteristics, thoughts, feelings, and behaviors of children at different ages, the better able you will be to understand and guide them wisely.

The purpose of this Appendix is to give the reader a broad overview of some basic concepts and principles of child development. The focus of the Appendix is on the emotional, social, and moral character development of children, rather than on cognitive or physical growth. It is felt that knowledge of child development will assist you to make more effective use of the skills and techniques presented in this book. You should also be more confident in your parenting if you know what to expect from children at different ages and levels of development. Armed with developmental information, you will be in a better position to be responsive to the needs of children at every stage of their development.

General Concepts of Child Development

The behavior of children is constantly changing and developing in lawful, regular ways. Not only is there a strong predisposition for children to develop in healthy, adaptive ways (mentally and physically), but each stage of development tends to build upon the previous one so that behavior becomes more differentiated and hierarchically integrated as a child matures. At times, children will move rapidly in an area of development, then long periods of very slow growth will prevail. Also, rather than developing in a steady, continuous straight line upwards, the growth of children tends to be spiral in nature, that is, children will move ahead a little in learning or emotional adjustment, then circle around or regress to an earlier level where they will reconcile their old and new behavior patterns, and then advance again to a higher stage of development once consolidation has occurred. Consequently, parents should expect backward moves in children's development and not become anxious or upset by them. It would be unrealistic, for example, to expect that a child would have no more "accidents" after one day's success in potty training.

There are many interrelated parts to a child's development, i.e., cognitive, physical, emotional, social, and moral. The close interrelationship of these behavioral domains is seen in the fact that retarded physical growth will impede a child's emotional and social development; also, emotional or social problems can interfere with the physical and intellectual development of children.

Developmental Stages

Although a child will follow his own individual rate of development in different areas, there seems to be definite stages or steps of growth that all children go through in the same sequence. For example, children tend to sit before they stand, to babble before they talk, to say no before yes, to draw a circle before a square, to play alone before playing with others, to be selfish before they are altruistic, and to be dependent before they are self-sufficient. All the different abilities of a child seem subject to laws of growth. Dr. Arnold Gesell of Yale University made some of the most careful observations of the growth curves of children. Knowledge of the behavior norms published by Dr. Gesell* and his colleagues should assist parents to develop realistic expectations for their children's behavior. Once you know a child's current stage of development and the next higher level, you will be in a better position to encourage the child to progress, e.g., you might provide him with challenges that are just slightly above his current level of functioning.

Children advance from one developmental stage to the next for two main reasons: maturation and environmental stimulation. Maturation means development which is a function of age or time; it refers to physiological changes in the body. No amount of practice on tasks for which a child does not have the necessary physical readiness will help him to master them. Thus, it would be foolish to try to teach 18 month old children how to read or try to toilet train 9 month old children – they simply are not developmentally ready for this. However, maturation alone will not produce the highest level of development in behavior. The child needs his parents to provide desirable growth-inducing challenges or developmental pressures. Optimal development, then, is a function of the interaction of maturation and environmental stimulation. Thus, *you must gear your childrearing practices to the child's developmental stage!*

How will you know when to exert some pressure on a child to advance to higher levels of development? You should have some general idea of what he is capable of by reading child development texts which describe the characteristics of children his age, by talking to his teachers, and by observing his friends – all this with an open mind. Your final decision must then be individualized for your child – based upon your knowledge of his unique rate of development in an area, his particular personality characteristics and cognitive abilities, etc.

Stability of Behavior

Behavioral stability means that adult behavior is predictable from childhood behavior. With respect to normal behaviors, research findings support the

* Gesell, A. and Ilg, E.L. *et al. The Child From Five to Ten.* Harper, New York, 1946.

common sense conclusion that, "As the twig is bent, so grows the tree." Once a child reaches about age 10, it seems that most normal behavior patterns tend to remain stable through adulthood. Thus, if a child shows strong achievement strivings in elementary school, he will probably continue to exhibit these strivings in adulthood.

Only when the behaviors of children are at odds with the norms of expectations of society is there a strong tendency toward change from childhood to adulthood. For example, passive-dependent behaviors tend to decline in boys as they mature, while aggressiveness has been found to diminish in girls as they develop into mature women. After reviewing the literature on child development, Professor Jerome Kagan of Harvard University concluded that children retain an enormous capacity for change when it comes to pathological behavior, and that they have a tremendous resiliency or capacity to bounce back from severe traumas or blows to their psychological security or self-esteem. These findings should be most reassuring to parents — particularly oversolicitous or overanxious parents. There seem to be few, if any, *irreversible* traumas that children can experience as a result of your childrearing.

Theories of Child Development

Most theories of child development describe an orderly, sequential process with the child developing more complex skills that build upon earlier ones. At each developmental stage there are usually one or two tasks that the child must accomplish if he is to mature. Among the major theories related to the personal-social development of children are those of Sigmund Freud, Eric Erickson, and Abraham Maslow. A brief description of each theory follows.

Freud's Theory of Psychosexual Development

According to Freud, children have a natural drive toward maturity which goes through a sequence of four stages. Arrested development at any stage can lead to psychological problems later on in life which must be "worked through" in therapy. The four major stages of development in Freud's theory are: (1) oral stage; (2) anal stage; (3) phallic stage; and (4) genital stage. Each stage is characterized by a different erogenous zone from which the primary pleasure of the stage is derived. Freud's theory focuses on a basic biological drive, i.e., to obtain pleasure — which he equated with sexuality.

The oral stage of development concerns the first year of life. The child's major need in life, feeding, is met by oral gratification (sucking, eating). The child is totally dependent on his mother at this stage for protection, comfort and security. If feeding and/or weaning problems develop during this period,

an "oral fixation" may result which means that during later stages of development the child may seek excessive oral gratifications (e.g., overeating, smoking)
to compensate for the pleasure or security he missed at this stage. At the
second stage, the anal stage, a major task required of the child is toilet training.
The child derives pleasure during this period from elimination functions. Parental anxiety and/or undue pressure during toilet training can lead to later difficulties in elimination, such as bedwetting, soiling, constipation. On a broader level,
basic personality types can result from unmet anal needs, e.g., an "anal reten-
tive" person is described as obsessive, constricted, introverted, and a miserly
hoarder of possessions. Freud sees the child at the anal stage as being very
egocentric, i.e., concerned with his own needs and possessions while showing
little or no concern for others. At this age parents begin to ask the child to submit
his will to others; they attempt to make demands and set limits on the child. This
leads to the negativism of the "terrible twos" which is a natural tendency of the
child to assert his growing feeling of independence and selfhood.

During the phallic stage (spanning the years from about 3 to 12), children
show an early tendency to develop Oedipal feelings. After discovering his
genitals at about age 3, the child begins autoerotic stimulation. Too much
parental restriction at this stage can lead to impaired self-confidence and di-
minished curiosity. It can also produce anxiety about the body and its natural
functions, particularly concerning sexual functions. Self-exploration of genitals
leads to primitive sexual feelings which the young child tends to direct to the
parent of opposite sex. A natural rivalry tends to develop then between the
child and parent of the same sex for the affection of the other parent. The
child soon learns that he cannot defeat one parent for the attention of the
other so he learns to suppress his Oedipal feelings and identify with the same sex
parent. The resolution of the Oedipal conflict signifies the beginning of the
latency period which constitutes the second part of the phallic stage. This
period lasts from about 7 years of age until puberty. The latency period is so
named because it is a time when sexual drives tend to lie dormant. The child
has many developmental tasks to master at this stage, including school achievement, peer relationships, and establishing moral or ethical principles. Upon
completion of the phallic stage, the child progresses to the final stage of development – the genital stage. Sexual interest in the opposite sex reappears when the
child enters this stage. This is the adult stage of functioning and signifies that
the child has successfully completed the process of psychosocial development.

Erickson's Eight Stages of Personality Development

Erickson was strongly influenced by Freud, but he advocated a strong social as
opposed to biological point of view in accounting for personality development.

His eight stages of development are related to the learning or developmental tasks that must be accomplished at each stage. Satisfactory learning of each task or crisis is necessary if the child is to manage the next stage satisfactorily. Erickson postulated the following eight stages of development:

1. *Learning Trust vs. Mistrust.* If made to feel loved and secure by his parents during the first year of life, the infant develops trust in adults, a sense of security, and a basic optimism. A child tends to develop trust in his relationship with his parents if they respond promptly to his cries, keep him warm, dry, and well-fed, and provide him with considerable amounts of physical holding and cuddling. From this basic trust comes a sense of security and self-acceptance.

2. *Learning Autonomy vs. Shame.* Between about 18 months and 3½ years, the child is faced with the task of learning control of both his impulses and elimination functions. Perhaps the biggest task of this stage is toilet training and parents are advised not to start this process until the child is physiologically ready (between 15 to 30 months) and to avoid shaming or punishing the child during the training. If handled well, the child will emerge from this "law and order" phase with a sense of independence and autonomy, with pride in his self-controls. The oppositional tendencies of this age help him develop a feeling of being independent from his parents and feed his new-found awareness of self as a separate entity.

3. *Learning Initiative vs. Guilt.* During the period of about 3½ to 6 years, children are exploring everything as a means of finding out more. They not only physically intrude into cupboards and drawers, but they verbally intrude into other people's interactions, demanding attention. Children also spend considerable time in dramatic make-believe play during this period. Play is a very serious business during childhood and through it a child learns to try out different roles, to imagine the consequences of different courses of actions, to relate to other people. If well-handled a child will not be made to feel guilty about fantasy-play or inquisitiveness, and will take the initiative in relating to others and exploring the environment rather than hanging back in a fearful way.

4. *Learning Industriousness vs. Inferiority.* During the grade school years, a major task of children is to learn to be industrious, to develop good work habits, and to complete tasks. They learn to respect the rules of a game and to develop self-confidence in their abilities, to do well in work and play — both in school and at home. They do their chores at home conscientiously and reliably. They also perceive that they are successful at making friends. It is very important that children this age experience some area of success where it is clear that they are achieving and pleasing their parents and other adults as well as themselves. Even if a child's

ability and interest lie in activities not valued by parents, they should make a special effort to encourage and support any areas of competence.

5. *Learning Identity vs. Identity Diffusion.* During the adolescent years, the child is engaged in the major task of resolving the question, who am I? He will experiment with different roles, consider different occupations, seek more and more freedom and responsibility at home, reject certain values and develop others — all in the effort to establish who he is and what he wants out of life. It is very helpful for adolescents to be members of a family where the parents are committed to basic beliefs and values, but where the children are given freedom to choose their own values and life styles.

During adulthood and old age, Erickson theorizes that a person goes through the last three stages of development: learning intimacy vs. isolation; learning generativity vs. self-absorption; learning integrity vs. despair. During the later part of adolescence or in young adulthood, achieving true intimacy in a relationship with another person is a major focus, while becoming successful in your job and as a parent is the challenge during early adulthood. If all the other stages of development proceed normally, one reaches the final accomplishment, integrity of your personality which leads to inner peace and happiness.

Maslow's Hierarchy of Needs

Like Freud and Erickson, Maslow conceptualized a hierarchical growth of the human personality. Concentrating on human needs, Maslow stated that there are some basic needs that must be satisfied before one can even think about developing his higher level needs. At level one Maslow places the physical needs of man, i.e., hunger, freedom from pain. Level two is associated with the basic needs for safety and security — both physical and psychological. Only when one feels confident that he can count on food, clothing and shelter, as well as the unconditional love of his parents, does one tend to reach out to others to develop close interpersonal relations, i.e., reach level three which represents the social needs of caring and interacting with others. Level four concerns the development of achievement needs by accomplishments in school and at work. At the highest level Maslow postulates the need for self-actualization, i.e., the complete realization of one's abilities and interests. Examples of fully actualized persons, according to Maslow, are highly creative, productive people who are free to do their own thing and who love what they are doing. After studying these people extensively, Maslow concluded that they tend to be vigorous, full of zest for living, humorous, imaginative, and open to mystical, transcendental experiences.

One common assumption of all three theories of development described above is that a child can move on to the next more advanced stage of personality development only after he has successfully completed the requirements or tasks of the previous level. This insight can provide parents invaluable understanding into the personality development of their children.

Developmental Tasks for Parents

The aforementioned theories described, from differing perspectives, the basic needs and developmental tasks that are common to children as well as the general patterns of development that are characteristic of most children at certain ages. Parents also face certain tasks at each stage of a child's development.

Infancy

Being responsive to the infant's needs is perhaps the major task for parents, e.g., paying prompt attention when the baby cries. You *can't* spoil an infant with too much attention, rather it gives security to infants to have their basic needs responded to with few frustrations. The sense of self of the infant is too immature to cope with many frustrations and delays. By being responsive to a baby's needs for food, warmth, physical comfort, sleep, and cuddling you develop basic trust in the child towards you.

Another task for parents is adjusting to the inevitable stresses of living with a new baby. During infancy a child is totally dependent upon his parents for survival. Infants make continual demands on their parents for time and attention. The disruption a firstborn infant creates in the household is hard to imagine — the infant just home from the hospital cries an average of an hour and three quarters a day. A colicky baby seems to be continually upset — both day and night. As a result, fathers often feel jealous of the attention mothers must give to infants. Many fathers tend to find fault with their wives during this period, which only compounds the tensions within the home. Hard work, sacrifice, and sharing responsibilities are the order of the day with infants around. They test the strength of your marital relationship as well as your personal adjustment.

The Preschool Years

By the second year of life, the child is no longer a helpless, completely dependent infant but begins getting into things and behaving in ways at odds with parental wishes. So now parents attempt to change children's behavior against their wills while the kids attempt to have their way despite knowing what the parents want. So a conflict of wills emerges and the parent's role makes a dramatic shift from primarily being an affectionate caretaker to being a disciplinarian or teacher. The feelings of affection and trust generated during the caretaker period will undoubtedly affect a child's receptivity to parent discipline at this stage.

The major task of parents of preschoolers, then, is to gradually socialize the child by setting limits. They must help a child learn controls by being firm but loving. Rather than acting like dictators and expecting instant obedience, parents should allow for delay and grumbling when a direction is given. Be firm but realistic. Children must learn early that there are two very different kinds of activities for them: those things they must do whether they like it or not, and those things they can do or not do as they like. This takes time sc begin early and don't expect self-control to develop all at once or once and for all.

Rather than saying no to everything a preschooler does parents should use distraction a lot. Young children thrive on variety and change of pace. Thus, when you see children getting bored or restless, head them off at the pass by providing new activities which will interest them.

Another task of parents is to encourage play and fantasy behavior while simultaneously providing the child with reality testing experiences. So help children discriminate between real and pretend objects and events without inhibiting their fantasy life or enjoyment of play.

The Grade School Years

Children this age must be doing things, they would rather not sit for long periods of time. During the elementary school years an important task for parents is to provide constructive outlets for the abundant energy of children and to ensure some success experiences. The school age child acquires self-esteem from what he or she can do, from being competent at school work, sports, and making friends. They are introduced to the world of work through chores at home, homework, and classroom assignments. Their work must be supervised to ensure that they learn correct work habits and attitudes. Also, parents should encourage children to develop special interests and skills by providing them with the necessary materials and instruction.

Although parents are still the primary source of support and influence for school age children, their world of social influence is widening. Another task for parents, then, is to learn to be part-time parents, that is, share their child with teachers and peers.

The Teenage Years

The parents of adolescents face the primary task of giving their children the necessary freedom and autonomy to find out who they are as persons. They must learn to think for themselves, develop their own values, and make their own decisions. By giving ever increasing areas of freedom and responsibility you gradually turn over to them control over their lives. Adolescents should have few areas of decision-making that are not their own. Your role as parent now is to be consultant rather than disciplinarian in that you give more guidance rather than external controls.

While granting independence you must still be available to offer affection, understanding, and advice. This is no easy task since teenagers not only show open rebellion, animosity, and criticism towards parents, but they are difficult to talk to at this age. Teenagers just don't want to listen anymore to parents since they see it as a way of being controlled and kept dependent. While letting go of your adolescents, you still must give them the feeling that you are on their side, that you have faith in them, and are pulling for them. The teenager is trying to go in two directions at the same time, namely, be independent yet stay somewhat dependent upon you. The more you encourage the independent striving by treating them as adults, the more they will act like grown-ups.

The adolescent is fundamentally insecure, which is expressed by restlesssness, addiction to fads, and resistance to authority. They face a number of serious challenges and important decisions, including vocational choice, heterosexual adjustment, formation of a philosophy of life, and development of basic values. Parents must give adolescents the understanding, respect, and confidence they need to face these important challenges. Parents should also allow them to rebel in relatively insignificant areas, e.g., manners or dress, rather than in areas of greater importance, e.g., behavior which is inconsiderate or harmful to others.

Children's Emotional Development

At birth the emotional reaction of infants is not well differentiated. New babies show a generalized excitement which encompasses situations of discomfort, fear and anger. As they grow older, infants' emotional expressions become more clearly distinguishable so that a 10 month-old baby will exhibit identifiable signs of fear, anger, and satisfaction. With further maturation, the child's inner drives and impulses come into inevitable clashes with the demands of reality outside the self. Not only is conflict an unavoidable part of growth, but so is insecurity and anxiety. Being relatively weak and vulnerable during most of their youth, the children naturally feel some tense and uncertain moments in coping with the new challenges that they are continually experiencing.

It seems that the golden years of childhood contain more conflict, aggression, anxiety, and lonliness than most of us can recall.

Aggression

Through the first two years of life the child is self-centered and has a low frustration tolerance. Seeking to have their own way, these children tend to resolve conflicts by becoming overly aggressive, i.e., hitting, grabbing, biting. Consequently, social conflicts among preschool children are usually frequent and characteristically violent. Fortunately, aggression tends to be short-lived at this age so that preschoolers will be locked in intense combat one minute and playing happily the next.

Much of human aggression can be traced to frustration; it is just impossible to rear children without frustrating many of their desires or wants. As children grow up they learn more adaptive responses to frustration than directly acting out their angry feelings. Parents must encourage more adaptive reactions by indicating to a preschool child that they will not tolerate aggressive solutions to problems. Among the alternate responses that you can teach a child are the following: to verbally express disapproval; to develop a future time perspective; to be empathic to the needs and feelings of others; and to negotiate conflict by a give-and-take procedure. Throughout grade school, children show increasing control of their emotions so that there are less and less frequent temper outbursts. Crying as a mode of expression also decreases.

Childhood Fears

Fears can be described as responses to immediate and evident danger. They are distinguishable from anxiety which is an apprehensive response to possible threat. What a child fears has been found to differ with age and experience. From the relatively few, simple fears of the infant (fear of sudden movements, falling, and loud noises, fear of strangers), the fears of children become more numerous, abstract, and complex with age. During the preschool years, fears of animals, the dark, physical hurt, and imaginary creatures (ghosts and monsters) increase.

The preschool period is a naturally fearful period of development and parents should not become unduly alarmed when a child wakes up screaming after a nightmare. Most of these fears will pass with age. Remember not to deny the existence of the fear ("There's nothing to be afraid of."); rather, be accepting, understanding, and help the child verbally express the fear and thus gain greater control over it. You might suggest ways of coping with the fear such as imagining oneself yelling and hitting the imaginary creatures until they run away. You can help prevent fears in young children by keeping your own fears under cover and avoiding the use of fear-inducing threats such as "The boogey man will get you if you don't behave."

At the elementary school period, fears of animals, monsters, and the dark decrease but fears relating to school — including worry about grades and fear of teachers — increase from ages 9 to about 12. In general, the fears of grade school children diminish in both number and intensity as they learn to cope with new situations and overcome feared events. However, they still harbor a great many more fears than parents commonly realize. Studies show that about 80 percent of the children this age are afraid of dying or being killed, as well as being afraid that someone in the family will become ill or have an accident. About 70 percent of the children this age express the fear that their house might burn down, or that they might be kidnapped. Since so many children express these numerous fears, there is no reason to assume that they are unduly anxious or emotionally disturbed. Only when a child's fears seriously interfere with his functioning, i.e., doing things that other children do, should a parent become concerned.

Although many childhood fears decline and seem to disappear, a fairly large number of these fears persist in one form or another into adulthood. One study revealed that over 40 percent of childhood fears continued strong into adult life, e.g., fear of snakes and certain animals, fear of bodily harm by fire, illness, or drowning; and fear of threat associated with the supernatural (the dark and being left alone).

A recent survey of 500 high school students revealed that they remain fundamentally insecure and list the following 15 situations as the most threatening to them, listed in descending order:

1. Being teased or laughed at (boys felt most threatened when their masculine image was threatened; girls, when their desirability or popularity was questioned).
2. Death of a parent.
3. Facial or bodily injury.
4. Divorce of parents.
5. Terrible arguments with parents.
6. Being harshly criticized in public.
7. People who seem insane.
8. Arriving at a party where there are mostly unfamiliar faces.
9. Being caught in a lie publicly.
10. Moving to a brand new community.
11. Violent or "bullying" peers.
12. Failing an exam.
13. Terrible arguments with friends.

14.   Being rejected by a member of the opposite sex.
15.   Becoming addicted to alcohol or drugs.

So adolescence is a time of dilemmas (being independent yet still wanting the security of parental dependency) and important decisions; insecurity and anxiety seem to be the rule, as opposed to the intense fears of early childhood.

Children's Social Development

During the preschool years, children's interactions with their peers show clear age trends: solitary play, parallel play, and cooperative play. For the first two years children tend to play largely by themselves, even when others are close by. From about three to five, children will copy the behavior of their peers. If peers are riding tricycles, a child will ride his tricycle also. By age three the child can engage in cooperative, give-and-take play with peers, not just parallel play. They can wait, share, and take turns, and accept substitute toys. However, they are still egocentric and show little consideration of other children's feelings. They have little empathy or capacity to put themselves in another person's position and take that person's point of view. It is this immaturity, not perversity, which makes a preschooler continue to pester her mother after she has been told that mommy has a headache and wishes to be left alone.

In grade school, the loosely knit play groups of the five-to-eight year olds develop into gangs or cliques. A gang is characterized by its longevity, solidarity, and group loyalty. A clique is a smaller, more informal, intimate social group. It exists not to compete with other groups but for the mutual satisfaction and good times of its members. The grade school child likes peers of the same age and sex. About ages eight and a half to ten, the "chum" or special friend period arrives. Intimacy with a chum sets the stage for later heterosexual intimacy in adolescence and adulthood. If there are frequent family moves during this period which interfere with the development of close friends, then later social development may be retarded or impaired.

Friendship means a sincere liking between two people. By age three or four a child is usually able to identify a "best friend." These early childhood friendships are less intense than adolescent friendships, but they nevertheless are important in that they overcome loneliness, self-centeredness, and boredom. They also offer support and encouragement, teach a child to solve conflicts by compromise, provide feedback about self, and encourage the sharing of personal experiences. For the school age child, the best friend or chum is usually the one who lives nearby, can play with him, share things, have fun together, and engage in the same kind of activities. The adolescent, on the other hand, seeks a more intimate kind of friendship, that is, the sharing of secrets and confidences, trust and loyalty, and the opportunity to talk and talk and not get bored.

It is evident that the friendship experiences during each of these three stages of development prepare the child for the next higher form of friendship.

Self-Esteem

A generally accepted theory relating to the development of self-esteem in children is that a child's self-regard is profoundly influenced by the significant adults in his life, especially his parents. The noted psychiatrist Harry Stack Sullivan maintained that a child's sense of self is developed by the process of "reflected appraisals." In other words, as significant persons appraise him so in time will the child come to value himself. Praise, approval, and acceptance by parents, then, seem especially important for young children since these reactions generate the beginning of positive self-regard in the child. If you are constantly saying no and disapproving of the child's behavior, then it seems likely that he will soon disapprove not only of his actions, but of himself as well.

Maladjustment in Children

There is no precise, sharp differentiation between normal and abnormal behavior. Most, if not all, pathological behavior in children has a normal counterpart at an earlier age level. Diagnosing maladjustment or emotional disturbance in children requires an intensive, professional study of the child, including his motives, temperament, typical social interactions and current stresses and pressures. A variety of surveys have indicated that about 10 percent of school age children in this country have emotional problems, although only about 1 percent of the child population receives professional assistance. One reason is parental resistance to seeking outside help for psychological problems although parents regularly bring their children in for physical checkups.

How can you tell if your child is experiencing an emotional difficulty that warrants outside help? Some indicators are that his or her deviant behavior has persisted beyond the expected age; the behavior is frequently displayed and easily aroused; and ordinary educational efforts to change the deviant behavior have failed. Other criteria of abnormality are the extent it interferes with the relationships between the child and other people — both adults and peers; the extent it may handicap a child at a later date (e.g., a learning disability); the degree and duration of regression or return to an earlier level of development that is present; and how much inner turmoil or loss of self-esteem it causes the child.

Development of Moral Character

Morality can be defined as the direct internalization of external cultural norms. According to cognitive-developmental theorists, there are universal ethical principles which are distinguishable from arbitrary conventional rules and beliefs. These theorists further assume that moral development — like intellectual and personality development — follows an invariant developmental sequence that is influenced by maturational and environmental factors.

Kohlberg's Developmental Theory

After extensively studying the development of moral judgment across different cultures, the psychologist Lawrence Kohlberg concluded that character development progresses hierarchically through three general levels. At the first stage, called "Preconventional", the preschool child responds to parental labels of good and bad but interprets these labels in terms of either the physical or pleasurable consequences of actions (punishment, rewards) or in terms of an elementary notion of reciprocity, e.g., "I'll scratch your back if you scratch mine." At the second or "Conventional" level, the grade school child perceives that following the regulations of parents and society is valuable in its own right, regardless of the immediate and obvious consequences of an act. The child's inclination is not only to conform to conventional norms of morality but to be loyal to and actually maintain, support, and justify these norms. The child tends to identify with the person or group involved in giving the orders or setting laws. At this stage, the child begins to experience some guilt after a transgression, rather than just fear of punishment. When asked why a behavior is wrong a child at this stage will say because it "isn't nice or good" or it's "against the law." At the highest level, called "Autonomous" or "Principles," there is a clear effort for adolescents and adults to define for themselves moral principles (equity, justice) that have validity apart from the authority of persons or groups holding these principles.

Kohlberg has found that the great majority of Americans reason about moral issues at the conventional level.

Piaget's Developmental Theory

A number of years before Kohlberg's formulation, Piaget also postulated three general levels of moral development. The first stage, termed the "Morality of Constraint", lasts until the child is seven or eight years old. It is characterized by blind obedience to parents, with adults regarded as omnipotent. The child views punishment in terms of such primitive concepts as "imminent justice" and "moral realism." The former refers to the idea that all bad acts will be punished by either human means or by natural or supernatural forces. The latter pertains to a child's evaluation of actions in terms of consequences rather than in terms of intentions or motives.

Between the ages eight and ten, the child goes through an intermediary stage of adherence to rules in which he either internalizes the rules without judging them, or alternates in his responses to situations. At the final level of moral development, rules merge into abstract principles around the age of twelve, and the child begins to evaluate intentions and circumstances rather than deeds or outcomes alone. Moral principles such as love, justice, and honesty come to form the basis for morality rather than rigid rules or fear of punishment. Moreover, cooperation and mutual respect among peers takes the place of the former unilateral respect for adults.

Summary

Both Piaget and Kohlberg describe a developmental thrust in the child to move from initially acting appropriately out of fear of punishment; to conformity out of respect for law and authority; to moral behavior based upon an inner conviction and belief in basic ethical principles. To help a child advance to the next higher level of moral development, parents should not only model the more mature moral behavior, but also discuss with the child the need for law and order and the rationales underlying such universal ethical principles as the Golden Rule, and Equality Among Men. Even more importantly, parents should realize that respect is the primary root of morality — respect for oneself, for others, for authority; if you are continually berating or belittling authority figures (police, mayor, president of the nation, teachers, bosses), how can you expect your child to respect them?

Studies have shown that by age ten, in most cases, the moral character of the child is well formed, although it will continue to develop through young adulthood. A further finding is that to a startling degree, each child learns to feel and act, psychologically and morally, as just the kind of person his or parents have been in their relationship with the child. So the early parent-child interactions seem to form a child's character to a substantial degree. It makes a difference if your interactions with a child are accepting vs. rejecting; approving vs. disapproving; affectionate vs. cold; responsive vs. indifferent; empathic vs. misunderstanding; respectful vs. disrespectful; kind vs. cruel; and enjoyable vs. grim.

The golden rule is the most universally accepted expression of good character. So teach a child to love, i.e., an attitude towards people which includes unselfishness, consideration and understanding of others, cooperativeness, kindness, and altruism. The child learns best to love by being loved; to be just by receiving just treatment from parents. The first decade of life is the most important one for moral development. The continuous daily experiences with parents determine a child's character in large measure. These experiences teach the child right from wrong and the value of self and others. Good character is based on love of self and others, then, and the joy of giving rather than fear of punishment. Good moral character cannot simply be taught in the schools; it must be learned and lived in the home. In this sense, the prime responsibility for its development rests not with teachers or friends, but with parents.

NOTES

1. Salk, L. The *New York Times* Book Review Section, September 4, 1977.

2. Freedman, J.L. and Fraser, S.C. Compliance without pressure: The foot-in-the-door technique. *Journal of Personality and Social Psychology,* 1966, **4**, 195–202.

3. Snyder, J.J. Reinforcement analysis of interaction in problem and nonproblem families. *Journal of Abnormal Psychology,* 1978, **50**, 528–535.

4. NIAAA Information and Feature Service. IFS No. 60, June 7, 1979.

5. Tuchman, B.W. The decline of quality. *New York Times Magazine,* November 2, 1980.

6. Rosen, B.C. and D'Audrade, R. The psychosocial origins of achievement motivation. *Sociometry,* 1959, **22**, 185–218.

7. McClelland, D.C. *The Achieving Society.* Princeton, N.J.: Van Nostrand, 1961.

8. Chance, P., Schlachter, T., Elliott, L. The roots of success. *Family Circle,* 1978, **91**, #5.

9. Stitt, S. *Human Behavior,* 1978, **7**, 36.

10. Eberle, N. Raising my children: What I'd do differently. *McCall's,* August 1979, 156.

11. Drabman, R.S. and Jarvie, G. Counseling parents of children with behavior problems: The use of extinction and time-out techniques. *Pediatrics,* 1977, **59**, 78–85.

12. Hollandsworth, J.G. and Cooley, M.L. Provoking anger and gaining compliance with assertive versus aggressive responses. *Behavior Therapy,* 1978, **9**, 640–46.

13. Gordon, T. *Parent Effectiveness Training.* New York: Peter Wyden, 1970

14. Leighton, L.A., Stollak, G.E., and Ferguson, L.R. Patterns of communication in normal and clinic families. *Journal of Consulting and Clinical Psychology,* 1971, **36**, 252–56.

15. Gordon, T. *P.E.T. Parent Effectiveness Training.* New York: New American Library, 1975.

16. Bugenthal, D.B. and Love, L. Nonassertive expression of parental approval and disapproval and its relationship to child disturbance. *Child Development,* 1975, **56**, 747–52.

17. Baumrind, D. Current patterns of parental authority. *Developmental Psychology,* 1971, **4**, 103.

18. Hodgson, R.W. Evidence of two kinds of fear arousal by threat appeals. *Psychological Reports,* 1977, **41**, 788–90.

19. Dobson, J. *Dare to Discipline.* Tyndale House, 1970.

20. Dreikurs, R. and Grey, L. *Logical Consequences. A New Approach to Discipline.* New York: Hawthorne Books, 1968.

21. Glasser, W. *Reality Therapy.* New York: Harper & Row, 1965.

22. Gardner, D.C. and Gardner, P.L. Goal-setting and learning in the high school resource room. *Adolescence,* 1978, **13**, 489–93.

23. Rosswork, S.G. Goal setting: The effects on an academic task with varying magnitudes of incentive. *Journal of Educational Psychology,* 1977, **69**, 710–15.

24. Sullivan, K and Sullivan, A. Adolescent-parent separation. *Developmental Psychology,* 1980, **16**, 93–99.

25. Dinkmeyer, D.C. Use of the encouragement process in Adlerian counseling. *Personnel and Guidance Journal,* 1972, **51**, 177–81.

26. Dyer, W. W. and Vriend, J. *Counseling Techniques That Work.* New York: Funk & Wagnalls, 1977.

27. Hoffman, M.L. and Saltzstein, H. Parent discipline and the child's moral development. *Journal of Personality and Social Psychology,* 1967, **5**, 45–67.

28. Hoffman, M.L. Child-rearing practices and moral development. *Child Development,* 1963, **34**, 295–318.

29. Sampson, R. Transmission of values within a traditional family structure. *Family Therapy,* 1977, **4**, 163–70.

30. Bienvenu, M.J. *Parent-Teenager Communication.* Public Affairs Pamphlet, New York, 1970.

31. Levine, S.V. and Salter, N.E. Youth and contemporary religious movements: Psychological findings. *Canadian Psychiatric Association Journal,* 1976, **21**, 411–20.

32. Simon, S.B., Howe, L.W., and Kirschenbaum, H. *Values Clarification.* New York: Hart Publishing Co., 1972.

33. Raths, L., Harmin, M., and Simon, S. *Values and Teaching: Working with Values in the Classroom,* Columbus, Ohio: Charles Merrill, 1966.

34. Platt, J.J. and Spivack, G. Social competence and effective problem solving thinking in psychiatric patients. *Journal of Clinical Psychology,* 1972, **28**, 3–5.

35. Spivack, G. Platt, J.J., and Shure, M.B. *The Problem-solving Approach to Adjustment.* San Francisco: Jossey-Bass, 1976.

36. D'Zurilla, T.J. and Nezu, A. A study of the generation-of-alternatives process in social problem solving. *Cognitive Therapy & Research,* 1980, **4**, 67–72.

37. Whiting, B.B. (ed.) *Six Cultures: Studies in Child Rearing.* New York: John Wiley, 1963.

38. Ebert, B. The healthy family. *Family Therapy,* 1978, **5**, 227–32.

39. Lerner, H. The taboo against female anger. *Menninger Perspective,* 1977, Winter, 5–11.

40. Wahlroos, S. *Family Communication.* New York: Macmillan, 1974.

41. Pikas, A. Children's attitudes toward rational versus inhibiting parental authority. *Journal of Abnormal and Social Psychology,* 1961, **62**, 315–21.

42. LaVoie, J.C. Punishment and adolescent self-control. *Developmental Psychology,* 1973, **8**, 16–24.

43. Chance, P., Schlachter, T., and Elliott, L. The roots of success. *Family Circle,* 1978, *91*, #5.

44. Jones, R.A. *Self-fulfilling Prophecies: Social, Psychological, and Physiological Effects of Expectancies.* Somerset, N.J.: John Wiley, 1978.

45. Roll, S. and Miller, L. Adolescent males feeling of being understood by their fathers as revealed through clinical interviews. *Adolescence,* 1978, **13**, 83–94.

46. Sheviakov, G.V. "Some reflections on the problem of discipline." In *From Learning for Love to Love of Learning.* Edited by R. Ekstein and R.L. Motto, Bruner/Mazel, 1969.

47. Rotter, J.B. Interpersonal trust, trustworthiness, and gullibility. *American Psychologist,* 1980, **35**, 1–7.

48. Reardon, M.E. What is a well-mannered child? *The Catholic Digest,* July, 1977.

49. Brownstone, J.E. and Dye, C.J. *Communication Workshop for Parents and Adolescents.* Champaign, Illinois: Research Press, 1973.

50. Chance, P., Schlachter, T., and Elliott, L. The roots of success. *Family Circle,* 1978, **91**, #5.

51. Burke, R.J., and Weir, T. Husband-wife helping-relationships: The "mental hygiene" functions in marriage. *Psychological Reports,* 1977, **40**, 911–925.

52. "Do you have what it takes to make a good marriage. *Ladies Home Journal,* October, 1980.

53. Biller, H. *Father, Child, and Sex Role: Paternal Determinants of Personality Development.* Lexington, Mass.: Heath Books, 1971.

54. Rogers, C. *Client-centered Therapy.* Boston: Houghton Mifflin, 1951.

55. Feshbach, N.D. Empathy training: A field study in affective education. Paper presented at the American Educational Research Association Meeting, March 29, 1978, Toronto, Canada.

56. Havens, L. Explorations in the uses of language in psychotherapy: Complex empathic statements. *Psychiatry,* 1979, **42**, 40–48.

57. Jourard, S.M. *Self-disclosure: An Experimental Analysis of the Transparent Self.* New York: John Wiley, 1971.

58. Wahlroos, S. *Family Communication* New York: Macmillan, 1974.

INDEX